UNQUIET VIETNAM

Kenneth Murphy

GIBSON SQUARE BOOKS

This edition published for the first time by Gibson Square

uk Tel: +44 (0)20 7096 1100
us Tel: +1 646 216 9813

info@gibsonsquare.com
www.gibsonsquare.com

ISBN   9781783341276

*Papers used by Gibson Square are natural, recyclable products made
from wood grown in sustainable forests; inks used are vegetable based.
Manufacturing conforms to ISO 14001, and is accredited to FSC and
PEFC chain of custody schemes. Colour-printing is through a certified
CarbonNeutral® company that offsets its CO_2 emissions.*

Printed by CPI.

Contents

For Wen Liao

献给廖文:

梦为远别啼难唤,
书被催成墨未干.

杜甫

Author's Note

The events recounted here should, perhaps, be described as 'truthful' rather than 'factual', though they are based on facts of my travels in Indochina. My reasons for making this distinction are simple: Vietnam and Laos remain communist countries; Cambodia flounders in a blood-soaked chaos. So the names of people and of places have, by necessity, been changed and disguised in some circumstances. I am obliged to all of the people I met for their hospitality, their many kindnesses, their insights and, in a few cases, their willing friendship.

Many friends were of help and support in completing this book: Rebecca Sternal goaded me into going to Vietnam in the first place, and Roman Frydman and Andrzej Rapaczynski covered my back, as it were, when I disappeared into the silences of Indochina. Norman Manea and Katja Krausova provided helpful comments and ideas at various stages of the manuscript. Through his consistent and continuing support, George Soros indirectly made this book possible. Although I do not know Nate Thayer, anyone venturing into the mire of Cambodian affairs nowadays owes him a debt of enlightenment for his Ahab-like hunt.

I

Alias Saigon

'Where you from? You look American. I have much respect for Americans' Ut Phung said, squatting like a weightlifter and taking hold of my bags. Despite his hurried movements, a withered left arm could not be disguised. After popping open the boot of his Toyota and storing the luggage, Ut turned his head in my direction once more. 'Americans,' he continued, 'have so many dollars to throw around. Maybe, one day, they throw some more to me.'

Crossing a border into a poor, communist country usually means more than clearing passport control, customs, and the visual frisks of uniformed men bearing rifles. Approach such a border checkpoint and you are almost certain to feel stress, sometimes fear, less often a sense of liberation. You are either at the beginning of something, or at the end of something. Once your passport gets stamped, your emotions are likely to remain ratcheted up a notch: you can find yourself speechless in a world where you cannot know the private grammar of even the simplest thing. How, for example, do you choose one cab driver over another in a strange country?

You scan the faces. Ut was smiling gently, thin lips cracked from the heat. That smile made him stand out in the jostling scrum of cabbies outside the arrival hall at Saigon's Tan Son Nhut airport. Ut's gestures seemed restrained, his voice dry and composed, and he gave the impression of a bemused detachment. Most of the others in that ragged bunch appeared crafty, slightly thuggish. Hysteria seemed locked up in their necessary smiles, their all-too-eager-toplease eyes. Desperation was also suggested by the condition of their taxis. There wasn't more than one or two without a door or fender bashed in, some body part rusting or amateurishly repaired.

Many of those drivers were in their fifties. I wondered if they longed for the days of the 'American mission,' when thousands of officers and civilians and journalists came to Saigon. Back then there were never enough hotel rooms and no cabby ever pined for a fare.

Needy or not, their shouts for attention expressed a kind of sneering pride behind which lay a submissive resentment for all the harassments and petty humiliations inflicted on them each day. As I watched, two drivers stepped up on the curb to get closer to the glass doors from which tourists and visiting businessmen emerged. A slim security guard in khaki and mirrored glasses (one too many movie cops for him), rhythmically tapping his holstered pistol, was on top of them. He ordered them back to their place. They turned their whole bodies in defeat. No reminder of their status was needed.

A newly arrived cabby strode to the spot where the others had been evicted. No one hassled him. A furtive flicker passed between his eyes and the now grinning guard. A deal had been struck. Within a minute, no longer, the driver had not one but two Korean businessmen in hand.

Watching that duplicitous drama, Vietnam began to unfold. Here was a country composed of two distinct classes: those with 'influence' and those too poor to buy any. Among the former, life would be 'normal;' among the latter, life must be hell. From years of travel in the old USSR and its successor states, I knew that under communism a job of even the slightest importance was a hatchery for parasites, with the fortunate, such as that airport guard, besieged by schools of unfortunates. If you wanted to operate a cab, open a business, get your daughter that job as a high school English teacher, you needed to run a gauntlet of people in order to 'facilitate' the deal, register the papers, put the thing through with the right departments, the right officials, all of them coveting a commission if not an outright bribe. Follow ordinary channels and you were lost. Weeks, months, years could go by with nothing happening. Cab drivers without influence, men such as Ut, must scramble; the select saw business directed their way.

Musing over this, sympathy for the two rejected men began to rise in me. It soon passed. I could not shake the feeling—not hard to arouse after twenty-one hours in the air and in airport lounges—that those cabbies and the other airport loiterers posed some vague sort of danger. They all appeared as sly, perhaps desperate, rustics wrestling with their frustrations and their newly acquired urban vanities.

In the swirling dust of the parking lot some of the nearby buildings looked like peasant dwellings; rolled up palm frond bedding mats—brightly coloured by stripes of red, green, and bamboo yellow—hung from windows in those low buildings, and from a wire mesh fence surrounding them. I could not trust my first impressions: dismal, on-the-make village sorts, dwarfs, twisted and mutilated people. But these were more than the dismissive observations of the practised traveller; I was suddenly wary of having left a settled world for the fluid, tropical atmosphere of Vietnam.

My disorientation became even more heightened at the immediate, unexpected, you-can't-help-but-see-them reminders of America's long abandoned rule of the southern regions of the country—the half-oval concrete aeroplane bunkers ranged in military lines alongside Tan Son Nhut's runway, now cindery like a furnace floor; the rusting US Army cavalry combat helicopters, baking in the sun, displayed to remind forgetful foreigners of what the country had endured for half-a-century; the list on a Vietnam Airways notice board of destinations for its in-country flights—Da Nang, Hué, Hanoi—the names echoing Gallic and Yankee imperial missions, battles and bombardments from long ago. I felt as if I had been dropped into a page of history. Those recognitions contributed to the physical edge given my nerves by the scorching heat and dust. Everything—the palm trees, the people—seemed to be growing out of that dust.

Ut's smile reassured. Moonfaced, a little stout (unusual in that crowd of hungry looking men), Ut wore an old polyester blazer despite the heat. Because of its age—wide lapels that had been out-of-date since the 1970s at least—he obviously took great pains to keep the jacket in good nick. His wife, it seemed, sponged, brushed, and pressed his jacket and trousers each morning. Unlike the other drivers, Ut's clothes fitted him at the waist and at the shoulders, and he carried himself with reserve and dignity. He had a fine, slight moustache and spoke English in a soft, persuasive way, his gentle enunciation laced with dated American slang. His conduct seemed ruled by a disciplined, survivor's pride. I saw him as a man who had probably worked for the United States in some capacity or other during the war. Those compromising ties had perhaps left no other work open to him but to hustle foreigners with their dollars and yens, francs and bahts into his cab. He would be interesting to talk with, I decided. Without haggling—Ut loathed bargaining—we fixed a price for the trip to my hotel; the five dollars for which he asked seemed reasonable. I was beginning to like the country. Alert to my satisfaction, Ut responded quickly: 'Maybe you will think about using me during your stay?', he asked as we set off.

A tempting idea: I needed an interpreter. I had secured only a few contacts in Saigon—officially called Ho Chi Minh City, but a name that no one, including officials, seemed to use—so there was no one, really, for me to rely on. My sleepless dreams on the flight to Saigon were of repeated and frustrating attempts to get the journey started— I had failed to secure a visa to communist and hermetically sealed Laos from either its Washington or London embassies. Now, having arrived in Saigon, the prospect of a long, solitary expedition across Indochina became depressing. Ut, with his retained Americanisms would provide me with that entry into the language without which I would likely be over-awed by the scale of Vietnam, pushed like a blind man this way and that by a pavement crowd.

*

DECADES HAVE passed since that night in April 1975 when the last American helicopters scrambled from the roof of the US embassy in a retreat code-named 'Operation Eagle Pull,' timed to begin when the tune 'White Christmas' was heard on the embassy loudspeakers. The searchlights illuminating those night-time evacuations were red, white, and blue. Because the last flights out had no room to spare for cargo, three-and-a-half million dollars and eighty-five million South Vietnamese piastres were destroyed in a bonfire in the embassy courtyard—'Operation Money Burn.'

I thought of those old reports, the entire phantasmagoria of America's evacuation—of air lifts and marines on the roof and stranded personnel and tarmac littered with shoes and broken toys—over and over again that first night in Vietnam. Then, the city must have appeared to the lucky evacuees as a line of concrete, wooden, and red tiled roofs fading away below as they headed for the Seventh Fleet's aircraft carriers cruising in the South China Sea. Now I could see skyscrapers and tall white/pastel blocks of flats like upended sugar cubes; Saigon was reinventing itself by taking on—all these years later—an American appearance once again.

My use of this special lens, through which the country remained somehow tied to the United States, was encouraged by sights in every direction. Vietnam had surrendered to revolution, but for every communist agitprop poster—the eyes only ever-so-slightly suggesting an Asiatic cast—of the sort once pasted in all Soviet-style countries, you saw a billboard of Juliette Binoche hawking Chanel, or Jennifer Love Hewitt selling Neutrogena skin cream, or huge signs for NEC computers, Hyundai cars, as well as terse warnings in Vietnamese which counselled that 'Aids kills: use a condom.' There were film posters for Jackie Chan kung fu movies and smaller handbills on trees and lamps. What romance of escape from poverty and communist conformity did those films promise the Vietnamese?

It certainly had little to do with the black-and-white Saigon I remembered from countless evening news broadcasts seen as a child. The decrepit wooden buildings and teeming slums of the Vietnam War era had given way to newish concrete houses along every street, the dates of their construction—1991, 1985 seemed to be the most popular vintages—chiselled near the top. With six million people, the city had tripled its population in a generation. Only the stream of Saigon traffic, jumpy with individual stops and swerves and with no clear driving lanes, harkened back to the city's wartime chaos.

Arriving in Vietnam by air brought the brief illusion that I could somehow be detached about the country. But detachment and distance seemed impossible in the rush of images that overwhelmed me as I arrived at the Majestic Hotel. Vietnam's landscape appeared as something of a living presence; something bare, frugal, and hard—a militarized place. Every sight appeared distinct and exposed. A palm tree, a hut, a road: all stood equal and isolated.

My responses to the country were based on hazy preconceptions.

The ideas that I carried with me were not sharp, definite images (as, for example, the face of my long dead brother is to me), the sort that can be summoned with only the slightest prodding of the will. No, what I have in mind is the kind of blinding stab of afterimage that comes when a camera flashes in your face or a light bulb sparks and dies.

Like any other American alive at the time of the Vietnam War, no matter what age, everything about that conflict is personal. Of course, what I most remember, much of it everlastingly clear, is a youth of friendships and no forebodings. I was a suburban child, pale, cared for, and for the most part unaware. My image of combat had been mainly formed by movies: *Where Eagles Dare, The Guns of Navarone, The Battle of the Bulge.* My only experiences of war were the games my brothers and I played. They were brilliant as only schoolboys can make games brilliant, with complex rules for movement, engagement, damage, resupply, manoeuvring platoons in the cornfields and woods behind our home in endless fights, often with diagrams and accounts written up afterwards. Thousands of miles away there was a real war.

In time, Vietnam became a central part of my education even though my teachers sought to dodge the issue whenever that disagreeable ghost might appear. Should some classmate ask a question or if (I recall two such occasions) a brother of one of us seated in the rows of low desks was listed in the morning paper as missing in action or killed, Mr. Moore would wave it away before it could be finished, crossing the words out in mid-air. I remember such days because of the calm that followed; the usual classroom antics having been rubbed away. On such days Mr. Moore would leave at the end of class, chalk dust on his suit, stately but shuffling. The look on his face would be one of not quite remembering; there may or may not have been tears in his eyes. The war was crowding in on his school and he feared it.

By then the Vietnam War, degenerating into gangsterism, was ferrying its pathologies home to America. The country's political class was cracking from the strain, and with the murders of Martin Luther King Jr. and Robert F. Kennedy in the spring of 1968 the whole country seemed to be going out of its mind, slaughtering its best as well as its innocents. The public was wearying of the weekly body counts—this week, eighty seven Americans, one hundred ninety and four South Vietnamese, seven hundred Viet Cong—though I have to say that my only clear recollection of the student protests and riots that gripped American campuses was of a crisp autumn afternoon in October 1969.

Skipping school with a friend that day, we went to see his oldest brother pitch in the Princeton/Rutgers baseball game. We wandered the Princeton campus in search of the ballfield, around and past the great 'Rockefeller' Gothic lecture halls and dormitories, the hulking bulk of the Firestone Library, the cool shadowed splendour of Nassau Hall—briefly the home of the US government after the revolution, which we did not then know. Suddenly we found ourselves in the midst of a mob of anti-war students chanting 'Ho Ho Ho Chi Minh' and 'Hey, hey, LBJ*, How many kids did you kill today' as they marched beneath the yellow and red maple trees lining Nassau Street, Princeton's high street. Unified chants; fevered energy.

Across the maple-shadowed lawn below Nassau Hall, we noticed twos and threes of bearded men, armed with sticks and bats, gradually moving toward the university buildings. By the time they got to the door of the president's office, they had turned into threatening dozens.

As I recall, there was continual talk of 'morality' and 'conscience' in the crackling, microphoned speeches, but, in fact, even the grade school boy that I was could see that personal jealousy and egotistical rantings were at the root of their actions.

The events had all the febrile energy of agitprop, and the protests may or may not have been on their way to getting out of control that day when suddenly one long-haired undergraduate, in flannel shirt and jeans, stood on the ledge of one of the buildings overlooking the main quad to shout 'Hey! Hey! The Mets have won the pennant!' Baseball, the great American unifier, worked its magic once more. In a few moments, not much more, news of the Mets triumph transformed that protest. Even some of the New Jersey State policemen on sentry duty joined the celebrations.

For myself, such sights, words, and experiences were strange and

* President Lyndon (Baines) Johnson.

exhilarating. But those Princeton protests were not my first encounter with the idea of the Vietnam War. I was, I suppose, seven or eight years old when images of 'Vietnam' first gripped my consciousness. Every night, or so it seemed, we watched that country burning on television: villages on fire, jungles on fire, Vietnamese on fire. Even now, if I close my eyes I can recall those grainy frames of explosions, flat as lead, as B52s dropped their bombs; the sombre voices of the newscasters, hushed, almost faint in their formality—like the sound of Father Grabowski in the blackness of the oak-panelled confessional on Saturday afternoons. You watched the TV, a bomb would drop or a shell be fired. You really could not be sure what was happening; you watched, the explosion would come, emerging onscreen like a photograph in development. Sound came later, standing apart. I think I was sickened by it the first time, but cannot be certain; it may have been fun. Then you saw bodies strewn about, usually Americans, sometimes Vietnamese. After a few moments, not much more, the broadcast would move on, and I would lose interest.

A family ritual: my parents, brothers and sisters, would gather in front of the television before dinner, my mother anxiously asking my father about how long the war might go on, and would it linger long enough for one of her sons to be drafted. Obsessively, my parents followed President Johnson's press conference chicanery: the dummy gestures, the satanic sweating, the dazzling lies. Sometimes I felt sympathy for LBJ, some days he seemed to be the only other person in as much trouble with my parents as I was.

Over the years I tried to follow with growing discipline our dinner table discussions about the progress of the war, about Westmoreland and Thieu and Cabot Lodge and General de Gaulle's warnings, about what John Kennedy might or might not have done had he lived. I was pulled this way and that by my parents talk, their love of America and their fears for a future that, with the war growing ever more unpredictable, might one day claim one of their sons.

After hours in the orderly world of the schoolroom, and the smiling discipline of the ballfield, that regularly reappearing newsreel of a land of mud-soaked men in ponchos, of naked children running from flames, made me aware of fear and uncertainty, and the lawlessness of the soul that makes them possible. Catechism classes taught me about a world in which sin was punished and good rewarded. The great virtues were indivisible, the priests would say; they were commandments that demanded to be obeyed. In life, we were told, you might know fear and defeat and maybe even disgrace, the world itself might fall into darkness, but those virtues would never fall or fail. Never. Devout Roman Catholics, my parents insisted on those classes. In the America they saw emerging they were counting on faith to steady us, as the quivering needle in the compass firms on the pole.

Those nightly newscasts, with their hypnotic power, delivered another message—that this was a world of appalling, random cruelties. Sometimes when my parents mentioned this or that government official—McNamara, the Bundy and Rostow brothers, Laird, Kissinger—the ripples in their voices suggested that here was evil incarnate. Each night I watched, with horror and fascination. Those broadcasts were an hour's escape into a new world. They formed an hour of confusion and expectation during which I became aware of uncertainty and transience. Through a kind of visual attrition, I began to believe not that the world was orderly, which was the lesson imparted by my parents and my catechism classes, but a place in which anything might happen. Nothing was inevitable.

So doubt came. I may, at times, have begun to believe a little more in heaven because it had become possible to see a glimpse of hell, but for a long while it was only that hell which I could picture with any degree of intimacy. Father Grabowski could not provide the same intricate images of heaven; only painted plaster saints and the wooden risen—not crucified—Christ hanging above the altar. Those symbols of faith were supposed to be primary symbols that could only be altered by adult life. Instead, their potency, if not yet the faith itself, was lost early on; I began to populate heaven with the appalling mysteries unlocked by television in its relentless quest to deliver to our comfortable homes images of our ravaged world as a place of the damned. Those reflections made me feel that no one was really responsible for anyone else, or anything else. We may not even be held responsible for ourselves.

That sense of meaninglessness was confirmed for me on a cold December afternoon when I was twelve. My family arrived at the cemetery after my brother's funeral mass. Inside the gates, a gang of workers idled about, leaning on a small yellow CAT earthmoving machine, and clapping their hands above a fire in a dented black cast iron trash bin. All of those workers were either black or Hispanic, and they reminded me of those nightly newscasts about Vietnam—so few of the soldiers were white, most were black or brown like the cemetery workers.

With the war winding down, draft avoidance had become routine. Everyone was doing it. Strings no longer needed to be pulled in the way they were for George W. Bush just a few years before. If you were middle class, you could get out of the draft easy. Anyone could get a college deferment. Professors were inflating grades to make sure no student flunked out to become subject to the draft. No one questioned any of this. President Nixon was not prepared to lose his base of support in the middle class over a war he had decided to finish. Let people who would never think of voting for him fight and die until the end.

Only the poor, or those who volunteered for whatever reason—and I did not know my brother's reason for volunteering to go, there was nothing gung-ho about him that I could recall—were drafted. Marx spoke about class war, but what America went through in Vietnam was the real thing. The working class waged war so that the middle and upper classes, who had wanted the war in the first place, did not have to do so.

Approaching the cemetery entrance, my father was staring at my mother; he wasn't merely sorry for her; he was horrified. It wasn't only that she was white and drawn but that her features, her mouth pinched at one corner, were set rigid in accusation. Why? Why? Her lips moved silently. She had no more idea than any of us as to why her son was dead.

In contrast to the cemetery worker there were our family friends, looking decorous in dark suits, shoes, and dresses. Standing between the workers and our family friends was our parish priest. Father Grabowski was stout and sourly masculine, sallow and sullen with the awkwardness of someone who devotes his life to Christ because he thinks himself too inadequate to live normally with ordinary people. The hem of his cassock was unstitched and coming down. His cardiac-patient's face was a ruin: my brother had once been one of his altar boys and now he was burying him.

A voluntary committee of sharp, henny ladies—their black clothing made them look ancient—took charge of us so that my parents could grieve in peace. Behind their jutting teeth they were protective, advisory—straightening our ties, whispering where to go, stand, sit, kneel.

We set off in a group, walking through a cemetery dense with stones. Recent monuments were protected from the weather by heavy plastic sheets fastened with belts and ropes, and rattling in the wind. One of our neighbors, who had a young Labrador puppy, covered the family sofas and chairs with this material; here it was the obelisks and headstones with their freshly carved inscriptions that were protected.

No melancholy pleasant winter sunshine; instead, the weather was dark, windy. At the grave a large crowd of mourners— classmates of my brother, colleagues of my parents—were waiting. There were numerous dark red tapers—they looked like the sort of flares you set up when your car has broken down on a roadside at night—leaning every which way. Some were sheltered in cast iron lanterns but gusts came down and shook the rest. The mourners were seated on metal folding and green canvas chairs around the grave, the college and high school students crowded up behind—the long hair of the boys tucked under ski caps. Small purple cyclamens— survivors of an early snow—stood forlornly in concrete pots around the grave.

Now the priest got the service under way. Efficient and gruff, Father Grabowski spoke, mumbled, sang. Now and then a howl came out. Heartache of his own. He was not a pampered priest. The type of metal chair about the grave is what you saw in his rectory. He looked like a big-bellied tramp in his black boots and great coat.

The lashed sheets of plastic over the surrounding obelisks and headstones clattered hard. In the scuffles of the wind the tapers blew out. Where they fell, there were patches of black soot in the grass. Old women rekindled them. I watched my father shiver, having respectfully removed his hat while Father Grabowski prayed. My aunt made a gesture ordering him to put it on again.

By now the gusts had overcome the last of the tapers, which had tumbled and were jumbled together in the black-spotted grass. From all sides came a rude rattle of plastic billowing in the wind. Just at that moment, six uniformed Marine Corps pallbearers appeared and snapped to attention. When they did, a bugler jumped out from behind a tree to take his place at the back of the guard of honour. Then came the hearse carrying my brother's body, winding up and around a circular road, its headlights dim in the sun. The next ten minutes seemed an eternity. I watched my brother's coffin being carried to the grave by the Marines, and watched the pallbearers lift the flag, trying to hold it taut in the winter gusts.

Of my brother at that moment I think I felt a secret thrill and envy. His life, the scraps that I knew of it, seemed worthy, complete. He had left something behind, people who would never forget him. What more is there really, I wondered, to wish for in life than to be loved and remembered? To go on living forever in the memories of others? Death at that moment seemed a pure act. So far from death, I had no fear.

The wind was blowing increasingly hard, toppling vases of white lilies set atop a mound of soil next to the grave, obliterating most of Father Grabowski's words. I was standing behind a line of canvas chairs, standing there and looking beyond the priest to a scattering of graves in the distance, graves so fresh that they had no headstones, just red plastic markers jutting out of the ground where the headstones would one day be.

Father Grabowski's prayers—*Our Father who art in heaven, hallowed be*—were sounds, not words, his voice shattering the quiet as the gleaming mahogany box hit the dirt of the pit with an echoless thud. The honour guard raised their rifles. Shots cracked the stillness. A bugler played taps. A bag piper from the local volunteer firemen played 'Danny Boy.'

Two pallbearers folded the flag meticulously until only the blue field and a few white stars showed. A young Marine captain then stepped forward to present the flag to my mother, who stared at him savagely, but seemed paralyzed, unable to put out her hands. After a few moments my father—an ex-Marine officer himself, now standing perfectly at attention—took the flag from the suddenly worried looking officer. My father transferred it from hand to hand as if it burned, all the while looking out across the expanse of graves. He was not seeing his wife, not his other children, not anyone. He was focused inward—inward where the coherence and certainty were supposed to be, inward where everything he had believed about his country had shattered, where none of the grief of that day would ever fade.

The service ended, the entire party walked slowly along the grave-bordered footpath to the main cemetery avenue. Again we saw the line of idle graveyard workers holding their hands over the crackling flames. Suddenly the weather took over, nothing but cloud and sleet, the old people seeking shelter or hurrying to their cars, Father Grabowski in his boots striding over gravel, rushing through the big gates. My father, blank-faced with the pride of the betrayed, guided my mother to the first car.

Back at home, my father did not enter our house. Instead, he sat down outside on the front steps in the bitter cold. I watched him through the curtain. He sat without moving, not even when my mother went out to comfort him, for over an hour. All that time he was leaning forward, his elbows on his knees, his face invisible in his hands. There were so many tears inside his head that he had to hold his head like that in his two strong hands to prevent it from tumbling down. Then he stood, bearing within him, as we all did, everything that we would never understand.

The Vietnam War, that madness that was at last ending half a world away, was over for us. A breach, however, had opened that would never close.

*

OF MY FIRST evening in Saigon I remember mainly images, indelible but hard to connect. It wasn't that things seemed absolutely strange; more disturbing is that just the opposite was true. Wherever Ut drove I was struck by unexpected recognitions. Everywhere it was possible to spy familiar eyes, noses, complexions, gestures, postures (the 'American slouch,' Evelyn Waugh called it). So insistent was that sensation that I began to suspect that, across the globe, men and women were deployed in only a limited number of body and facial types. That sensation was both pleasant and unnerving. Eyes, hands, mouths on the people who passed by appeared utterly familiar. Take a second glance, however, and you realized that those resemblances misled.

Once, indeed, in a crowded street market set under giant peepul trees I undoubtedly saw an Amer-Asian grown to full maturity. Unshaven, with long dank hair and dressed in flapping Ho Chi Minh pyjamas, tall with sloping shoulders, he drifted in and out of view, passing saffron-robed monks, moving stealthily between shanties enclosed by lines of damp laundry. It was mid-afternoon, the sky practically cloudless. Palm crowns and poinciana blossoms were hanging motionless because that day's monsoon rain was late.

My own conspicuousness was on my mind at that moment, because a few of the street hustlers had withdrawn into the shade of the market stalls to hiss at me, a sweating American. But if it wasn't for my height advantage over the Vietnamese in that market, I would never have seen what that Amer-Asian was doing.

Staring down, as if viewing open heart surgery, I watched that man, who—like me—was the wrong size for the place. At that moment, unnoticed, the man was pushing a small trader of pipes and pots against a market stall. The Amer-Asian pressed the Vietnamese man forcefully, belly to back. Not a word passed between the two men; the Amer-Asian would no more speak than a tiger would. Suddenly, the Amer-Asian spun the trader around, almost effortlessly, all the while holding his prey tight against the stall with a forearm.

A breeze came from the river then, carrying the smell of rain, stirring the fronds and blossoms and the dead air. Monsoon clouds were closing off the sky. This incited the Amer-Asian to act: he hurriedly took out his penis—a large, uncircumcised thing—and displayed it to the trader. Over a forearm and fist, the trader was forced to look at it. He made no cry for help.

The interval seemed long. The Amer-Asian's expression was not overtly menacing, but had a serene masterfulness. For whatever reason, he was showing his prick with a lordly certainty. Then it was returned to his pyjamas in the same hurried way in which it was removed. The session, the lesson, the transmission, the warning or whatever it was, had ended.

It was at this moment, with a quick turn of the head, that the Amer-Asian saw me watching him from above the crowd. He acknowledged nothing, but began to weave his way out of the market, gently urgent, stooping forward. The monsoon rains began to batter. The ruts and potholes soon filled to overflowing. The Amer-Asian waded through the ruts until he made his escape.

This was in one of the most crowded slums along the Saigon River and the glimpse of that man made me inquire about him. A local communist party official told me later that he was probably a *hawkwai* (a Chinese word and as degrading as the word 'nigger'), the bastard child of an American soldier and a Vietnamese woman, probably a prostitute. For decades such half-breeds had been consigned to a new and virtually untouchable caste. Many of the older ones nowadays formed an odd community of practically nameless and unemployable fugitives.

The idea of them—of that savagely sunburned man in pyjamas navigating the market stalls that day, briefly exposed—filled, me with curiosity, horror, and pity all at once. Decades after the war's end you could still see Vietnam's walking wounded. In America, most of the veterans were themselves again, for what it was worth, the psycho vets of the idiotic *Rambo* movies notwithstanding. But the most specious lunacy had been conceived, written, and enacted in Vietnam and a good many of these vets never recovered. Some soldiers became mystics, some Communist sympathizers, some junkies; at times, certain people were all three at once. That Amer-Asian, however, never had a chance. His mixed race made him an outcast from the moment of his birth, and an outcast he would remain. I suppose that I saw him as a Vietnamese version of William Faulkner's character Joe Christmas, that tragic figure of suspect race in the novel *Light in August* who was meant to carry all the lingering burdens of slavery, America's original sin. Seeing that man, I knew that if I was going to understand Vietnam in any lucid way, I would need to come to grips with its outsiders.

It was lovely dry-season weather the week I arrived—New Year's week. Red banners proclaiming '*Chuc Mung Nam Moi*' (Happy New Year) streamed everywhere. By day the city quivered in a silvery film of fumes and heat.

Traffic moved slowly because of the surging crowds; it was as if some invisible human sluice gate had been opened. Then, as suddenly as they had been trapped by the crowd, the beaten up blue and yellow buses, the motley taxis and motorcycles, the bicycle rickshaws, would start moving, and the city would seem to work, waiting for the next human tide.

At night the streets were equally packed with people, in a sacred evening promenade that turned Saigon into a hive. Boys and girls cruised about on motorcycles, a bouncing froth of light-coloured, lightweight clothing in the clear night air. They seemed a kind of Asian replay of Italy's *dolce vita* era with its Vespa scooters and naughty flirtations. The men seemed hard and sleek and empty-headed, their laughter as cold as their eyes. Those evening cruises, however, did reveal the great beauty of the women. Girls sat daintily on the back of those Honda bikes, legs crossed, smiling demurely— a dolce vita beauty too.

Watching the crowds float by you were soon deafened by the babble and the violent noise of the traffic—that sustained, dry roar sounded at times like the roar of a football match or bullfight—but it was sight, not sound, that enticed. Among the young, a certain regularity of feature, bold jaws and brilliant brown eyes, appeared to be standard issue. There was a classic Vietnamese type of man, grave, dark, sallow, a skeletal muscularity; and there was the small, quick, famished, and mischievous sort. Some faces were round and some aquiline; some men were powerful and others chinless with birdlike beaks. Only the old, bent and beaten, carried themselves badly.

There almost seemed to be a racial difference between Vietnamese women and men. Perhaps the difference had social origins: the women, whether driving a motorcycle or perched on the back of one driven by father, husband, or boyfriend, legs crossed, had a formal, prim appearance, whether or not they were dressed in a traditional *ao-dai** or in tight blue jeans. In daylight, many wore long gloves and silk veils to shield their skin from the sun—among women, the lighter the complexion, the more marriageable you became. Sociable and talkative among themselves, girls and women exuded great personal pride. Trained from early childhood to play a double role, women displayed themselves, but only allowed their eyes to meet the eyes of a strange man fleetingly. Their decorum was Victorian.

So many beautiful women were gliding past but they were unap-

---

* *ao-dai*, a long slit tunic, usually made of silk, worn over trousers.

proachable. No glance was returned. No smile recognized. By ten o'clock, they were gone. The only women to be seen after that were raucous lottery-sellers, old beggars, and fierce girls at street-side counters, bars, and kiosks. The town was coming into the possession of men once more and in hundreds of ways, sitting about or walking, they claimed it: male voices, rumbling or shouting, ruled the warm night. Only in the side streets around city hall and the new Saigon Trade Centre tower could small groups of women be seen once this transfer took place: women standing in unlit doorsteps, eyes glittering with a desperate expectancy. One of them idled her scooter alongside me for a moment. 'You fuck girl?' came the brisk, practised question. I shook my head and before I could finish the bike was throttled. She then raised a finger to her nose and blew air through the free nostril. It was a whore's gesture of contempt, I supposed. For a moment, I thought she might blow her nose on me. She looked me in the eye: 'No fuck?' she called shrilly, trying to reach down and touch my belt. Again I shook my head no. 'You fuck little boy then?' I hurried away, but when I turned, she was still staring at me with her vacant smile.

At ten o'clock on that first evening the city hall was outlined in white illuminations. After the exploding of bottle rockets and the screeching of whistles, a procession trailed up from the lower quarter of the city near the river and passed into the main plaza near the cathedral. Shining like a ballroom, it dominated its part of Saigon like a wily old commissar. Drums rumbled; horns defiled; rockets sparked into popping stars. Strange happy emotions drifted through the night air like smoke.

Ut stopped his car on Dông Koi street, Saigon's swagger capital, and we entered a small restaurant. Incredible faces on every side, some as boney as feet. The city's new young rich—children of the nomen-klatura (itself a divided class, with comrades from North Vietnam squatting hierarchically atop comrades who emerged from the Viet Cong)—were out showing off, men in *faux* Zegna shirts, girls carrying shiny, knock-off Prada bags. The bar room was lime green, brightly lit, and filled with men playing cards. You could admire the bellies of the fat among them; they carried their burdens with the air of a cocksure martyrdom. There wasn't just one or two of those obese fellows; there were enough to form almost a distinct class of their own, and they were not without aggression. Wealth turned the glory of personal abundance into fat; it was a simple, unmistakable element of self-assertion.

There were mirrors all around the restaurant's walls, and above three electric fans with wooden blades that resembled propellers spun from a rusting, tin ceiling. Most tables were communal, five jutting from one side of the room, six from the other. A broad aisle divided them, but the crowd was so thick that the waiters had difficulty getting through. Those tables were long and old and plain, built to last. Their tops had been seasoned by drippings and spillages from thousands upon thousands of bowls of steamed and fried fish. At the bar, a big Korean businessman with a purple birthmark on his neck swilled beer through rotted teeth, a young girl standing next to him. She was wobbly on her feet but kept her head straight, like a hotel concierge. She was nice-looking with short black hair. She was drunk.

With Ut waiting outside—he refused to join me for dinner—the restaurant's owner showed me to a café table on the street. As I sat, a teen-aged paralytic worked his way on his hands toward me. Not more than three feet high, he had a scarred bandit's face and little yellow baby feet twisted the wrong way. One of the Vietnamese patrons leaving the restaurant handed him a few dong notes; within seconds two small boys, neither more than ten years of age and silent as cats in their approach, jumped on his back and, after a horrifying struggle, stripped the money from him. The cripple made no complaint; stoically, he shovelled himself back across the street. Here you were subject to jungle law, every man for himself, tooth and nail.

The more clearly you see the world, I thought, the more you are obliged to pretend it does not exist.

On the sidewalk next to me two tables were pushed together. Seated at them were six boisterous Vietnamese, slouching and drinking; one or two chain-smoking Camels and Marlboros. These were Vietnamese-Americans. They were larger than local Vietnamese, big hands, broad shoulders. Compared to most Vietnamese men, they seemed ready to burst out of their shirts. There were Pepsi bottles on the table for the pretty, quiet Vietnamese girls, their backs ramrod straight, seated in silence and self-removal at the side of each man. In their exquisite *ao-dais*, their hair pulled back straight with orchids, they looked like ceremonial figurines. The girls appeared dispirited and I immediately began to see them as part of a vast servitude, anonymous and unending. Nothing amused those Americans. They looked bored, and polished their gestures of contempt. One inspected his reflection in a mirror, sucking his teeth. A chill passed through me: they looked like another pack of scavengers on the hunt for the weak and crippled.

There appeared to be no shortage of Americans in Saigon, but these were the first Americans of Vietnamese birth I had seen. The loud shouts and antic movements with which they barked their orders created the atmosphere of a frat house party. Eavesdropping, I could not but hear their deadening table talk, but it at least betrayed their mission: they were on the hunt for brides.

My food arrived and after I thanked the waiter in English, one of the quieter men in the group turned to me. 'You're an American?' he asked, 'Want to join us?'

'I'd like that.'

'Do you believe this girl,' he said, touching the arm of the pretty girl on his left. She was wearing a tight fitting lime coloured *ao-dai* with a white silk blouse underneath. 'Do you get to meet girls like this?'

'It's impossible. They won't talk. I was told that if you want to ask one out for a meal or even just a walk, they won't go unless you want to marry them.'

'You've got that right! But that's why I'm here. That's why we are all here.'

He then told me that all of them lived and worked in various high-tech jobs around Santa Clara; they were chip engineers and computer programmers and website designers at places like Intel, Cisco Systems, Netscape, and Sun Microsystems. Bonuses and stock options had made them rich. The pressures from their families to marry were unbearable; mothers and fathers, boat people and refugees from 1975, wanted their boys settled down in the wilds of America. Not with American girls, mind you: *they* couldn't be trusted. Not even Vietnamese-American girls were trustworthy: who could tell what values such girls now held, their mothers would say, shaking their heads; they could be as money-grubbing as any California bottle blonde. No, the answer to the marriage problem was back in Vietnam, where girls as reliable as mom could be found. The men had been in Saigon for four days already, in suites at the Saigon Sheraton; no successful matchmaking had yet taken place. No wonder the girls at the table looked jittery; the fortunes of their families were at stake, so no wrong moves. Conversation with those Americans, like others I would have on my trip, derived its candour from the certain knowledge that none of us would ever see each other again.

Another Vietnamese-American, in jeans and a Stanford baseball shirt, staggering a little, approached the table.

'What happened Nye?' a man seated at the head of the table asked him.

'I went up to that sonova bitch and said, "Look, I'm not giving you money just because you introduced me to your daughter." But he just looked at me kinda dumb. Like if he stood there, all pathetic, I'd hand over the money. They think we'll just marry any of these girls. That we're gonna pay just to look'

'The hell with that. You did the right thing. There was no point in seeing him anyway. My mother had arranged lots of contacts through her uncle, you knew that.'

'Well, why should I trust your mom? She doesn't really like me,' said Nye with a leer.

'Damn straight there,' a third interjected.

One of the girls tried to speak. 'Isn't his mother nice?'

The man at the head of the table glared, taking off his San Jose Sharks baseball cap. 'No one spoke to you, did they?' The girl cast her eyes to her feet, saying nothing. Then she turned her head toward me. She was very young. Sixteen, no more than that. Pure, expressionless features. Suddenly I was in anguish. I sensed her predicament. As Rilke said, life offers no classes for beginners; the most difficult things are always asked of you right away.

Nye now looked for a place to sit. There was no other chair at the table, so he stared possessively at a table where some Vietnamese men were sitting quietly, and grabbed one of the chairs without asking.

'Sit down before you fall down,' another one of the Americans shouted.

'Get me a drink, you shit,' said Nye.

'Your ass I will. Get your own.' He pulled out a lumpy wallet. 'I've only got fifty thousand dong to my name,' he said, drinking his beer and smiling between pulls on his bottle.

Voices grew louder, more insistent. The Vietnamese girls seemed to shrink in embarrassment. Nye got up and went to the bar, wrapping his arm around an elderly Vietnamese man standing there. Spying this, a young Vietnamese man who had one wall-eye lifted Nye's arm off the old man.

'Hey, Nye!' came a shout from the table. 'We don't want to get into a fight tonight.'

Nye shook his head and tried to buy the old man a beer but was ignored. One of the other Americans came over from the table and slapped Nye on the back. Surprised, Nye tumbled to the floor. His purple, green, and yellow Hawaiian print shirt was open to his navel. His friend helped him to his feet and back to the table, where he promptly started to paw at one of the Vietnamese girls. Silently observing this scene for some time, other Vietnamese men in the restaurant began to grumble and speak to the waiters in agitated tones. The silk shirts and oily long hair of some of those men had probably been modelled on some star from Hong Kong's kung fu cinema. The care they took with their appearance was a sign that they had shaken off village ways and had become successes in Saigon. Two of the younger ones in that bunch looked as if they were ready to fight.

Seeing this, the loudest of the seated Americans shouted: 'What are you looking at?' to a table of Vietnamese men.

'Come here, buddy,' said Nye to the Vietnamese in his thin, petulant voice.

Fearing what may have been about to happen, the girls became nervous, fidgeting and hugging little pastel-coloured silk handbags. Two stood as if getting ready to leave.

'Hey!' Nye shouted to one of them.

'No wedding bells for anyone who goes,' another of the boys quipped to general laughter from the men at the table. The girls sat down, calm, demure, silent, and defeated.

***

UT LIVED in Saigon most of his life. His family migrated to the city from a village in Camau, the southern tip of Vietnam, when he was three, during World War II, and he had been to high school, a rare thing for Vietnamese in those days. Once a clerk in the office of a trading company, Ut had early in his life decided to attach himself to the Americans. He read American books; his slouch was American, too. Intelligent, imitative, and simple hearted, his admiration for Americans sprang from the observation that they were a people who had a lot of money and were, by his frugal standards, careless about it.

A man of practical talents, Ut had forged to perfection the art of living on little money. He had the art of being inquisitive without being offensive, of ingratiating without appearing servile. He had the art, too, of landing on his feet wherever he went. He was without prejudices, and had a knack for avoiding trouble. When he wanted to be, Ut was as discreet as a cat.

Ut, it was clear, did not believe in any ideology, but this did not alienate him from people who did; on the contrary, their commitments attracted his interest. Similarly, he didn't believe in God, but his wife went to mass each Sunday and prayed for him and he would smile at her prayers. Ut believed in doing things habitually and well.

Today Ut lived in small rooms in Cholon, formerly the Chinatown of Saigon. 'But most of the Chinese left years ago,' Ut told me, 'the government was then practising something it learned from the Americans: Vietnamization. It made life hell for the Chinese, they were enemies within, and when they started to flee in boats—Hong Kong did not seem so far away to them but how many of them drowned in the sea?—the government moved local people like me into the houses the Chinese abandoned. We were filling in the empty spaces.'

Life runs in cycles, and Ut was probably well aware that he had, years ago, run through the best of his luck. That didn't seem to matter. At home, he probably remembered past days. But he was young then, years ago. Now, every morning at six Ut went to Tan Son Nhut to greet the first overseas airline flight of the day. If unlucky, he waited for the next flight, then the next, and the next.

Once he went five days without a fare, which meant that he did not eat much those days. 'My stomach was grumbling so much it must have thought my throat had been cut.' Of course, Ut had other ways to make a buck. Hotels gave him a cut of any business he delivered. My hotel, the Majestic, located on a wide boulevard that runs along the Saigon River waterfront, would probably have given him ten dollars for bringing me to their door.

Ut was also an expert local fixer and most afternoons and evenings he made the rounds of the massage women, restaurants, bars, and brothels to see what price they were paying for customers. In his dealings he was like a disgraced doctor or one of those lawyers for criminals, someone with a stain who knew all that there was to know about a city's underworld. His hand was certainly capable of better things than this, but something within him—sad wisdom, a necessary surrender—held Ut tight in Saigon's shadows. He kept the addresses for all of Saigon's subterranean places in a small worn notebook. Some nights he visited gambling dens, which he could later tout to visiting Korean and Taiwanese businessmen on the prowl for a game. Though he carried little business cards for every massage parlour and gambling room in Saigon, Ut did not drink. 'In the American war I was in every bar all the time. Your MPs knew me. Bartenders tried to keep me out. I had dollars, no wife then, and I wanted to live like my soldier friends. Sometimes I got so drunk that my friends put ice in my ears to awaken me. When the war ends, I changed.' Ut brooded for a moment. 'I knew when they let me back to Ho Chi Minh City,' he drew out Saigon's official name with practised disdain, 'it was not possible to go back to my old ways.'

So Ut tried to maintain good relations with every shady business in that vast city. Alone, once inside the gambling houses, he just stood around shuffling his feet, refusing to risk a dong, gazing wistfully at the cash on the ground or on a table.

No matter how much those shrewd gamblers relied upon or liked Ut, they seemed to look down on him as a clown and parasite. Ut did not seem to mind their condescension, though the inner wounds for a man who had once held a responsible position, in the old American dominated economy must have been great. Still, Ut seemed to hint that their ill-treatment gave him a sort of advantage over them. 'In the end, they know that I know what I am doing. They respect a survivor, and I am that.' So armed, Ut could not really be insulted by them, by anyone really. In situations that I found painful to see— phlegm landing on his shoes, with what degree of deliberateness I cannot say—he always behaved with a kind of deadpan, Mr. Bean jauntiness.

Those inner resources, that instinct for survival, Ut attributed to his savvy family, and his years wheeling and dealing with the Americans. Ut, even now and after all the afflictions, seemed immensely proud of that 'American' period of his life.

'I would have thought that having an American past was still something to keep quiet about,' I asked.

'If you have any past that is not *theirs*,' he said sharply, 'it is something to keep quiet about. I will introduce you to someone who has a deeper history than mine. She is better, too, at being careful.'

*

THE OLD lady poured green tea from a porcelain teapot and looked about warily. She was stooped, slightly so, untrusting and alert. She wore a necklace of jade: her Chinese grandfather brought the stones in Shanghai and had the necklace made by a local jeweller to present it to his wife on their fifth wedding anniversary in 1936. Over the years, all the family's other treasures were sold off or used to bribe officials; those shimmering green stones were all that remained of her family legacy.

The family villa in Saigon was once one of the city's showplaces. Her parents also owned a dry season country home in the highlands near Dalat. They'd visit for weeks at a time, riding elephants and swimming in the hot, dry autumns, then return to Saigon for the rainy seasons.

Madame Mai poured tea with an air of priestly stiffness. She was performing the sort of chores that others once routinely did for her. Hers was one of the rich old intermarried families—part Vietnamese, part Chinese, a smattering of French blood—who made their money out of smoothing business relations between the three races of old Annam. Now old, tiny, and delicate, a little lame from rheumatism, she used a walking stick that had a dragon's head knob carved from ivory, inlaid around its edge with mother-of-pearl. I admired her instantly for the tenacity with which she had clung to a life and a way of life that she loved.

In 1975, she said, the new communist government gave her three weeks to surrender the family property. Three weeks to abandon lands and houses and furnishings collected and held for generations. That grace period, she was told, would allow her to put her possessions in order for a proper reckoning by 'the people.' She never worked as hard as she did in the next forty-eight hours, stripping the Saigon house. She took out everything she could, even copper plumbing. Even the marble baths. She would sell them for whatever price she could get. Saigon was so chaotic in those days that she knew she could get away with it; if asked, she would say that the house had been vandalized by Americans. *They* wouldn't dare dispute that. But she was not going to just give *those people* her mother's home, her grandmother's home, to live in as her family had lived. *They* were going to get as little as possible from her.

A stab in the back is what happened, of course. And by a man who had worked for her father for twenty years. Always helpful. Oh, yes, always polite, always solicitous. Her mother had looked after one of his sons when the boy was once sick, and the man only started to show his true self when the Americans began their retreat. He tried to stop her father from selling the furnishings from the Dalat house, furnishings her father had agreed to sell to a Canadian diplomat posted back to Ottawa. The servant wanted the family's things for himself. So he turned in her father to the Viet Cong; her father disappeared; she never learned what happened.

It was terrible. Other servants disappeared. The house in Dalat, she heard, had been set ablaze. Throughout that April she expected to be killed in her bed. And what did they do when they got the Saigon villa? Ruin it. Chickens in the flower garden! What use were flowers to *them*? They didn't even repair the plumbing for their own use; they merely constructed an outhouse where a fountain once stood.

One local party man even travelled to the 're-education' camp where Madame Mai had been sent to complain in person about conditions in the house. The ceiling fans didn't work, what should he do? Where were the keys to the attic, the basement, the cupboards? They didn't know how to live in such a place; they couldn't be bothered to learn. Half the time they were too drunk to do anything properly.

Destroy, destroy, destroy. That's all they wanted. That's all they knew how to do. They'd be in the house a year, she remembered thinking, and it would be a ruin. And it was, too. Years later she went and saw what had been done; the place had been ravaged. One by one, possessions, even architectural details, had been stripped and carted away. Ash and cinder were everywhere: what beloved things, she wondered, had been burned?

As she spoke, Madame Mai's eyes temporarily closed and she touched a distended vein in her temple—as though remembering yet another irreversible loss. After her eviction, Madame Mai moved a few cherished pieces of furniture into a small apartment in the city's outlying 11th district, which she returned to after nineteen months in the camp. 'The old Cau Lac race course was near, and so when I went out for walks I could remember my childhood, dressing up and going with my father to watch the horses.' It was a pretty apartment, and of course in no time at all *they* wanted that too. The district party boss came to her door four times. There was nothing to stop him: no law, no personal discipline, no party discipline, certainly no code of honour. No respect for her at all. He said that the party demanded the furniture she had salvaged so that it could be used in its district head-quarters and she replied: 'You have taken enough.'

The third time the party boss appeared he came with his wife, who nosed through the black lacquer and mother-of-pearl inlaid chest and even patted the mattress on her bed. They left for a moment and then returned, backed by four Viet Cong men in uniform with holstered pistols. 'It is too much for someone who lives alone. Don't you agree this is too much for one person? Aren't you frightened having so much when others have so little?' the party apparatchik said, solicitously.

Yes. She was frightened; she was frightened of him. All the same, she wasn't going to give him the satisfaction of seeing her scared and intimidated. But what could she do? She could not sell her things as she had before. Besides, the dong was worth practically nothing and possessing dollars would send her back to prison if she were caught with them. But *they* still wouldn't get her things. At least not from her, anyway. Her neighbour had a son who was an officer in the regular army and she offered the things to him. The boy and his army chums came with a truck the same day to haul the furniture away.

The next morning the party boss returned. Enraged, he ordered Madame Mai's arrest. They marched her to the party headquarters where a 'trial' would be held. Some of her friends went to the officer and explained what had happened. Perhaps he would tell them what really happened? 'You surprise me,' said the officer, 'I know nothing about this matter.'

So it was back to prison, a camp felling trees in a forest near the Cambodian border. Chutes of rain soaked through the hut that imprisoned her, she recalled. It had a mat on the floor and she shared it with four former prostitutes. She was released after a year.

I asked her if she ever thought of fleeing. The 'boat people' were everywhere in the news back in those years. Anyone, everyone with some dollar savings was escaping. Surely she could have gotten out, too?

'I wasn't going to go away,' she told me. 'I belong here. They will have to kill me if they want to get rid of me. Besides, where would I go?'

Not surprisingly, those experiences made her cautious, but this didn't stop her daring to become one of the first private business owners in the city after the party relaxed its stranglehold on the economy. The air conditioner factory she operated—she secured the start-up capital from family friends in France—was an immediate success. 'How can you fail making and selling air conditioners here?' she laughed.

Prosperous again, she was as superstitious as she could be. She saw signs that things were going wrong everywhere. Every so often, she admitted, she had dreams that frightened her. Even when she tried to put a better 'spin' on her dreams—how quickly American jargon gets around the world, thanks to CNN—the next day she would still shift one of the factory's employees from one job to another just because she sensed the need to do so; or she wouldn't receive guests or meet with business partners. No one but employees would be allowed to enter the factory; no one would go out of her office in the Tân Bình district. 'People complain. They can hear us moving around inside here, but I won't let anyone go to the door.' Her mother, she said, was even worse. 'She would have a dream and

the next morning we would pack our things and be off to Dalat for a
month.' Madame Mai kept a surplus of good luck charms on top of
her desk, fingering them every now and then as she spoke.

*

THE CITY that for a generation symbolized Asia more than any
other seemed exotic to many Vietnamese: decades after reunification
people from the north still held Saigon to be not merely foreign but
suspect terrain. They spoke of people from Saigon and the south as
if they were members of an alien tribe. There was nothing
mysterious in this. History had made the Vietnamese one of
mankind's great secret societies, a race long before they could be a
people and a nation. Among the Vietnamese, safety only seemed
possible when cultivating private distinctions. You were not in the
country very long before you began to discover that—north or
south—you would not dare to ask two or three Vietnamese to meet
without telling each the names of all the others who might arrive at
the meeting. Vietam remains too full of enemies and feuds for even
the most casual of encounters to be lightly tolerated.

    If not exactly foreign still, Saigon remained haunted by its past.
The Gallic appearances and common usage of English deceived you
into thinking that a modern openness existed. Instead, everywhere
there was the furtive whispering you find in isolated villages when a
stranger appears. Ask the whereabouts of this or that place, this or
that person, and you would receive 'I have no information' as the
most common reply, if you received a reply at all. To savour the
possibility of a looming treason seemed to be a private delight of
many.

    There was a special Vietnamese vanity in that insistence that life
was all duplicity. Naturally enough, you began to play your part and
act as if you were deceived. In buildings, shops, restaurants, bars,
any outspoken or demanding voice disturbed; more than that, it
offended. It was more than rude, and like speaking your mind openly
here it stripped the mystery from any encounter. The eyes of
everyone you met—cabbies and cadres alike—conveyed that
morbid wariness.

    Reasons for this were not hard to guess. Today the war, despite years of *doi moi* (meaning economic renovation, a Vietnamese *perestroika*, and just as incompetently managed here, it seems, as by Russia's Gorbachev), remained in the fabric of life throughout Vietnam, fixed in both the emotions and the economy, dominating not only collective and individual memory, but visions of the future. There came a point at which almost every conversation—personal and private, commercial, or casual—referred to the war. Communist party officials would relax on the rooftop verandas of their large houses, enjoying the cool twilight air and the scents of flowering trees, and looking out toward the hulk of what was the American embassy and would suddenly interrupt the flow of conversation to tell you about the day *it* happened: the combat green helicopters rising from the American embassy roof and the bodies sometimes falling back to earth on that April day in 1975. Their descriptions were rarely remarkable, but they were remarkable things to hold in the memory. Younger ones among the cadres remembered how they climbed to the tops of trees and buildings to watch the panorama of fires leapfrogging across the city, like children watching a fireworks display. In their retelling, a certain glow—heroic and dreadful and dizzying all at once—suffused those years.

Saigon under the French boomed; manpower poured in from throughout the Vietnamese empire; from China, too. At one point in the 1920s men outnumbered women by two to one, so prostitution thrived. Orphanages were soon established by Sacred Heart nuns. The harbour heaved with all the ships. Saigon became something of an international city. If, in that era, imitation of the West didn't run deeper than the *colon* aristocracy, then the Saigon of the pre-World War II decades with its *nouveau riche bourgeoisie* (French, Vietnamese, and Chinese), its administrative high society, its demimonde lively enough to attract the likes of André Malraux, became sufficiently Western to lavish more than a degree of contempt on other parts of the Vietnamese empire.

The conventional view was that America's intervention in Indochina was as imperialist as the French 19th-century land grab, but in observing Saigon this increasingly came to seem an absurd jibe. Like George W. Bush's invasion of Iraq in 2003, the American mission was purely sententious and military; nowhere was there evidence of the *civilizing* preoccupations of a colonizing power—

sewers and other forms of drainage, railways, structures and infra-structures built to last. In Saigon, the US embassy and the old Abraham Lincoln library exhausted the services of the lone official architect sent by Washington over the course of the war years. Those two buildings survived all sorts of bombings because that architect incorporated a rocket-screen into a decorative feature of the outside wall. This, however, was a slim achievement compared to the French-built post office, the Roman Catholic cathedral, the several *lycées*, and the solid old planter clubs like the Cercle Sportif Saigonnai. That most elite of *colon* clubs survives nowadays only in pieces of club crockery. Old and broken tea cups are now used for sugar and condensed milk; when they go, the name will have vanished.

Planning and maintenance characterize even the briefest, most brutish of empires; apart from instituting a legal system, there are not many other imperial virtues. America wasn't pledged to plan and maintain. All the American buildings spoke of indifferent improvisation and temporary design—prefabs, huts, shelters of plywood. In the decrepitude of these buildings that I encountered, a willfulness was revealed: as in Iraq in 2004, America didn't intend to stay in Vietnam any longer than was necessary to stop the Asian dominos from falling, and so no vision of the country, except abstract notions of political and military order, were ever formulated, let alone articulated, by those making policy in Washington. Most of the American-built structures were dilapidated or falling down—some looted, some pulled apart for lumber or sheet metal—and, seeing this advanced state of decay, you sensed that in a matter of time, perhaps merely a few years more, there will be little physical evidence that over fifty-thousand Americans had died in that country. There remain, I was told by Ut, poisoned rice paddies between the straggling fingers of the Mekong Delta, and scores of blondish, freckled, and black-skinned men and women scattered in sidewalk crowds. Before my eyes, those unusual features were being submerged.

II

Victor Hugo, Saint

THE NEXT EVENING I made use of a formal introduction I secured before arriving in Saigon. I dined at the home of Phuc Tien, editor of the magazine *Saigon Times* who was probably the only Oxford graduate in Vietnam, having attended Greene College on a Reuters fellowship.

Locating Phuc's home wasn't easy. Despite the presence of foreign consulates and scattered ministries, Saigon's third district was ghetto-crowded, with every kind of smell and noise. The brown-black smoke from cars using kerosene-adulterated fuel was like a hot fog that seared the skin and felt barbed in the lungs. As darkness fell irregularly spaced floodlights created the effect of a canopy that appeared to press down on everything. It was far too noisy to talk to the taxi driver.

Frustrated at the cabby's inability to negotiate the maze of side streets to find Phuc's address I paid him off and hurried out of the taxi. Streets ran parallel to the main road in numerical order. Turning away from the lights and smoke of Nguyen Vân Trôî Dong, the district's major road, I entered an area where narrow lanes opened onto narrower alleys lined with little low houses. Some way off, the main street glowed and roared but the lights in these lanes and alleys were dim, the paths overhung with shadows, the noises domesticated and subdued. This was no unregulated slum; the lanes were too straight and paved, and—even though the scale was small—there was a harmony of layout and building that suggested an official plan. Phuc later confirmed that this was one of the city's first post-war municipal developments. He lived here because it was one of the more 'serene' parts of Saigon.

Phuc's house was an open-fronted concrete structure, thirty feet wide, spacious by Saigon standards. Exterior concrete walls were painted grey; inner walls were painted sky blue. The front room where I was received was fifteen feet deep with a doorway at the back leading to the kitchen, where his wife Khué was cooking. Near that door shoes and slippers were stored on a shelf built into the concrete wall.

In the space above the kitchen was the sleeping loft that Phuc used as his home office. Exposed wiring ran from the kitchen into the loft where an Apple PowerMac computer stood on a plank desk. These lofts were vital to Vietnamese urban life. Without them, houses could not provide the space that a family needed, and Khué was well advanced in a pregnancy. Phuc's was the first such sleeping loft I had seen, but I came to notice them all the time, in cities and in villages, over the coming weeks; and began to understand how so many large families—in no way merely the poor—managed to live in one or two small rooms. Every night, all over Saigon living rooms changed their function; various portions of a house like Phuc's— essentially that main drawing room—became a place for sleeping. With a sleeping loft you utilized the volume of the room.

We had been talking in the lane outside Phuc's home. He seemed agitated, slightly embarrassed and certainly distracted as we spoke about his home. At first I thought that he found it indiscreet, or discourteous, to be talking in the open about where he lived with all those curious ears listening. Then I realized that there was something else he wanted to discuss, but he could not bring himself to say it. Finally, Khué joined us outside, asking her husband: 'Have you taken Ken yet?'

'No, not yet,' came the sheepish reply.

'Is there a problem?' I asked. Phuc fell silent, standing in the lane in that dim light, in his patch of crowded Saigon, saying nothing. At that moment he seemed the wrong size for the place; indeed, for a Vietnamese he was a big man, the same height as me, with shoulders as wide. He was freshly dressed, as if for relaxation, in a flowery printed shirt and grey khaki trousers. Above his broad smile was a wispy, Mexican bandit's moustache.

'Not a problem. Just a formality. In order for you to come into our home, we must inform the area party secretary. I went to see them before coming home earlier, but they asked that I bring you to see them. You don't mind, do you?'

'Not at all. It'll be interesting.'

'Maybe for you,' he said, in a half-joking voice tinged with uncertainty.

The three of us set off, the lane sloping down from both sides into a shallow, dust-filled trough. The cries of the street were unforgettable; the air split and bludgeoned by them. In one or two windows women sat sewing, or nursing babies.

When we arrived at the neighbourhood party headquarters, Phuc knocked at the door as children in the lane mocked me, threatening with kung fu stances and awkward kicks. It seemed traditional play, in no way intended to offend. It was a difficult moment for Khué though, trying to shoo the children, keep their dignity, and yet preserve courtesy to Phuc and myself.

The door opened. We entered a vestibule, removed our shoes, and went up cinder block steps to a gallery which ran right around a sunken paved courtyard. After the dust and heat of the lane, the tropical night seemed benign, perfect even. I would have liked to pause and ponder the courtyard with its lone orange tree and pale awning. But a bare-footed soldier was seated cross-legged a few feet ahead in the gallery with a submachine gun. We turned into a concrete-floored empty room and sat down in silence beside an electric fan. Three other men in the room smiled, at once expectant and encouraging.

'He is coming,' Phuc said, 'Stand.'

We stood to attention as the district party leader swept into the room in regal display. He was a smaller and slighter figure than Phuc. Hungry-looking, his cheeks were sunken, and he had distrustful brown eyes set above a mouth with such large gaps between his teeth that, when he smiled, he took on a hobgoblin's aspect. His beard, neatly trimmed like a moustache, made it hard to guess his age. His two button suit was a pale fawn colour, and made of the thinnest cotton, which he wore with an open-necked shirt. His fingers were stubby and, unusual among Vietnamese men, their backs and his forearms were rich with silky black hair. The other party cadres in the room appeared to fall forward behind him—a flurry of solicitousness. Allowing one or two to shake his hand, he gave each a benediction, an exultant hiss escaping his pursed lips. Following his lead, we took our seats. The seats were small like all the furniture. Nothing was big save the district leader's authority. He said nothing; only seemed to stare unflinchingly ahead as if reviewing the troops. The other officials sat erect, with servile grins.

This was no interview, Phuc said; I was not to ask questions. Suddenly, a door blew shut and we were in darkness: the electricity failed. The room became hot with resentment and embarrassment. Breathlessly, patronizingly, he grunted to his aides, who bowed and scraped and fled the room. Another cadre thought of testing a fuse and the lights and air conditioning obediently returned.

The district leader announced that he approved of my visit to Phuc's home. Yes, he approved of contacts with Americans; yes, there was uncertainty in such meetings, but they are beneficial so long as they did not serve 'backward political interests.' As he spoke, he sweated and rolled his eyes. He puffed his chest authoritatively, like a bullfrog, and sweated some more; ritual hospitality held him uneasily curbed. Appalled at his arrogant pose, I still felt that there was something genuine in his bullfrog's rage: the hopeless bewilderment of a party hack having to accept a representative from a world he despised. There was never a chance that he would say no to my visit: I knew it, and he knew that I knew it. His real problem was that, like everyone else in the party machine, he was caught in a maze of friends and enemies. People who were his friends milked him; people who were his enemies watched his every move for deviations. He was inclined to hate me, and saw the decision that he had to make about me, so seemingly simple, as a distraction and, worse yet, a risk.

Back in Phuc's home, all was friendliness and warmth. Khué had prepared a feast. The scale of the meal delighted, then caused me to fret. What was Khué thinking? An American appetite: how could she possibly tame it? How much might I need to consume? How much would I demand? How could she even begin to guess? *These Americans, their appetites could be unlimited. Take, take, take.* There were Vietnamese pancakes and a chicken salad with lime and red onions. There was a beef dish with mint wrapped in spinach leaves. There were crisp fried insects and fearsome-looking, but mild-flavoured, dragonfruits. Mounds of cherry-sized plums sat in the middle of the table; some of the other fruits looked so strange that, at first, I thought they might have been fish. Phuc offered me a piece of jackfruit, which tasted something like a cross between a pineapple and an over ripe melon. You dipped the yellow fruit into a blend of salt, sugar, and mixed chillies. The combination of sweet fruit and piquant dip was exquisite.

*

OUTSIDE THE Cao Dai temple at Tay Ninh palm trees stood like Lakota warriors with feathered headdresses, huddled together in furtive conversation. Those palms and the other trees about had no beauty—they could have been an exhibit in some pictoral dictionary for the words 'barren' or 'parched.' Because of their size, I thought that their voracious need for water might be the cause of the extreme dryness you saw everywhere. Some of the palm fronds seemed burned, like cigar ashes about to drop. One or two had small flowers, but even this did not give them the slightest hint of beauty—the flowers were a sickly pink, like the frosting on one of those factory-made ice cream cakes. Dusk cast a slight, humanizing touch on that sooty desolation, as if for a moment the world was under examination by God's empathizing eye.

It is hard to say how seriously the Cao Dai took their religion because the faith seemed to be a matter of every believer making up his or her own rules and saints as they went along. Some Cao Daiists were married by Roman Catholic priests, some by Cao Dai monks, some in official communist party ceremonies. Some had their children baptized; some did not. In temples some lit chai sticks before their favourite ikon, and others brought bottles to the temples—old medicine bottles, old Coke bottles, green, clear, bottles of every type, glass and size—and elderly female monks filled them with what may or may not have been holy water, which believers then took home. For most of the faithful, the primary contact with their religion came on public holidays like Tet, and at funerals. Cao Daiists celebrated something like the Catholic funeral mass, but the main site of the ceremony was at the grave. Coffins, ornately carved of a creamy stone like ivory, were opened and everyone peeked in for one last look and some chanted quietly. Old women dropped to their knees and butted their heads against the coffin or some nearby monument. When the mourning ended, they looked dazed and walked about in slow circles. Before the coffin was covered they dropped little sheets of ersatz paper money into it.

In the centre of the compound was the great Cao Dai temple, the Vatican of the faith. Half-a-century old, its facade was covered with figures—the Cao Dai Pope and high priestess most prominently. When you looked closely at the individual faces of the statues and carvings, you saw the expressions of the old bearded European prophets and saints. Move away from the terracotta facade and the effect became more Oriental.

Before the church door a kind of carnival of the faith was in progress. The scene was grim, and the people—a beggar's opera crowd— looked as squalid as any I had seen in Vietnam. There were the usual market women hawking food: a few melons and bananas, steamed rice, sugar cane; pottery and basket weaving in ugly shapes and colours (there were no tourists to attract, really, but they were ready): hideous little toys and trinkets, second hand medallions were lying among the vegetables. Everything a family might possess was for sale.

In a cleared space a young lunatic pranced, with muddied face and matted hair. He was dressed in a long Ho Chi Minh nightshirt, blue, ragged and ratty. As he strutted and pranced he looked dehydrated and exhausted. A little band of grinning boys tormented and goaded him; not one of them was more than ten.

At noon a bell rang and you entered the temple for the service. The faithful entered in silent lines, their pecking order distinguished by their robes—aquamarine, scarlet, saffron—each believer holding out his or her arms and sliding silently across the stone floor toward the altar. Before the altar the aged high priest was laying out full length, forehead pressed on the stones. A long day's journey through the heat had brought the faithful here, but the mortification in this procession was only beginning. Here was the atmosphere of a Lenten fast in a poor village in Spain or Portugal, and I suddenly realized that maybe this was the population of heaven—these elderly, beaten, ignorant yet hopeful faces. Five minutes, ten minutes passed and the arms of the aged worshippers were still outstretched. A young woman in white robes—she looked like a novice nun—moved her way up the nave on her knees, and behind her in the same attitude was a young man. It was a slow, sad procession toward the cluster of Cao Dai saints at the altar. I would have thought that life here was mortification enough for anyone, but like those destined for Catholic sainthood the Cao Dai faithful sought out greater happiness than allotted to them in this world, and the road to such happiness was pain.

In 1995, in the northwest Mekong delta and in regions west of the Bassac river, a place where Vietnamese settled among Khmers a century ago, colonizing a vast (mostly uninhabited) wasteland of scrub, mountain, and marsh, the communists unleashed a purge on religious cults. Since the days of the Nguyen empire, the Bassac region had served as refuge and breeding ground for all manner of prophets, magicians, and faith healers, and for the secret societies that flourished in the tangled undergrowth of Vietnam's fusty Confucian world. In the 1830s, one charismatic shaman named Phat Thay Tay-An predicted that 'men from the West' would destroy the Vietnamese empire. Widely propagated, his teachings incited two savage (and savagely suppressed) local rebellions against the French, one in 1875, another in 1913. The hostility of 20th century governments, of all ideological stripes, to newfangled religions and sects was but a continuation of the old ruling caste suspicions that sects were *ipso facto* subversive, demanding to be crushed. Throughout the 20th century, anti-government agitation in the region arose not among the educated, but from society's depths—peasants and low civil servants touched only by colonialism's backwash. Bitter at the wealth others displayed, Vietnam's impoverished and culturally adrift lived in a no-man's land between mushrooming cities and the hermetic villages of the forest.

In 1925 a group of second rank civil servants discovered, aided by a medium, a spirit revealed as the Cao Dai, or supreme god of the universe. Within a year the group became a full-blown sect celebrating the 'third amnesty of God'—the first amnesty being that of Christ and Moses, the second of the Buddha and Lao Tzu. Taking the Masonic eye of God as their symbol, the Cao Dai worshipped all the world's religious leaders, elevating such figures as Jeanne d'Arc and Victor Hugo, as well as the Taoist gods, into their panoply of saints. Their first grandmaster, a shopkeeper, modelled the new faith on the Catholic Church—owning land, dispensing welfare, engaging in education and public works. Twenty thousand believers in Cochin China joined the Cao Dai in the faith's first year, including many officials of the imperial administration.

Sudden, miraculous, the growth of the Cao Dai revealed how fractured traditional society had become under French rule. From self-sufficiency, the peasantry became dependent on absentee landowners, Chinese merchants, French administrators, and the vagaries of the international rice market. Many fled the land; villages lost their sway— why worship your ancestors or the mandarin-genii when those household gods held no power over your future? The Cao Dai and a cousin sect, the Hoa Hao, posed a seductive alternative: a way to restore spiritual communion between man, heaven, and earth.

Today, the army, not communism, holds Vietnam together, giving the country some rest after decades of drift and rhetoric. Since 1985, with the help of foreign (primarily Asian) investors, Saigon had sprouted new hotels; main roads were repaved; the beginnings of services appropriate to a modern economy had begun to appear. From this period of relative tranquillity there grew up an educated generation, the first Vietnamese generation in fifty years to know peace and stability. But stability, combined with an absence of belief, provoked restlessness—which was expressed in the return of the sects that were, like the Cao Dai, more than ritual; for they spoke of the injustices done to the peasantry and the satanic ways of foreigners.

The modern world, we know, is filled with all sorts of strange sects, people who move around America's west and south, Canada's eastern provinces, Switzerland's rural cantons; men and women who receive information only through the most tenuous chains of rumour, hearsay, internet clutter and trickle down. Such people seemed comprehensible in Indochina; for to look at the life of one man or one woman is to wonder how, with so little to hold on to over the decades in the way of law or country, anyone could withstand so many direct hits on his or her personality.

*

NGAN HA must have been in her late seventies, small and slight in the Vietnamese way; in the street I might have passed her by. Within her own home, a few miles from the Cao Dai temple, detached from the Vietnamese crowd, her aging beauty shone; and it was possible to see the care with which she dressed—blouse, sash, silken trousers. It was also possible to see beyond the ready Vietnamese smile (after only a week in the country I often found these frozen smiles disquieting) to her exquisite manners, and to see in that ferocious will to endure—her family lost all its money and social position when they fled the north of Vietnam with the country's partition—the representative of a high and vanished civilization. Ngan Ha retained the disciplined pride of her ancestors, and that aristocratic pose had been transformed into a kind of courageous scepticism. Her face was serene and open; she held her head high, with a slight backward tilt; her bones were fine, her eyes bright, though depressed in their sockets, and her lips were classically shaped over perfect teeth, though stained by cigarettes and tea. She spoke English well, in the hoity-toity way of foreigners when they address Americans in 'English' English. But she was not being superior; only singing songs from a better time. It was all part of the ritual of welcome; among aristocrats even the downtrodden were courteous.

Ngan Ha described herself as one of the 'statistical Catholics' of Vietnam, but she had received no religious training. Her family was among the hundreds of thousands of Roman Catholics who fled Hanoi when Vietnam was divided into north and south in the 1950s. She had absorbed her religious knowledge as a young girl. Ngan Ha was not sure if she believed in an afterlife; and she seemed doubtful that such a belief was in any case doctrinal to Catholicism. Nowadays, she was dabbling in the faith again; the day of my visit was Ash Wednesday and I could see the priest's blackened thumbprint on her brow. In the life of the Church with its rules and rituals, she began to find and reconstruct for herself something like the old feudal community that no longer existed.

Ngan Ha belonged to the old nobility, but nowadays that only meant that she was not of the peasantry; the skills required of the nobility in the French colonial era were not high and so the family slipped into a kind of genteel poverty. Her grandfather, as a noble, was given a modest white-collar job in the French administration; Ngan Ha's father was a bookkeeper for French planters. It was possible for Ngan Ha, as a noblewoman, to go to a French school. Fees were low, and Ngan Ha, it turns out, did not have to pay any thing at all. The schooling was good; some graduates went on to the Sorbonne in Paris. Early in 1942 the Japanese occupied Indochina. The message from Radio Tokyo was that the mighty Imperial Japanese Army would bring the French colonies and protectorates of Indochina their independence. So, just as they nowadays welcome Japanese businessmen, many Vietnamese welcomed the Japanese soldiers as liberators.

Because Petain's collaborating government at Vichy reached an agreement with the Japanese for the French to continue administering the three provinces or *pays* of Vietnam—French prefects would act under Japanese tutelage just as their compatriots were acting under Nazi control back home—French teachers were allowed to stay on in their posts, but they now were joined by a few select Vietnamese. A new headmaster was appointed, an old man from Japan. For six months classes continued in the same manner as when the school was under undoubted French control. Then—it is amazing how life goes on, even during the most tumultuous upheavals—Ngan Ha enrolled in a 'higher school, not quite a university,' which was not far from the family's villa in Hanoi. Even more Japanese administrators were to be found there. But the Japanese could not master foreign languages. Recognising this failing, or so it seems, the Japanese appointed more and more Vietnamese to teaching and administrative posts, though the Vietnamese, like the remaining French, worked under Japanese supervisors.

Slowly, over time, the Vietnamese teachers—inspired by Japanese propaganda about liberating Asia from the white, European empires—began to use their classes to preach a mild Vietnamese nationalism. Japan's lightning victories over the British, Dutch and French, stripping them of their Pacific empires, shattered notions of European invincibility. Yet, despite emancipation from colonial rule, the goodwill felt toward Japan dissipated fast. It was clear to Ngan Ha that Vietnam's economy was being subverted to assist the Japanese war effort. European racism had been replaced by the Japanese sense of themselves as Asia's master race. Two incidents occurred at this time that made Ngan Ha declare her opposition to the Japanese. University authorities ordered that all male students shave their heads, and that classes be segregated by sex. Here was the barracks discipline of the Shinto monastery.

One day on the parade ground—male students faced mandatory military training—a student was slapped across the face by a Japanese officer. All the Vietnamese felt humiliated. That afternoon, Ngan Ha and her friends held a protest demonstration in that same university courtyard where the military drilling took place. Twenty of them, teachers as well as students, were arrested by the Japanese secret police and taken to jail.

Confined to cells, the students learned of people being tortured for anti-Japanese offenses and even for listening to Free China Radio broadcasts from Chiang Kai Shek's redoubt in Chungking. Ngan Ha's group—four other women took part in the protest—were treated like political prisoners; they continued to be disciplined in the way of the Shinto monastery. Men were beaten with bamboo staves, but it was only a ritual humiliation. Soaked, the bamboo staves split at the end; they didn't rip the skin nor do much more than sting; they made only a showy cracking noise, Ngan Ha recalled. The women were kept in solitary confinement, verbally abused by the guards. No one touched them, there were no sexual assaults, though Ngan Ha and the others feared such at every moment.

After a few weeks of this, Ngan Ha and her group were released and expelled; Ngan Ha never completed her education. The students got off lightly because Ho Chi Minh and his supporters—some now armed and living in the northern hills near the China border—were quiet, and the Japanese, who did not take the nationalists seriously, also did not seek to antagonize them unnecessarily. Ho never believed that Japan would lose the war, or so Ngan Ha said; he didn't even believe it when word arrived that atomic bombs had been dropped on Hiroshima and Nagasaki. It was only after the Japanese surrender, when British and French officers under Lord Mountbatten used captured Japanese troops to keep order in the colony, preferring to re-arm the enemy than to trust the Vietnamese, that Ho began to plan for immediate independence. There were desultory talks with the Americans and the French about a timetable for independence over the first two years of peace, but these were 'worse than useless,' Ngan Ha said. Years of fighting with the French followed.

Ngan Ha was now without hatred or bitterness of any sort. The events of her life were simply too big; there was no one to blame. She harboured no ill feelings towards either the French or Japanese or Americans; she respected all of them as peoples who, in the end, honoured a bargain. The Japanese had the reputation in Indochina of being hard negotiators, but Ngan Ha had been told that the Japanese were more generous nowadays than the French. Ngan Ha was without rancour and I could see that she had won through to a kind of peace. Despite her permanent smile, her grace, there was an Indochinese sadness in her, and it was the sadness of a woman who felt she had been left alone, and was now—after the French time, the Japanese time, the American time, the ten years of Ho's orthodox communism, the decades of desultory, Deng-style economic reforms—without a cause.

More than once the world had seemed to open for her and her family, only to close just as quickly. With her husband, who served the French as an administrator but avoided service with the Americans, she laid low during the early communist years. Though often brutish (many friends disappeared for two or three years of 're-education'), Vietnam's unification appeared to revive the country. Ho Chi Minh's puritanical communism, however, wasn't what she wanted for her children and grandchildren. Now, over the past few years, Ngan Ha sensed that something new was happening, something that she also did not understand. The country was opening to investment, and everywhere there were businessmen: Taiwanese, Japanese, Koreans, Thais, Australians, all sorts of Europeans. Lately, even Americans had appeared. Ngan Ha feared that she was losing her grandchildren to this new turn of the screw. They insisted on speaking English, even in the house; they no longer wanted to live with the family but to find flats in Saigon. Ngan Ha's son and daughter had sensed that the world was changing; Ngan Ha had seen so many changes that she feared that she could no longer learn the rules when an important new game was afoot. She advised her grandchildren to ride out the changes, to commit themselves to nothing, but all five of them wanted to join the new world, to join and see a little more.

At the end of her story, just before we separated, Ngan Ha said, 'I've been lucky. I haven't been like so many others, switching to another wavelength under pressure.'

'Another wavelength?'

'You know how people are here. Perhaps you don't. If they feel frustrated in their work or career or lives, they put on another face.'

Today, with Vietnam at peace for decades, with the coming of new industries and new types of learning, with the arrival in Indochina of personal computers and all the paraphernalia of today's high-tech civilization, the world was growing stranger and stranger to people like Ngan Ha, who had survived so many changes over so many years. And like anyone who had seen her world collapse, Ngan Ha feared it would happen again.

After returning to Saigon to hire a boat for a journey into the Mekong delta, I spent my last evening in the city walking in Cholon, the old riverfront Chinatown. Everyone Ut and I passed seemed to smile. Sometimes an old face—leathery skin, somewhat starved, old but ageless, with deep-set, yellowed, fixed eyes—would accost me with a look: 'This place is not what it seems. It is cursed.' That look would make me shudder, but in an instant, after having averted my eyes from so ferocious a gaze, I would turn and look again and the face had vanished. In vain my eyes searched the milling crowds, the traffic rushing by on Hondas and Vespa scooters: through the sharp, slanting light the fading features of the city's fading French buildings. The geometry of Saigon's architectural and human perspectives—the styles of successive imperial overseers, overthrown and absorbed and claimed as their own by the victorious Vietnamese—were perfect for losing things forever.

We walked for about an hour when I came upon a bookshop filled with young people—boys in white shirts and ties, women in white blouses and dark skirts that ran to the knee. There were books in English on business and technical subjects—computers, management, engineering. There was also a large section of English language books on mystical or occult subjects—Taoism, the *I Ching*. To old and young alike, it seemed that this was how the new global civilization appeared: technical skills and magic incantations, an

imported civilization without a real core. Whether people were
moving forward into the new civilization like Ngan Ha's grandchildren, or backward, like Ngan Ha in her decision to return to her
girlhood Catholicism or, again, like the Cao Dai cultists of the
Bassac river valley with their ersatz versions of the old faiths, they
were entering somebody else's world.

Saigon, late that last night, with the young wanna-be westerners
back in their homes, cramming for the future, seemed a city of
matchless decrepitude: muted colours, hard tough boys and girls,
trash. A tropical city, a venal city, one that flourished in times of war
and chaos. No city so often abandoned and betrayed could retain a
shred of romance or illusion. In daylight, Saigon could be beautiful.
That last night, soft and quiet as it was, the city seemed sinister.

III

The Tribunal

I HAVE ALWAYS found a magnetic enchantment in rivers. The Mekong was no different, and I spent a lot of time poking about it during my travels. There was nothing at all romantic about this; at times I felt as uneasy about the Mekong as Joseph Brodsky did about other Asian rivers:

Rivers in Asia are longer than elsewhere, more rich
in alluvium—that is, murkier. As you reach
for a mouthful, your cupped fingers ladle silt,
and one who has drunk this water would prefer it spilt.
Never trust its reflection. Crossing it, cross it on
a raft built with no other hands but the pair you own.
Know that the gleam of a campfire, your nightly bliss,
will, by sliding downstream, betray you to enemies.

More than other rivers the Mekong hypnotized, as it flowed warm and dirty and drowsy. At early morning deep in its delta, and going upriver toward the forests of Cambodia, it seemed, secret and remote—unreal, like a river of myth or in a dream.

Ut expressed little interest in the country through which we floated. Bush, scrub, marshes, swamps: the disorder of it all did not arouse any response in him—except, as he said, there was too much of it. Only as my own expectations began to erode did I begin to gain a dim understanding of that wilderness and how it might frighten a man like Ut, who had escaped it. This came at moments when I was overcome by a feeling that this was a place where nothing could ever really be done. At such moments I began to understand the weariness that infected most peasants. Such a moment came to me on the journey upriver from the Mekong's delta, for centuries the heartland of Vietnam, now merely a rice bowl.

In villages we passed, Ut informed me, only one child in five might go to school after age eight. The cost of school—50,000 dong a month for high school (a little more than $3 at the time), and 30,000 for grammar school—lay beyond the reach of most parents. Men and women tilled the paddies, hardly exercising any modern skills, using the simplest tools and sometimes no tools at all.

The few factories also demanded no skills. The jobs they offered were child's work and children, being cheaper than adults, got the jobs—from the age of nine they were available for a monthly salary of 60,000 dong.

Generation followed generation here. Men were as replaceable as those huts made of grass, scavenger's iron, and palm mattings (green when new, quickly weathering to a yellow grey/black) in which three and sometimes even four generations of a family lived. Men and women knew what they were born to do, and accepted their fate. Every family lived in its own area, defined immemorially; and the pariahs, the scavengers, the madwomen and black-skinned, kinky-haired Amer-Asians lived on the fringe of the village (racism flourished even after the American armies had left, but now it was not the 'gooks' who were despised, but the bastard children of white and black Americans).

When viewed from the river there sometimes rose above village huts the two storey brick or concrete structures of families who might once have owned much of the surrounding land; but this was not social grandeur, it was more like a monument to the squalor and the defeat out which those houses had arisen. Such a family would have been dispossessed by the party; the property given to the local cadre now in control. Decades of war and revolution and the old arbitrariness of power had not changed; nothing seemed likely to change.

Most of the time the Mekong flowed brown, like Earl Grey tea, the sky above it like the wall of some huge blue house, immovable. At an estuary and in those places where the river broadened, the far bank dimmed to a lean hot blur. In narrow channels, branches of the trees on opposite banks almost met overhead. We seemed to be passing display cases of fantastic drapery and millinery, unfolding in absolute silence. Sometimes there was a break where the case had been smashed and the trees uprooted, at other times there were muddy coves where tree ferns made a shade for herons.

Every mile we went upriver thoughts of human possibility dwindled. A thatched hut built upon a platform of stilts would appear, and brown children would be seated, naked, watching the wash of our boat. The children seemed without curiosity or recognition. They sat fixed and still, river light wavering over their bodies. At such moments the Mekong seemed to have become a world trapped in time. It was like the sterile weariness I sensed within Ut in Saigon, where the absence of opportunity left him only a dignified muteness that exacted a heavy toll each day.

It was not that things were stagnant. Electricity had come to the Mekong and its delta. After half a century of sacrifice the communists had at least brought the peasantry that. Imperfectly conceived schemes—new roads, irrigation projects, and catfish farms—were being planned. A few foreign factories arrived—assembly plants for bicycles and Honda motorcycles. But the difficulty, of a peasantry trained only in loyalty and the doggedness of guerrilla war, lay in the people themselves: not just with the mediocrity and epidemic corruption of the leadership provided by the cadres—which they didn't bother to mask—but also with the people lower down, whom modernity was supposed to benefit. How could a people, generation after generation forced to finding consolation only in obedience and survival, be made, suddenly, to want to achieve, to want to *do*?

Noiseless dusk enveloped like a veil as our boat shut its motor and petered in toward shore. The heat felt like a tongue on the skin as I stretched my stiff legs and rubbed the red lumps on my arms made by swarms of river insects. Yawning wretchedly, a man grabbed the bowline and pulled us toward shore, scratching his oiled hair. Ut paid him twenty thousand dong, and the man blinked, grey-lidded like a fowl, in thanks.

The dock was on a dark, marshy bank smelling of dead crayfish, mud, discharging sewage pipes, oil, and tropical weeds that emitted the mould-filled vapours of a compost heap. Lights from the town of Hông

Ngá sent shafts of gold cascading into the still water; these flickered in the pooled gloom like a constellation of river stars or schools of darting golden fish. In the distance, women were standing knee deep in the water, naked above the waist, their arms weaving soap through their hair in an ecstasy of twilight. Standing in the blackness, I watched. Nothing, not a horn or a shout disturbed. For a moment I could hear the women breathing, the silence was so complete.

Turning from the river, the lights of the town raked the black mountain shapes of the forest beyond. Hông Ngá lacked the honking, electronic cacophony of Saigon's nights. Instead it tinkled and clanged with small hard noises, like a forge. Packed tight—sometimes no more than a foot existed between them—houses looked like one-storey concrete jars with corrugated lids. You expected such population density in places like Saigon, but in Hông Ngá, a place where nothing seemed to happen, it was surprising and demanding: overcrowding on such a scale demanded manners; anything less than perfect order, and the place would spin out of control.

After paying off the boatmen Ut led me down a rutted lane shrouded in darkness. Old men playing mah-jong looked up and stared; old women shouted. Babies screamed in the arms of emaciated girls. Young toughs stared down blankly at children. Two girls with sores on their lips, like dark and sticky honey, had insolent boys hanging about them. The eyes of those girls were sad and beautiful, reddened like grapes. The sweet-sour smells of the women, the heavy acrid smells of the men hung in the air.

The small house where we would stay was no different from the other jar-like houses, with a long wire fence running from the front to the back of a yard where the family's oxen were stabled at dusk. An earthenware basin of water was set under an eave beside a door closed save for a slit of orange light from within. Inside were two rooms, one a kitchen area with a chimney corner, charcoal fire smoldering on a heap of white ash as a black pot bubbled. On a metal bench along the white stonewall was a girl, shredding a chicken, singing softly as she ripped strips of yellow flesh from feeble bones. Outside, the air was on fire, but within that cool, cellar-like structure it was like plunging into a dark natural spring.

Dao, the proprietress, was a dark, delicate woman, her black hair drawn back as tight as her smile. Her eyes were small, inky bright like wild berries, and set in a straight, candid gaze. Ut greeted his cousin affectionately. After filling the room with blurred words and rumblings, he then escaped for a moment, returning soon after with six large bottles of cold Tiger beers, which we drank with a dozen eggs fried in oil, some small steamed fish, and spicy casava mixed with rice. More steamed white rice was brought in a large blue bowl, and some pint-sized green bananas and mangoes, which Ut placed against his chest and pared with a penknife. This was a family feast. Bowls of food were passed from hand to hand with gentle ceremony.

The room was whitewashed and had a small red-framed portrait of Ho Chi Minh on the wall opposite the door. Next to it was a wooden crucifix, from which the body of Christ had been prised off. At a table in the corner, in the shadows near the cooking pots, were other members of the family: two sons and another little girl, this one in a green satiny kind of dress that hung loosely over men's trousers. The boys were motionless, sullen, but the girl was active. She talked all the time and was prompted in this by the others, who seemed to find everything she said entertaining. From time to time one of the boys smirked, as though inviting me to look at the girl. Squealing at one stage, the girl ran up the back steps to a sleeping loft, squealed some more and, pounding her feet, provoked fresh bouts of laughter below. She bounced down the steps again, displayed for the others what she had brought down. Then she turned and for the first time I could see her face.

She wasn't a girl at all. She was tiny, not more than four feet tall, middle-aged and probably mad. She showed us, as if we were co-conspirators, what she brought down from the loft: a bowl of dried out rice with the rotting indigo-veined flesh of a small bird's embryo nesting atop it. Was this a gift for her family? For us? Ut couldn't say what she intended. He listened while she jabbered, but said nothing to her. Then she broke away and ran up to the loft once more, this time in silence. Through the loft's entry I watched her dance and swoon; her pale shadow, changing size, could be seen against a white sheet divider or screen in the room—the sheet was fixed to wire netting—like a figure in a shadow puppet play.

I said to Ut, 'Is she a member of the family? An aunt or cousin or something?'

Ut said, 'Oh, no. She's not of our family. Just someone from the village with no place to go.'

As we talked, the mother made preparations for sleep. A clean sheet was spread on a string bed in the front corner of the room, a courtesy for me. From somewhere in the darkness outside Dao's husband came in to assume the role of host.

Phuoc, a small man, though not as small as his wife, looked frail and unwell. Dao seemed a capable and determined woman; her husband a man who, though once all muscle and discipline, had with age become little more than someone shuffling around the house, in everyone's way, getting drunk on his home-made hootch and brooding on the past. He once owned a brick factory in the city, but the cadres had commandeered it decades ago. Now he washed bicycles. He was dark, with a long, silvery goatee. That beard was the old man's lone remaining vanity. In Vietnam different groups of men wore different styles of beard, and Phüoc's beard was that of a mandarin's beard. The more you thought your world had shrunken; the grimmer life became; the more you insisted on holding onto what you were and what you had been. That was the defiant message of the crucifix on the wall and of that dandy's beard.

Phuoc said he was sixty-one. Before Ut could translate that for me he responded by saying that he knew that he looked much older, and what he said was certainly true. At first I had thought him Dao's father, not her husband. Westerners did not look as old as Vietnamese, Phuoc said. He knew: he remembered the French and the Americans: some of them were seventy but they worked as hard as boys in a field. Phuoc had aged not only because of the conditions of his life, he said, but also because of what had happened in his life. Still, he liked being sixty-one: his father died at thirty-eight. I began to feel affection for him.

We drank more beer, formally offered—bottle by bottle—and tried to make general conversation. Ut did not guide me as to whether my questions were intrusive or pressed. As we spoke Dao was bringing pots and tools from outside into the house. I wondered about this, and asked Phuoc whether there were many thieves about. It occurred to me that the openness of life here, the communality of it (as of a commune), made people not only vulnerable to communist party watchdogs who could know their every move if they so desired, but to more traditional types of social predators.

The old man said there were thefts every day. There were fights between thieves and homeowners. Sometimes violent ones. If a neighbour's child was the thief and you hit the child trying to protect your property, you could start a feud. 'Were these blood feuds?' I asked.

'Some people are Viet Cong; others hate them,' said Phuoc. 'They are not the right kind of people. Because of their reputation, if someone steal's from them, or if someone attacks one of their children who is stealing, anything can happen.'

'What happens when there is violence?'

'The court is full of such things. We will go tomorrow.'

The municipal court in Hông Ngá was located on an ominous street that was little more than a concrete alley, a passage of aqueous light that was almost impassable because of the throngs of people who walked up and down it, in an endless, scraping parade. Each man and woman seemed trapped in a bubble, surrounded by their own impervious atmosphere. Bump into one, even if you shouldered him or her violently, and nothing would happen; no notice would be taken. The only people who seemed aware of anyone other than themselves were a variety of medicine men in strange frocks scattered and waiting about the alley. One or two were selling live lizards; a dozen were tied to a large stone. Ut told me that the lizards were for strength: you bought and killed the lizard and then ate a certain gizzard.

At the end of the lane was the smell of carnage. A boy, trundling a wheelbarrow of slaughtered pig heads, approached and passed. We stared down at scores of dumb victims. The mouths were pink, the nostrils moist. When we looked up we saw the bloody arms of the workers slashing away. Wherever they moved, skin magically parted, and warm insides poured out. Everything was swiftly decided and divided. An animal brought into the lane a minute or two before disappeared in an instant. Watching this slaughter, Ut pulled his blazer tight around him as if there was a nip in the air.

Next to the court building an old black cat was sitting in a shop window, staring fixedly at people entering and exiting the building and waxing her tail. 'She's the biggest cat around,' said Phuoc, 'I've watched her many times. One night I saw her catch and eat a rat.'

We paused and stood in front of the building. Trials were public events here. The party insisted on that: how else were people to learn their civics lessons? Phuoc greeted a man who may or may not have been expecting him. The man was middle-aged, with a calm, observant, and strong-jawed face, with a boxer's flattened nose. He was also small, one of those men who could sit in a chair and not have his feet touch the floor. His world, too, was small; a market city on the edge of the no-man's land wilderness of the Vietnamese/Cambodian border.

Because people bowed and scraped to him as they passed, it soon became apparent that he was a policeman, perhaps a senior one. That cheerful smile probably convinced people to talk to him too readily, and I guessed him to be a good listener, one of those people who probably believe little of what they hear but who look and act as if they believe every word. 'My friend says to go inside to watch,' Phuoc said as he parted from the policeman. 'If you want to talk or ask questions, we can meet with him later.'

Outside, the building's purpose was impossible to misunder-stand—a forbidding bunker, it was a punishment merely to look at it. Within, the courtroom resembled an open-plan, village schoolhouse, where all classes and ages studied in one large room. A place, then, without drama. Safe, even cosy. On the front wall was a large portrait of Ho Chi Minh, framed group photographs and individual photographs of the ruling politburo, the blood red Vietnamese flag with its yellow star hanging above everything. Along one wall was a row of straight-backed chairs. The remainder of the room was filled with wooden benches, arranged like church pews. Along the back of the room three armed guards were in scruffy fatigues My first impression was of young gang members lolling about in wait for the trial of their chief to begin. The room was packed.

Through a side window you saw a double door leading to an inner court where prisoners were led into the yard. They were tied up in twos, thick ropes attached to their wrists. The free end of the rope was held by a khaki-uniformed guard. Their movements did not seem extraordinary, but routine, even friendly. In the courtyard bustle, no one stared or paid too much attention to anyone else. Prisoners chatted derisorily with the guards. One or two stood chewing betel nuts and spitting. Their vacant expressions suggested the paralysis of boredom, not fear. One man, however, had helter-skelter eyes. Two bare-footed prisoners, who brought up the rear of that roped parade, looked mentally defective. They were tied not only at the wrists, but ropes were also knotted at their upper arms, which made them move like marionettes. Still, the whole thing seemed friendly, no one overtly nervous or afraid.

On a raised wooden platform at the front of the room sat the tribunal, a gathering of local party officials who, collectively, acted as judge and jury. They stared ahead, waiting for custom, one or two fingering grubby ledgers. To the side of the desk the court recorder or stenographer pecked away on an old, manual typewriter. The dock where the accused would be kept was a little railed pen in the middle of the room set below the magistrate's table. Two air conditioners roared, drowning out most of what people said, and making much of those trial sessions inaudible to the public, even those seated on the nearest benches.

Many people, peasant women and old men, were seated in the pews. At times I could hear an angry mutter or two. At the back of the court three old men were playing cards and talking softly. A shoeshine boy started to wipe my shoes but Ut shooed him away.

That casual atmosphere seemed incongruous, it made the grave appearances of the depressed looking men being ushered in seem out of place, like actors taking their roles too seriously. As the proceedings advanced, it was hard to know what was going on. People spoke loudly in Saigon; but in that room everyone mumbled. Within that gathering babble, it took some time even for Ut to comprehend what was being said and to relay the information. After a while it became clear that most of the cases involved theft, which meant that the police were not obliged to produce witnesses.

Tied together, three boys were brought before the magistrates's bench. They were watched over by a lean, stork-like man, who paced before them with his hands behind his back. Ut spoke to one of the boys; they seemed happy to discuss their misadventures.

The boys worked in their father's pipe shop and had been charged with theft. They claimed that their neighbour was lying about the whole thing, and had beaten up the youngest of the boys as well. They laughed, seemingly lost and bewildered by their surroundings as the stork-like guard fiddled with the rope that bound them together, smiling and shaking his head as he did. Seated in the row behind them was the neighbour who had pressed the charges of theft against the boys. Stout, he smiled from his stomach upwards, and had unreliable eyes.

In progress at that moment was a hearing involving a man from Saigon charged with a murder by stabbing. The trial made headlines. It was followed by everyone in the court. But the event itself seemed private, unimportant. Barefooted, the accused wore leg irons in addition to the rope manacles all the prisoners had lashed around their wrists. He coughed persistently and though he walked with a strut he was gaunt and stooped, as if he had tuberculosis. Narrow, motionless, almond-shaped, his eyes were unnerving. He was aware of the stir he created; everyone seemed to know that he was a man marked for a firing squad, someone high above the Hông Ngá court's usual suspects, and he was dressed like an outlaw chieftain for his final public performance. Although his long-tailed shirt was grimed around the collar, a decorous yellow and red cotton scarf was knotted about his neck—a man standing out when he should be submissive; asking to be convicted. There was no question of Ut stopping him for a chat.

Noticing his manacles, Ut said: 'You see, we are so poor that only serious criminals get chains. I'm told that it is easy to escape from the courts. The ropes must be why. I think the chains are reserved for political prisoners and killers.'

Momentarily, the magistrates left the room to consult in private on the murderer's case. From another door, a young woman prisoner was led in on a rope. On spying her, a gap-toothed old woman with two young boys at her side—they were seated on the far side of the room—stood and tried to make eye contact, but the young woman ignored them or didn't see them and instead looked at me, a stranger. The young woman's face was round and flat, set atop a craning neck; her skin rough, her hair lacklustre, her eyes empty. Awkward and frayed, she had obviously not been getting enough to eat.

She had bought some property, Ut said, but it wasn't really clear what sort of property it was; she carried the precious documents of ownership in a red plastic envelope that she held in her small hands. A local official claimed that she raised the money to buy the house through selling herself as a prostitute. The party tried to be merciful, about all this, the cadre explained. For three days she was hauled before the party's district committee where, despite every opportunity, she refused to confess to the charge. Not even her neighbours could shame her into truth, he exclaimed, making a big show of their collective disappointment. The local cadres threatened to take her sons away and stick them in an orphanage; still she refused.

What can you do with a woman like that? The cadre shrugged and smirked. The local party leaders of her village were washing their hands of her; it was up to the tribunal. She responded that her conditions were desperate; the bones of her children were brittle, wasting away because she could not afford to feed them. She had only 'two clothes.' Her sons and her house were all that she had. She said that she lived ten kilometres from Hông Ngá, that her husband was dead.

Ut seemed taken aback by this last bit of information. It meant that she had no man, no protector. Still, Ut doubted her story, at least in part; perhaps the husband divorced her because she was indeed a prostitute, or at least a part-time one. 'In the villages, many girls will go to Saigon for some weeks to see family but really they will become prostitutes.' In any case, it would have been more of a disgrace for the woman to admit that her husband had left her, alone and unwanted.

Abruptly, the murder trial resumed and proceeded at a sharp pace. The defendant had been arrested two days before. Despite his shackles, he listened in a swaggering way as a police official read from his file. The defendant said he was at ease because he had done nothing. But the straining of his neck from his manacled arms, the blank, glazed stare of his eyes, became hateful. The magistrates and the prisoner stared, each seeing in the other an enemy who wished only to destroy. Each saw the opposite of himself. A terseness came into the policeman's voice as he read the evidence against the accused. He said that the knife that had been found in the body was owned by the accused; that the man who had been killed was a man of good character who believed in the party and its principles. The defendant owed the deceased the equivalent of four hundred dollars for a motorcycle. No one else in the area would have wanted the man killed. The accused now seemed resigned, accepting, and still. In advance, he was dying a little bit already.

Many of the people who testified against the defendant, PháÅc informed us, were professional witnesses, they appeared and reappeared in various cases; saying whatever the party bid them to say. Phuoc had sat in the court gallery many times; some of the faces of the witnesses became familiar to him over the years. There were others in the gallery who also recognized Phuoc: two women—their faces marked by sun and labour—smiled at him from across the courtroom. These were Hông Ngá's Madame de Farges, they loved the legal atmosphere, as did Phuoc; the court building and its trials was their amusement arcade.

One of the magistrates now ambled away from the table and stood beside Phuoc, staring at me. The two men knew each other slightly, or at least recognized each other. I relayed a few questions through Ut. How did the man feel about these trials?

At first, he seemed to have misunderstood my question. He claimed that he was not corrupt. He did not plan to do the job much longer; he was moving up in the city administration. As he spoke, the murderer was led out of the court, a gentle shove in the back administered just at the moment he was taken out the door. It was now the woman's turn to receive the court's verdict and the magistrate returned to the bench.

The woman offered her documents. They were declined. She shrieked momentarily, caught herself, and spoke more calmly. Title to the property was clear, she said, and she had given three hundred thousand dong to the party cadre to 'register' her claim—she expressly did not use the word bribe, Ut said. But the man took the money and guaranteed nothing. The tribunal of magistrates did not seem to care. The magistrate farthest from us leaned over the table and looked deeply into the woman's eyes. His mouth gaped open and he spoke a few slow words. His eyes stared and glared at her. Distended in his thin face, his teeth were as pronounced as in a stage prop skull. They gave him an air of grinning diabolically. The woman sank in her seat, staring up at the magistrate, blank-faced. Then she turned to face that old woman who was probably her mother, and to face her children. There was a look of pity in their faces, of dumb questioning. The woman was taken away.

IV

Cinnamon Ships

DAWN IN DA NANG: the sun arose with tropical suddenness. Within minutes, the light that flashed off the South China Sea was intolerable to the eyes.

In the dining room of my hotel near the Han River port I drank a bowl of treacly Vietnamese coffee—tar black and sweetened by condensed milk—and ate steamed rice and shredded fish followed by papaya. It was a stale, decayed sort of place, with fraying lace curtains weighted with dust, and what Americans call a 'wet' bar, with a rubber surface, at the far end of the room. Three young men were quarrelling loudly beside it. They were all dark skinned, oily haired, and agitated. One of the three had offended the others, and he was now crying and trying one excuse after another on his mates. When nothing appeased them, he shot up his arms, squared his shoulders, let out an angry cry, and stormed out of the hotel.

Finishing my meal, I found the lobby barred by ladders, pails, and boards. An invasion of plasterers had taken place during breakfast, so the hotel was in turmoil. After two days on a motorcycle journey up to Da Nang along Highway 1, I was keen to stretch, so I started exploring the city, aligning my senses to the smells of the place, and my stomach to the taste of its seafood. Mornings in Italy smack of espresso; Spain in the evening reeks of olive oil. Da Nang too, smelled of oil, and the fumes of that oil, which was used by mothers to light their cooking fires in the street and for burning in the lamps of huts along China Beach; it hit out from all directions with a solid blow that can be revolting, at least at first. Like the stares that had, at times, so bothered me when walking the streets of Saigon, I was gripped by it at first but later came to take no notice.

Before arrival, I had assumed Da Nang to be a provincial city of a few hundred thousand. Instead, perhaps a million people huddled in its small, low concrete houses. There were the usual Catholic churches, official looking colonial buildings, and villas with their small barred windows set high and out of reach, like prison gratings. From the chill and damp of their Central Highlands plantations French *colons* used to come down to Da Nang to warm themselves in the sea. Decades later, American Marines bartered to get posted to China Beach.

In the centre of town, near the harbor, was a sun-drenched plaza with giant red poinsettias sweetly patterned in it, and in its middle the yellow mass of a colonial era mansion, a stout and pompous little place that now housed a collection of artifacts from the Chams, a people who had inhabited this part of the land of Indochina before the Vietnamese people pushed down from China. The museum's door was burned and drowsy like an old peasant's face. I enjoyed the way the sun scorched the building's sandstone till it was ripe as sunflower.

The streets of Da Nang were as white as those of Saigon. The bustling lanes were grey gulfs of wind blown heat. Everything was covered with a fine white dust. Women balanced containers of fresh and dried fish, melons, sugar cane, baskets of oranges and sacks of ducks at both ends of long timber poles perched on their shoulders, the strain showing in brisk, mincing walks that emphasized their feminine daintiness. On one corner a man with a scale was selling a tasteless white local cheese.

Behind Da Nang to the north and west, conical mountains rose steeply. From their peaks you looked down on a flat-roofed city that had forsaken its Oriental character to become a planned grid-like metropolis, as anonymous as any American middle west city. From above, the main arteries of the city appeared shaded by the thick branches of peepul trees under which much of the population seemed to sit—day and night.

How dated everything looked. Not merely out-of-fashion like Ut's polyester blazer with its wide lapels, but tired and worn out. Da Nang seemed to be the place where, what remained of America's mission in Vietnam after April 1975, came to retire and die—jeeps became creaking taxis, the shells of trucks were transformed into storage bins, Quonset huts sliced into roofing shingles, old artillery shell casings served as stilts on top of which sat fishermen's huts. Such resourcefulness incited both respect for Vietnamese ingenuity and a kind of nostalgia. The Marines who so dominated the area in the Sixties probably left most, if not all, of this stuff behind or even as junk, and when South Vietnam's army disintegrated, the more enterprising among its soldiers commandeered the jeeps and trucks for themselves and their families so that, today, those mechanized ghosts prowled the pocked roads of the city and its outlying flat lands, rattling, throttling and wheezing in a kind of anonymous, domestic afterlife.

*

THAT EVENING a warm wind blew. I ate an early dinner, and when paying took out of my wallet something I had almost forgotten. Not knowing what to expect, I hailed a taxi motorcycle and went to call.

The apartment was in a central district, yet the driver had some trouble finding it. The address was straightforward, but even a policeman could not direct us. After prowling about for fifteen minutes or so, a street vendor pointed to the right street. It was narrow, descending a sloping hill. We laboured down it, searching for numbers. At last the taxi stopped before the right one.

An elderly man was standing in the yard and the driver handed him my letter of introduction. The man read it quickly, breathed an audible assent, smiled and then looked up to me as he offered his hand. 'I am Huu,' he said, 'I welcome you to my home.'

Huu was short, half a head lower than me, and slightly stooped, yet possessed an underfed dignity. Huu's hair was long and grey, his eyes had the changeless brown of the Mekong in a dark ochre skin, his eyebrows bristled. His face was thin, his teeth yellow but full and straight, giving a scholarly discipline and, teamed with the steady inquiry of his eyes, a shrewdness to his speech. His canvas shoulder bag gave him the look of a contemporary undergraduate. He told me that he once knew English perfectly, 'but now I do not get the chance to practice so much.'

He led me into the ground floor of a building, out through a sandy yard, and down through a passage to another building. The old man must have been well known in the neighbourhood; although his walk created little stir, people watched and were respectful. From squatting positions, some stood as he passed. Why were they so reverent?

It was only later that I learned of the old man's story. Huu was once part of the highest levels of the government of the Republic of South Vietnam; for three years he was deputy governor of its central bank. After the communist victory, he was imprisoned for nine years, from 1975 until 1984. Somehow, with his formal manners, I had missed the political, powerful side of the man as well as the results of his near decade of imprisonment, years when he had not been allowed to read or write anything, years when his family kept away from him for their own safety. Over the years he had learned to disguise that side of his character and even now he didn't want me to see it: like the young people who only wanted to get on with building modern lives for themselves, Huu wearied of carrying his past into the future.

Huu did not come across as an old-fashioned Vietnamese mandarin of the sort I had met, those who had transferred class loyalties from the French to the Americans but could not change their allegiance a final time and accept the communists. Instead, he was a modern professional—skilled, humane and reflective. He had studied mathematics at the University of Bordeaux; and taken graduate economic courses at the University of Michigan. Nowadays, his languages and intellectual skills were of use again, and so he taught economics classes to students—not at Da Nang University, the government would still not allow him to teach in any sort of publicly recognized and sanctioned capacity—but to that university's best students, who paid to hear him talk three nights a week in the breakfast room of the tiny Bamboo Hotel near his home.

We turned off the path and faced an old two-storey building. At the back we ascended a flight of stairs to a gallery like structure at the top. That verandah ran the width of the building, and the floor was laid in an old French way with large tiles. The room at the end was where the family lived. Two young women in the room had their faces buried in books.

I was invited to remove my shoes in a narrow, slightly sunken entrance just inside the door. A pile of books stood in one corner. Six people, it seemed, lived in a room and a half: grandfather and grandmother, father and mother, two daughters. They were people who appeared to take everything as a matter of course: the system, their powerlessness, their poverty, their hopes. They simply tried to make the best of everything: to keep food on the table—and, whatever the food was, to turn it into delicious morsels. Their possessions—dishes, clothes, linen—were clean; the furnishings dusted and polished or patched. The amazing thing was that they were people who did not seem agitated by the congestion of their lives. Tired, yes: hysterical, never. The grandparents and parents, it seemed, were always on their feet: cooking, washing, circulating among the generations. The only time they were seated was meal time. The girls, studied. Kien, the elder of the two, though you really could not tell the sisters apart, was an English language student at Da Nang University; her sister was in her final year of high school. She needed to be up at four in the morning each day, for the high schools in Da Nang conducted classes in three shifts, there were so many students. She would be home by noon to make way for the next shift; she returned home to chores and more study.

Their flat was open to other flats. Lack of privacy, a bane of life everywhere in Vietnam, had its redeeming side according to Huu. It stripped away your illusions about human nature. By the volume of a fart you could tell who was occupying a toilet. You knew the sounds people made in bed. Your neighbours would confide their grief in you. Even if they didn't, you learned of them anyway. One day you might find a neighbour, or they could find you, dead on the floor.

All objects, of course, have their shape and weight, their colour. But there is also another dimension where objects define and absorb the identities of their owners: a small, tea-coloured music box where the family's savings were hidden; an old photograph in a silver frame of three young men, Huu on the left, linen suits blazing white, their eyes narrowed, the Washington Monument floating behind them. Huu kept it atop an old armoire, to be seen whenever someone came into the room. Nothing could alter the lives captured within those objects, no revelation, no crime. They seemed to me like leaves drifting in the street.

Huu was fluent and intelligent. He seemed above the confusion of life, as if protected by a mandate. He spoke briefly of America and of the war with the United States, and he did so without bitterness. Wars were not of his doing. He considered them almost poetically, even though the collapse of the Republic of South Vietnam had shattered his career and made him an outcast. He described the American retreat in 1975 vividly, the endless hours of waiting as the Viet Cong encircled Da Nang, the huge US transport planes thundering low, in and out, over storms of fire.

'It must have seemed like being killed yourself.' I said.

Huu smiled.

'You would think so,' he replied, 'and I, myself, did at first. But no, it was not. It was in the end like being born again, I decided. I started life for a second time.'

Small finger extended, he would stroke his nose during our conversations in a characteristic gesture of disbelief and thought. Despite having been a deputy governor of the Bank of South Vietnam with close ties to the Americans, Huu stayed on in Vietnam; stayed on in the winter of 1974-75 when everyone knew that the war was ending but pretended it was not; stayed on after the American flight when he still did not have to stay; stayed on when he could have fled in boats with so many thousands of others after the fall of Saigon. For that decision, he was sentenced to nine years in a re-education camp. He tried to be unrepentant with his new masters, at least for a short while. The price was high. He held out his hands; the fingers, the bones, had been crushed and twisted into a kind of congealed mash. But not all the guards were sadists, Huu insisted. One provided him with extra rice. Water, too. Some days were missed, but not many. Anyway, Huu saved up a small reserve. The guard was mostly dependable. He hid the rice in his cap. It smelled of scalp.

How many times, I wondered, had Huu been prepared to die? How did he feel when his life was permitted to resume? Those questions came to me near the end of dinner, during which Huu spilled a glass of beer over himself when he tried to drink. Pieces of food fell around his bowl, dropped by dead fingers. Huu appeared not to have noticed. His calm behaviour, his lack of complaint, spoke of his scorn for the present life of his country. His family now saw him as a symbol. But of what was he a symbol? Huu said that he did not know. Was it the mere fact of survival, I asked? He hadn't really done that, Huu replied, since so much of his younger self had disappeared. His life was not surviving, he sighed, it was only outlasting. He had lasted.

That gift of survival, of simple doggedness and cussedness, is what connected me to Huu. My father and grandfather were men like Huu, their rough-hewn perspective goading generations of striving for whom everything is unshakeable duty, for whom there is a right and a wrong way and nothing in between, a parent whose compound of ambitions, biases, and beliefs is so unruffled by nuance that you cannot escape from those certainties without a battle; men quick to be friendly and quick to be fed up; men for whom the most serious thing in life is to keep going despite everything.

In his decrepitude Huu also reminded me of my father, who had just died of cancer. He reminded me of what happens when strong men learn late what it means to be sick and not healthy, to be not strong but weak—what physical shame is, what humiliation is, what the gruesome is, what extinction is, what it is like to ask 'Why?' when you have never asked that question with any profound intent before. I was the son of such a man. I couldn't help but love Huu.

In their frequent, fevered proclamations of national unity, it seems, the communist party really seemed only to confirm the absence of that unity.

'Reeducation' was the party's chosen instrument to stamp out the doubtful, especially those, like Huu, who were known to have had 'collaborated' with the Americans. First purity of doctrine, and later (and unofficially) purity of race became the communist programme, hence the emptying of Cholon of its Chinese population which Ut had spoken about. Rows with the huge neighbour to the north made ethnic Chinese particularly vulnerable and suspect. Like Stalin's purges, 'reeducation' was a euphemism for trials where there were no named accusers and no precise charges, where confessions were 'spontaneous for no question of guilt or innocence ever arose. Vietnam's attempts at a coercive uniformity followed the infamous model of all ideological tribunals. Within its first year it became the arch-destroyer of the free-minded, for though it began as a search for capitalist traitors and false converts to communist ideology, it quickly became the party's prime political instrument, nipping off intellectual life at every point where free thought could have flowered. None of the other aspects of socialist rule—nationalization, atheization—was pursued with such remorselessness. Apologists for the severity of 'reeducation' say that its terrors and imprisonments are exaggerated. Or, they were inevitable, given the savagery of Vietnam's wars. Take your pick. Most Vietnamese— those who survived and those who evaded its clutches—think it a peculiarly un-Vietnamese abomination.

*

DESPITE WHAT fate had imposed upon him, Huu was ambitious for his granddaughter and wanted her to do well at university. And just as, many years before, Huu's father might have asked someone from the French administration to talk to Huu about learning and the wider world, so now Huu asked me to talk to his granddaughter Kien and to deliver to her the message that it was essential to do well, to get on with languages and with her books, to be always serious about her studies. It was not that Kien was fond of play, Huu assured me. She rose before dawn that very morning to buy the fish we ate at breakfast. Some play was good, I tried to assure him, and must have sounded spoiled and vacuous in doing so.

Huu had a simple plan for getting me to have a private talk with Kien. She would be the one to take me to Hôi An and pass me on to a distant branch of the family. During the trip, and in Hôi An, there would be plenty of time for us to talk, he assured me.

Like so many plans, it did not start well. Bright and happy when she turned on the engine of her motorcycle, Kien started sobbing as I got on behind her, and ran back into her home without turning off the engine. I waited, then returned inside where Kien looked at me with heartbroken eyes: 'You don't understand me!' she cried. Her father and mother held her for a few moments, consoling her. Then they spoke rapidly together in Vietnamese; it was the first time they had not spoken English in my presence. Whatever was said, it was all decided quickly: the whole family now went outside into the street and each—mother, father, sister—made a big show of saying farewell to me. Huu was the last to embrace me, and as he did he whispered in my ear: 'It was nothing you did that made her cry. She was afraid people would see her with you, and that there would be talk. With such talk, no man would ever want her. So, now, everyone knows that her family has blessed her presence with you. Everyone on the street knows that you are a family friend and that Kien can be trusted with you.'

The sun was high when we departed but it was still the coolest day of my stay in Vietnam so far. We left Da Nang through a part of the city with roads so new they had numbers, not names. Russians, I was told, had called the place 'little Sochi' in the years when Vietnam was in the 'socialist camp,' and it had that Soviet seaside sterility, little pieces of Muscovite giantism transplanted to a tawdry beachfront town, like Blackpool or Coney Island. Once out of the city, in the distance we could see the bone white crags of Marble Mountain and along the flat road to Hôi An, twisting over and round folds in the landscape, giant poinsettia trees glowed a crimson red in the unfiltered sunlight.

We stopped for a drink at a roadside hut selling cocoanuts and beer, and sat down beneath one of those immense poinsettias. I asked Kien about the concert the next day. She said that she loved music, both classical and rock and roll; the names of the bands that she recited were so up-to-date that I could scarcely recognize them. She wished she could play an instrument, any instrument; she wished she had enough money to buy a cd player. I liked her joy of music, so I could not find it in my heart to give her the sober lecture that Huu had in mind: I couldn't see how, in the conditions of Vietnam, anyone would want to do any really serious reading or study anyway; study with the idea of really learning and not merely getting credentials to secure a safe job.

I asked Kien what sort of job she hoped to have, and what sort of life she hoped to lead. Her soft eyes became startled. Of course, there was no misunderstanding the question; she was dismayed, I think, to have heard her grandfather's eternal question from me. Everyone in the family hoped that she would teach in a high school; it was a safe job and it would not threaten her chances of being married. But now she heard of women who were doing other things, she said; she might want to work in a business. All of her efforts, however, would count for nothing without connections; everything depended on 'fate.'

Huu would have been devastated, as I was surprised, to hear Kien's talk of fate. That unruly old man had been a rebel against tradition all his life, and he was young at a time—the 1960s— when Vietnamese traditions were being undermined left and right by the greatest revolutionary annihilator of tradition the world had ever known: American material power. His granddaughter, however, was very much a young woman of communist Vietnam, with ideas and ambitions not above those of any other young person in Da Nang. I believe Huu imagined that he had imparted to Kien a wider vision of her possibilities. I didn't say this to Kien. She was only in her first year at Da Nang University; years away from having to make decisions about taking her job. Her world, and her way of looking at the world, might change a lot before then.

Yet somehow I knew that even if tradition swallowed her whole, Kien would be all right. Her love of music spoke of something spirited and strong in her; studies and marriage would fall into place when the time came. It was not completely what Huu would have wanted me say, but it would probably have pleased him all the same. Something about him had made Kien more than the durable sort of Vietnamese woman I had observed so often.

When I first lived in England I was taken by the master of my Cambridge college telling me that it was the women who had really won the Battle of Britain; winning it through pluck, improvisation, and indomitable will. I imagined that much the same was true here; the women planting the rice and raising the children amidst all the horrors of half-a-century of war. Kien carried that sense of indestructibility, but she seemed to have more than that. She was strikingly herself.

*

THE THANH family home was in the Fai Fo district of Hôi An, within the perimeter of a coastal enclave conceded centuries ago by the Vietnamese emperor in Hué to isolate Chinese and Japanese merchants who were, uninvited, seeking to conduct trade with

Vietnam. After the sprawl of Da Nang, the neat, pastel houses of Hôi An seemed a kind of toytown.

For a millennium, Vietnam had fought off the incursions and rule of China. But from the Chinese empire the Vietnamese people acquired a sense of their own superior values; they believed that their independence was owed to the principles of order first formulated by China's sages and administered benevolently by a learned mandarinate over a harmonious whole. Everyone whose misfortune it was to live beyond Vietnam's borders were 'barbarians.' If such inferiors insisted on coming to the land of the Viets, they were required to make their approach bearing tribute and performing, again mimicking Chinese custom, the *kowtow* in token of humble submission.

Before the arrival of the Japanese in the 16th century, the foreign ministry of the Vietnamese Empire was authorized to conduct diplomatic relations only with China, the great neighbour to the north. No relations with other countries were wanted or deemed necessary. Aliens desiring to trade, preach, or otherwise establish contacts were dealt with by a ministry for the control of barbarians.

The house that we sought was reached by crossing a red Japanese-style covered bridge at the eastern end of Tran Phu street, near the sleepy Thu Bon River, where straw-roofed sampans and sailing junks drifted, as they had for centuries. The wooden bridge was built in a slight zig-zag form to thwart evil spirits who, unable to manoeuvre angles and barriers, would crash at the turns. A pair of monkey statues guarded one entrance to the bridge, a pair of stone dogs the other; in the centre stood an altar to the Shinto god of rain and wind. Everywhere you looked you could see this central fact of traditional Vietnamese life—fear of the host of demons, ghosts, and devils who could visit evil upon men. Foreigners, as indicated by the phrase *foreign devil*—sometimes modified by *long-haired*—were, it seemed, ever associated in the Vietnamese mind with evil spirits.

At 4 Nguyen Thi Minh Khâi stood a shadowy two-storey, three hundred year old structure that had once been a warehouse for goods shipped to Japan as well as a family home. A Japanese turtle-shell shaped roof overhung a balcony. Vietnamese 'eyes'—those round brightly painted wooden pegs that jut from above many doorways of the oldest homes of Hôi An—watched over the entrance on a street side.

The house had been in the family for eight generations; eight people now lived within it. Suong, the granddaughter greeted Kien with a smiling, slight bow and showed us into an entrance hall of solid, Victorian bric-a-brac. Darkness made the place seem the home of a shut-away old scholar, a place held together by the precious discrimination of an aesthete and collector who loved the smaller harmonies, the politer measures. The quiet aesthetic harmony of a thousand details—tattered books lining library shelves, statuettes and enamel boxes, bits of precious stone, ornate little dishes, antique nautical devices, tiny objects sculpted of jade—spoke not of decoration and ornamental bric-a-brac, but of possessions bound up with pleasurable living and, yes, *morality*, with the aspiration to achieve significance through connoisseurship and thought. In such an environment, even sipping green tea could be part of a great cultural enterprise.

From the back balcony I looked out over Hôi An. The sun slunk in from the west and caught the raised garden that contained remnants of the elegance of the pre-war generation: yellow splattered orchids and blood red hibiscus. Walking about, I passed a weighty wood planked room half above ground. A century ago, it would have been packed with cinnamon and other spices, porcelains, oils, Chinese herbs and medicines, and from the ceiling large poles of silk strands would have drifted, like the bodies of giant, luna moths.

Seated on a barrel in the room that day was an old man, propped up and cushioned by a comfortable round stomach. He had spectacles on the end of his nose, and was reading a small, blue soft-covered book.

It was a startling thing to find anyone reading so determinedly in a Vietnamese town, for life did not offer hours of leisure. Kien introduced us and I asked him what he was reading. He replied enigmatically.

'There are some books that people ought to read,' he answered with barely an upward glance. Then he continued to read.

I said it must be interesting.

'It is,' he said.

I asked what the book was about.

'It tells you many things that men must know,' his eyes looking up and full of tantalizing amusement. It was then that I noticed that the right half of his face was mostly of yellowish scar tissue.

'Something about Ho Chi Minh?' I asked, sensing that this was a moment for political correctness, Vietnamese-style.

The old man's eyes became alive with little flashing black suns of excitement. His lips trembled in his yellow oval face. He cried: 'Ho? Not worth any time reading. I read him when I had to. Now no one insists, so we don't,' he exclaimed proudly, looking about the room at the younger members of his family.

'So, who are you reading?' I pressed.

'Mauriac. Very sad. He is good about faith, about living in truth.' His head swayed from side to side as his eyes ran across the page. Then, with the satisfaction of completing one of Mauriac's morally agonized paragraphs, he let out an involuntary 'Ah!,' inserted his silk bookmark, and slapped the dog-eared Pléiade edition shut.

Tran Q Thanh was a blithe, emaciated little man whose family has been notable in Hôi An for two centuries. Bowing slightly, he quipped wryly that his family was the first and the last Vietnamese commercial dynasty. 'All the other trading families disintegrated or were taken over by the French or had their vessels confiscated by the Japanese during the war,' he said with family pride. 'Some took their business into the grave, some lost out in our many wars, and some could not adopt.'

'What did your family do?'

'We sold.... and before the river silted over and the business was gone for everyone.' He spoke with enormous pride at the sagacity of his ancestors, who had somehow contrived to hoodwink history.

Tran, hovered over by his lovely granddaughter, Suong, spoke slow, broken French. 'I am out of practice. I need no one else to keep up with my reading,' he said, tapping his copy of Mauriac's *Thérèse Desqueyroux*, 'but to speak, there is only my granddaughter, and because English is most important for her we speak nothing else. She *will* be a teacher in the high school.' Shifting gingerly about, he began to tell me of his great, great-grandfather who had built the family's fleet of three spice ships, which commanded much of Hôi An's trade with Japan in the nineteenth century; he showed me sepia tinted photographs of the boats in the 1920s, his father in a white Panama hat, the boats being loaded by coolie labour.

The house was crowded with people popping flashbulbs—tourists paid a $1.00 fee to enter, but the state took ninety percent of what was earned in that way. The Tranh's received the remainder. The tourists would be told to leave in less than an hour. It was the tourist trade that kept historical Hôi An in working order, and old families like the Thanh's in their ancestral homes. How many of those visitors, I wondered, had noticed that small man with his grizzled, wispy beard, his quick Gallic movements, and the steel spectacles? Tran's physical appearance had absorbed the ruling peasant style of Hôi An, and there was something rather horrifying and foreboding in that. In the bustle of the retreating tourists, Suong served tea in beautiful old porcelain. Her refined movements were like pure notes, unhurriedly played.

The family, undoubtedly, possessed a gift for survival. In the history of their perseverance I began to see something of the social and political life in Vietnam over the last five decades. Despite their local eminence, the family was isolated in the life of Hôi An, and in the life of the country. They were cut off not only from social life by their standards, what used to be called breeding, but from the values held by society as well. The Vietnamese, no doubt thanks to their decades of French tutelage, possess a kind of immense cultural snobbery unmatched in Asia outside of Brahmin India, and the perennial calamity of the country's political and religious differences was that people shut their doors against not only their opponents, but their neighbours as well. Over time, it became something 'not done' to read too much, as the Thanhs did, or to have too much pride in something that was not handed to them by the ruling party. For people like the Thanhs, family pride was at the bottom of their isolation, a pride that fused with the country's old survival instincts to become something ineradicable in its elegance and in its tenacity. The problem was that, in a society like Vietnam, ideologically good behaviour inevitably became socially good behaviour, creating socially 'right' and socially 'wrong' people, people who needed to keep in the back of their minds the fact that a world turned upside down once could be upended again, and again and again.

Tran was saved from complete self-absorption by that same

immense family pride. An old sick man, he could sit at his desk and stir his memory to recapture the ecstasy of the age when his family went down to the sea in ships. Or sitting in the high-backed Chinese chair between the dulled mahogany and teak furniture (an eclectic collection of 19th century Japanese, Chinese, and Vietnamese styles), the occasional more modern table, and the little porcelain ornaments and picture frames, he could look at old faded photographs, testimonials to dead uncles educated in Paris: Gan with a great Van Dyke beard, and brilliant Nhien, who died young— somewhere before the Pacific War and the Japanese Occupation. There were diplomas from the Sorbonne, and high school reports (Nhien coming top of every class) and a letter from the lycée master in Hué to his father and yellow clippings from *L'Impartial*, a French language Saigon paper of the time, about the degree conferred in Paris, on which Nhien's name was underlined in faded ink. Most remarkable of all the clan was the great grandfather, Trâû Gan Thanh.

In families of no importance, so much becomes lost: entire histories, there is no room for it all in the attic and closets and desk drawers. In such families there are only the generations surging forward like the tide. But every now and then, houses in Pennsylvania, the Dordogne, or Staffordshire surrender astonishing secrets. After half-a-century of wars and purges, you did not expect to find in Hôi An any record, not even an oral history, of such adventures.

The sea stories passed down through the generations from Trâû Gan Thanh were a bit disordered and repetitive. Perhaps Trâû began to retell them to his heirs only when he was old and ill, or perhaps others, returning to the Vietnamese cult of secretiveness, discouraged him from passing down a clear record of the family's old mercantile life. For a time he put down on paper all he could remember: ships and men at sea, the ports, the inland journeys. The feverish ports of the China trade were not places that raised his spirits; the violence, the opium tricksters, the bed bugs in flophouses, the crew men disappearing or returning drunk or drugged. He despised Japan, with its militarized ports and aggressive naval policing, but he had also seen the cherry blossoms and Zen gardens of Kyoto and the riotous autumn colour of Hokkaido. He told stories of his youth on sailing ships, riding the bowsprit, sails slack and white waves cutting through a dark sea.

He remembered stories of Hong Kong, Canton, Shanghai and the opium coast; the boarding-house masters who drugged sailors and delivered them to crew-starved captains and their ships. Dutchmen from Java were the worst of these. Once, two deserting Japanese sailors were grabbed in this way, but when the Japanese navy threatened to board all the ships coming out from Macau's harbor unless the men were returned for court-martial, the Dutch captain complied, handing over the wretched men in chains. There were the easy Singapore girls; the rough justice of the Penang courts. He remembered one Chinese crew decked out in dazzling silks, burning joss sticks, bowing to the sun while flying-tackle whizzed around their heads, and he remembered the hulks of the Russian Black Sea fleet, after crossing the surface of the globe, burning off the coast of Port Arthur under the cannonades of the Imperial Japanese Navy. He even recalled the rats that did leave a doomed ship, swimming races among sharks in the South China Sea.

The last barrel of cinnamon shipped to Yokohama, the last bolt of silk sold in Hong Kong, the last porcelain imported to Haiphong, the fair and foul winds, the last of the sailing junks and the first of the oil-fired engines—tales of all these things were handed down to his heirs, from generation to generation. And, always, there were the cinnamon ships easing their way down the Thu Bon River to the open sea, past the rushes and palms and tiny houses set atop stilts. Finally, he remembered his younger brother Nhien's voyage; from the dock it was the last he would see of him, standing still on the bollard, smiling and waving goodbye.

V

Down the Perfume River

THE TRAIN to Hué was filled with students returning from their families in Da Nang to their university. That university was said to have slipped badly since reunification. There wasn't any money for books; students hung out the windows of crowded classrooms to hear lectures. Those students travelling on the train with me, however, seemed earnest, bright, and friendly. Many had come from villages, but already they could speak a passable English and, like Kien, they knew about the latest movies and MTV music videos. They had the enthusiasm of people to whom everything in the world was new, and they felt, too, that the tide of history was at long last running Vietnam's way. Such enthusiasm, I thought, deserved a better-equipped country.

One young man was quiet and had an eggy complexion. He wore a narrow brown tie that looked a bit like packing tape. There was the nicety of the postman about him, and it was he, I learned near the end of the trip, who had gone around apportioning the time each student was allowed to take in talking to me to practice speaking English— fifteen minutes, no more, he would be watching the clock. Another boy followed him like a small dark dog. He was a boy with the bushy eyebrows of Denis Healey or Leonid Brezhnev. One girl had several small cloth cases; another was carrying what looked to be a Vietnamese version of a Harlequin romance novel. An older man in the train had a case that he opened to reveal a stack of religious pamphlets. A strange smile sparkled in his eyes. Later, I saw the girl who had been enchanted by the romance, and whose dark hair shone like some luxuriant fern, asleep with her head resting on the shoulder of her friend, the missionary's pamphlet open in her hand. Those nice students all accepted his offers, and put the books politely in their bags.

Talking with those students made the train seem alive, like a huge, moving being, the floor trembling beneath as the carriages climbed into the highlands, the thresholds between cars creaking with every metre. There was a sensuousness to the train's movements, in its twists of will as it rose into those eerie, blue mountains, their summits covered in mist and trailing smoke from slash-and-burn fires. There was drama in the ringing of the train bell, mystery as the train leaned into slow, lurching curves, the metal squealing like messages being passed along the line. Once or twice the train rippled noiselessly around a bend or onto a spur, like a straying spirit.

So numerous were the passes and tunnels along the railway that we seemed, at times, to be moving through a catacomb with countless sepulchres. Every once in a while you felt as if you had infiltrated a great, green enamel tomb. So vast were the vistas through which the train passed that there were moments when you could forget that Vietnam was mostly a narrow coastal strip of a country. Hugging the shore of the South China Sea, the line, sinking for long pauses into profound ruts, scribbled whitely among the cool, bluish trees, bumping and rolling. At times, the train was so close to the ocean that you could hear pounding surf and watch little black specks, sampans bobbing in the distance.

There was a gentle motion to that sea; the land coming down to meet it in heavy ore-like masses beneath an infinite azure sky, clear as wind. Along the headlands, white beaches were rooted on the sea's edge like teeth on a jawbone. Here and there in the frothy breakers men stood in the waves, spinning web nets to catch shrimp. It was a complex beauty: smoke filling the bowl of one valley, blue giving way to black and then the green of flat paddy fields bathed in a pewter light, all of it suddenly giving way to the immensity of the sea.

I gazed in wonderment, my head resting on steel. I was unprepared for that beauty; in all the thousands of words and images I had received about Vietnam, why hadn't *that* been conveyed?

Perhaps soldiers fighting in battle cannot grasp such magnificence. It made me sad to think of the glories they had missed, for we live for such visions; in later years they become part of our sacred past.

Five hours in that smoky train left my eyes playing tricks on me. Stumbling down the cracked concrete steps of Hué's pink colonial era train station—a plucky survivor, photographs taken after the Tet offensive of 1968 made it look like the Alamo—I spotted the man who was to be my guide in the old imperial city. A cigarette dangling, a gray forelock drooping, Nguyen Tat Dong was posed in a dingy trenchcoat like Humphrey Bogart in *The Maltese Falcon* or like Albert Camus in one of those famous *Paris Match* photographs.

The practiced boredom made Dong stand out amidst the furious early evening activity of the station, though he was half-hidden in a corner near the exit where the ceiling came down low. Everything about Dong was aquiline, nose, chin, forehead, eyes. The silence that enveloped him was aquiline, too. Yet, standing almost motionless, something seemed restless; he shuffled his feet, his hand fingered something hidden in his raincoat pocket, his eyes moved in soft, darting glances.

Dong noticed me with a dismissive lift of his left eyebrow and a quick calculating stab of his eye, then seemed lost in thought even though, in front of him, two dogs were attacking an enormous cat. A noisy crowd gathered around the beasts as if placing bets on a cockfight. With disciplined cool, Dong avoiding looking to see what the fuss was all about. Moving toward Dong, I stared at the dogs, but did not watch to the finish—I recall now only that one of the dogs, a gray cur, suddenly became still.

Dong's hands were not Bogart serene but speckled with liver spots. He trembled noticeably. That trench coat seemed a size or so too large (perhaps he never owned it new), and he wore it with rakishness. Lovingly preserved, the coat was more than wrinkled; it was ripped and stained, its tatters patched with locally made, mismatched fabric. Because his Burberry coat was missing its trademark tartan lining, Dong placed a newspaper under his shirt for warmth against the chill, dank Highlands air.

Reaching for my bag, Dong greeted me with a slight, formal bow. His manners were impeccable. That aloofness was at first difficult to bear, because I felt as if he was circling me, eyeing me from one side and then the other, taking my measure in the way that a good tailor does. In the end, a few short questions were settled as we drove to the Morin Hotel, which had once been a French department store, but now renovated for a hoped-for tourist invasion that never seemed to come.

*

SUSPECTING THAT I would be hungry, Dong waited as I bathed and unpacked in order to take me to Ong Tao ('Kitchen God'), supposedly the best restaurant in Hué, located in a small house not far from the grounds of the old imperial palace, that fortress citadel now sporting a huge red flag with a yellow star waving above it in a flat sky.

The cramped entrance lane before the restaurant was flanked by what smelled like latrine blocks and washing sheds. Motorcycles roared through outside, although the lane's narrowness did manage to keep out carts and cars. The latrine blocks were without doors; in one of the washing sheds little boys were bathing. Along the high banks of the Perfume River—its water the frozen gray of lead—women and girls were washing clothes. On the river that cold day, girl divers, small and bony, could be seen dropping from sampans to the river bottom, to emerge with trays of muddy sand to be loaded onto the boat and sold.

The chef was named Hoang Xuan Minh, and he was a living link with the fallen empire, his father having served as the last emperor's last chef. Hoang considered himself the keeper of the tradition and rituals of the imperial table. His restaurant was located outside the old citadel, a French colonial fort of standard construction.

Hoang was hunching between three tiny concrete grills set on the floor as we arrived, using chopsticks to turn tiny, oblong meatballs wrapped in shiny mint leaves. He was small, grimy, with bleary eyes and a grey, Mao-style shirt. Fussing over the grills, he assumed the air of an Aztec priest ordaining a ritual over a sacred fire. He appeared mesmerized, his concentration absolute, his touch as light as a brain surgeon's.

Dong introduced us, but Hoang did not pay attention; he seemed to be lecturing to himself. 'The cooking of Hué makes the country one, it makes the country whole,' he said in soft English, rambling along and stirring pots of dark, pungent fermented fish sauce and plucking spices from a clutter of masonry jars on his shelves. The room was layered with the smoke of charcoal, the flowery scent of minced banana blossoms and lotus seeds, and the strong, peppery smell of mint.

A bell on the door tinkled. Hoang scrutinized the two Vietnamese women who entered; the sharp look on his face suggested his desire to make certain that they weren't about to steal. He seemed to be the type of shopkeeper who believed that everyone entering his place intended to rob him. Hoang may have had good reason for his robbery phobia. Restaurants were frequently entered by petty burglars, a state of things for which he was himself partly responsible; in talking to customers he could not hold his tongue and spoke of his family's ancient connections to the imperial household. Who knew what sort of valuable trinkets he might have about the place?

Seated, Hoang spread before us two of the house specialties: *Com co dau*, rice steamed in lotus leaves and *Com cau lau*, a dish of mussels and their broth mixed with banana flowers, peanut sauce, fish sauce, garlic and rice. Before serving his mussels Huang displayed them in a steel bucket, swaggering with pride. The mussels were so black they glinted; so plump they were almost globular. I ate the mussels and drank the broth; it was rich, invigorating, free of grit and not at all briny. Dong drank with cautious, bird-like sips interspersed with little whimpering sounds indicating pleasure. Colour poured into his face; his eyes brightened; the trembling of his hands subdued. I hadn't realized Dong's ravenous hunger.

While garnishing a plate of stir fried vegetables, Hoang said that the finished look of this particular dish must remind you of the sky: red tomato slices represented the sun, wafer thin slices of star fruit symbolized the stars, figs cut into quarters represented the quarter phases of the moon. On the bottom of the plate, slices of green banana, knotty with seeds, embodied the fallible earth. Shredded purplish basil, yellow-tinged morning glory leaves and hair-thin slices of red pepper were meant to look like clouds, tinged by the sun. Such meticulousness, the time and effort required to turn out a dish that was such a work of àrt, inspired awe; such standards must have been almost impossible to maintain in the hectic, desperate bustle of Vietnamese life.

Hoang sat with us. He scratched the back of his neck, and then thrust his hand into his shirt to scratch his chest and ribs. When I asked him how many years he had run his restaurant, he said that in 1975 the 'regime' evicted his father from the inner sanctuary to a small house near the citadel, within the small coolie village that surrounded the old imperial compound. His father almost immediately turned the house into a business, and the family had been serving food ever since. When his father died, Hoang continued to practice the imperial style of cooking. No one from the party ever bothered him. 'Our restaurant was protected as a cultural institution,' he said, as he arranged grilled minted beef around a tart salad of shaved green papaya. 'They respected the discipline, the execution of what we do here.'

Of the emperor, Hoang remembered only a slim man, with large, cunning eyes. Where the usual Vietnamese meal would bring you ten or twenty dishes at once, the emperor's meals were served in procession, over fifty courses, said Hoang, each prepared by one specialist chef. Hoang's father prepared steamed duck, and steamed duck only, joyfully, every day for the emperor's table for nearly half a century.

Hoang remembered few other things about the emperor. The bows to him across the palace grounds, how holy bonfires were lit on holidays, how the emperor said grace before meals, how his voice was sonorous and harsh, how French officers would show him new weapons in a special yard near the fortress that guarded the palace along the Perfume River. And he could remember the quarrels among the chefs, quarrels about money. Sometimes courtiers came to their home just outside the palace compound, and then their father would talk in a language, French, that Hoang otherwise never heard in his home. Sometimes Catholic priests and missionaries would come speaking a zealous religious jargon. After such people had gone he would often hear his father say, 'Keeping these people quiet is only a question of knowing their language.' Nevertheless, Hoang's father always spoke wistfully of men who somehow found themselves free of subjection to a tight social order.

There was also, he remembered, an equerry from the palace who lived next door. He used to visit and speak and tell stories against the French and against the other palace functionaries. Hoang's father, at such moments, used to look powerful, austere, like a god.

But Hoang's memories were few and confused and the emperor they represented was only a fragment of the man whom Hoang thought about now. The emperor himself, however, was now a vacancy rather than a man; he was all the things Hoang did not know. But Hoang had poured himself into the unknown mould of that vacancy. His faith in tradition was the one pure thing he had to hold on to in this world. It shut out the party broadcasts on television, radio, and blaring loudspeakers in the town; it foreclosed the cellular telephones that his children wanted; it had no room for the new elite who were his patrons.

*

VAST, GRAND, its dragon-roofed temples and bridges of marble set faraway from the population centres of the empire in the Red River delta of the north and Mekong delta of the south Hué had been supported by a mass of hardworking peasants for centuries. Ancient and supreme on the Indochinese subcontinent, boasting a love of order, respect for learning, and contempt for war, the Vietnamese empire was reported by French travellers in the seventeenth century as a kind of utopia that seemed to have found the secret of rational government. Of course, even to foreign eyes the paradox of mass penury was puzzling. Some observers were troubled too by the recurring phenomenon of corruption and dynastic decay.

When, at the end of the 17th century French ships surged against Vietnam's shores, eager for tea and silk, they found no reciprocal enthusiasm. A past-oriented society, safe only in seclusion, sensed a threat. The imperial government raised every barrier through refusals, evasions, postponements, and prohibitions to foreign entry or settlement or the opening of formal relations. The earliest French merchants failed to establish themselves—in part because of the poverty of Vietnamese trade in comparison with that of the other Oriental countries, in part because of native resistance.

But Jesuit missionaries persisted and founded a strong presence. Otherwise, for a long time successive governments in Paris considered Vietnam unworthy of subjugation—it offered beauty but few commercial advantages. By the middle of the 19th century the British, Spanish, Portuguese, and Dutch had made extensive conquests in Asia, and French naval commanders in the Far East began to see Vietnam as vital to their imperial mission. Like American commanders in Vietnam a century later, they were concerned not so much about Vietnam itself but with China, where France was engaged in commercial competition with the other Great Powers.

Against French armed frigates Vietnam's antiquated coastal cannon were useless. The French occupation of Saigon in the south, and the surrounding provinces, provided French warships with a base on the Pacific and the opportunity to search for a southern river route into China. By 1873 the French had conquered most of south and central Indochina. Twenty years later, when they decided to make their move against the north in a bid to take control of the entire peninsula, the imperial armies offered little resistance to the French Expeditionary Corps. After the death of Emperor Tu Duc, the French installed their protegé, Dong Khanh, on the imperial throne in Hué.

During the chaos of insurrection in the south against the royal court, the French took over the collection of customs dues on behalf of the imperial government. As a result of greater efficiency Hué enjoyed a larger income from this source than ever before. The city experienced a building boom. New temple complexes were built all along the Perfume River. The French system of tax collection was then extended to all ports, then to the collection of domestic duties and taxes as well.

The French divided the areas to be taxed into a loose federation that included the kingdoms of Laos and Cambodia along with the three provinces or *pays* of Vietnam: Cochin-China, Annam, and Tonkin. For decades the French concentrated on promoting the production of a few goods—rice, rubber, silk—and in transforming a subsistence economy of starving peasants and landlords into an economy that produced surpluses for the international market.

To encourage the creation of large plantations and the

development of mines, the colonial administration began, at the 19th century's turn, to construct roads, canals, railroads and market cities, all financed by an increase in taxes on the peasantry. The result was a surge in the number of landless and impoverished people—people soon eager to accept plantation employment or work in mines under exploitative conditions.

The colony provided an easy living for some five thousand bureaucrats, usually those of mediocre talent, among whom a French survey in 1910 discovered only three who could speak a reasonably fluent Vietnamese. The colonial administration, requiring as interpreters and middlemen an auxiliary bureaucracy of dependable Vietnamese from the native upper class, awarded jobs as well as land grants and scholarships for higher education almost exclusive to converts to Roman Catholicism. Traditional village schools were eliminated in favour of lycée educations which, for lack of qualified teachers, reached barely a hundreth of the school-age population and, according to one French writer, left the Vietnamese 'more illiterate than their fathers had been before the French occupation.' Public health and medical services hardly functioned with one doctor to every thirty eight thousand inhabitants, compared with one for every three thousand in the American-occupied Philippines. The first colonial governor substituted the Napoleonic Code for the traditional village judicial system and created a Colonial Council in Cochin-China whose minority of Vietnamese members were referred to as 'representatives of the conquered race.' The French had gradually transformed a landowning peasantry into landless sharecroppers.

Saigon was built as the central market for all the French-run southern territories. As the 'Paris of the Orient' grew, Hué declined. Because the mandarin class for the most part had fled north at the time of the conquest, the French recruited a new cadre of administrators with no experience of traditional government and shallow loyalties to the imperial system. The French centralized the administration of the three *pays* along western bureaucratic lines.

Protests against French rule began with its inception. But few educated Cochin-Chinese possessed either the disposition or the resources to take up arms. They no longer retained ties to the pre-colonial imperial government. Their fathers and grandfathers vowed allegiance to the French colonial government even before the old empire gave way. Over several generations of French rule, Vietnam's upper class had severed all but their economic ties with country people—and for the maintenance of those ties they depended on the French. *Assimilés*, they mimicked their conquerors and looked to Paris for inspiration.

While the collaborating class enriched itself from the French table, others began to throb with the nationalistic impulse of the 20th century. Sects, parties, and secret societies were formed. Agitators led strikes and demonstrations that ended in French prisons, deportations, and firing squads.

In 1919, at the Versailles Peace Conference, a young man named Ho Chi Minh, graduate of Hué's leading lycée and a university student in Paris, tried to present an appeal for Vietnamese independence to the Great Powers but was turned away. Ho was in Paris to study, as a French education was prized among his family. So to approach the demi-gods at Versailles was a bold, headstrong thing for him to do. But from Hué he must have carried with him a sad, overpowering sensation that Vietnamese culture was rotting, was becoming more archaic and disconnected, was literally shutting down; and the ethos of his mandarin class, once great travellers of the empire, of imperial China too, was becoming lethargic.

The rebuke from Clemenceau, Wilson, and Lloyd George was shattering. Ho soon joined the Indochinese Communist Party, then being organized by Moscow, which sought leadership of the independence movement in the French colonies of Annam, Cochin-China, and Tonkin. Ho, his level of commitment to the new ideology never clear, accepted Kremlin support. For he was sure of one thing: if Gandhi had tried his ethos of passive resistance in Vietnam, Ho Chi Minh later wrote, 'he would have long since ascended to heaven.'

*

IT WAS HARD not to feel the undoing of Vietnam's imperial culture in Hué. Hoang, for all his discipline, determination, and unbending standards, was a man on the defensive. Dong, too, appeared a man isolated from his country's causes and concerns. The transformation of these bourgeois gentlemen seemed part of a more general movement downward. But appearances existed in order to be maintained. I was invited, and would go, to the home of Dong's brother for dinner and there meet the entire family.

Minh, the brother, possessed none of Dong's ersatz Hollywood style. He was, instead, a proud, toothless old mandarin; his lower jaw swivelled from side to side as he spoke. His hair was thinning on top, but at the back of his head it was long and frizzy, and he had a light, cinnamon-coloured goatee. My first sight of him was opaque: I saw only the outlines of a face and a hand holding a book. Then, a little light fell on his cheek and was diffused over alert eyes. Minh's hand was holding the book in such a way that only a raised thumb could easily be seen. He wore a pair of spectacles that were loose and lopsided and that slipped down to the end of his nose when he spoke. When he took them off to eat, he had the unruly, unfocussed stare of an emeritus scholar who has ruined his eyes on the small print of obscure texts. Although stooped, he moved rapidly, his head thrust forward and held to one side.

Entering his brother's house, Dong bowed in greeting to his extended family and then slumped in a chair. He let his glance take in the little space that his family had maintained as their own—the black lacquer chairs and table, the drawing room without any sleeping gear to be seen, the hanging shelves with books in French, Vietnamese, and English. Old, heavy, decomposing curtains hung over the street-side window in the room. The pattern of the red-blue-yellow Chinese rug was clouded by use. Only in a garage sale would you see a similar agglomeration of used, worn things. Those furnishings marked a long struggle against poverty and the shrewd fortitude and connivance of generations. In Western families, such single-mindedness usually became tortured, perverted by incestuousness, but in Dong's family home I recognized the obsessive independence, the tough if eccentric spirits of a family that lived by its own code. That little space was, like Hoang's restaurant, a redoubt against an alien world.

The two brothers represented, in their own eyes and to those who knew them, the highest synthesis of Vietnamese and French culture. Years ago they had been admired and envied because their jobs in the French civil service had been secure, in addition to having, with their imperial and French connections, the highest badges of breeding. Their salaries back then, compared to what even those who worked at the highest level of the imperial government earned, were good, among the best in Vietnam. Bureaucratic work was not hard; all that really seemed to have been required of them was that they be men of culture and well connected, elegant members of the colonial team.

Minh had wanted to be a teacher when he was younger. As he spoke, his granddaughter, Phuong, smiled: she was at Hué University studying to be a teacher. The other grandchildren, boys and girls, all younger than Phuong, seemed indifferent. Their distracted faces said it all: they were not interested in the past; they disdained it; and were interested only in today and its promise of change.

At one stage, Minh thought of being a Buddhist monk. Then his wish to prove himself in the world led him to take examinations to join the French civil service, and a job in the agricultural administration for the Central Highlands. When the news came that he had gotten the job, everyone in the family congratulated him. His grandmother was anxious, 'Don't you realize if you take this job you will become a different type of person?

The colonial government had been created to meet the needs of the French, their life styles, their economy, their ways of eating, sleeping, 'and shitting,' chirped Dong. The French who came to Hué had looked upon their time in the city as little more than a stay in a hotel; everything would be provided for them, down to the last towel and spoon, in preparation for the time when they would return home to France and buy themselves a house and wash their own clothes. Here, however, servants were provided.

The commercial aspects of French rule were merely an extension of the civil administration, where a select group of Vietnamese was separated from the rest and made into an integral part of the system of governance. Dong was one of these; he administered the transport of tea and rubber to the coastal ports. The object was to make this collaborating class identify more with French interests than with Vietnamese interests. This was done in a subtle way. Some Vietnamese could rise to the point where they would have Frenchmen serving underneath them.

The civil and commercial administrations were strictly hierarchical. There were 'workers' and there were other types of workers. 'We, the officers, had many comforts. Our children would automatically go to the lycée; our wives had money to shop in the Morin for clothing from Paris. We all enjoyed the luxury life. I would be a hypocrite to say otherwise. And I must say that way of living has left a mark on our needs over the years since then,' said Minh. 'But I also felt like I was living a Jekyll and Hyde existence. French clothes, French language, French job, during the day. When I returned home, the family was still what it had always been. The clothing, the food, how we spoke: everything was Vietnamese, the Vietnamese of our court. But when I went out among our people, I was repelled by many of them, the smell of sweat on their bodies.'

'When the French left, I stayed in my post and was promoted until I was the chief administrator for the province. The French left, but we did not change. All the rules, how we dressed, we even continued to speak French in running the office. The main virtue of the comforts of that style of working was that it prevented you from thinking. If you started thinking, it would cause you discomfort. This damaged some of my friends, permanently affecting their ability to be themselves, and imprinting on them a kind of pretence. Many people were simply incapable of holding their own without the French umbrella. They were humiliated when they had to run their posts on their own.'

'And when the war came?' I asked.

'Our jobs were more or less sinecures,' said Minh. The new government in Saigon would try to humiliate us by taking away certain symbols of our authority, and ordering us to work in this way or that way. Everyone would know of our humiliation. The orders from Saigon were made visible. Then things became corrupt: we had to pay to keep our jobs. Resignation was unthinkable. It would have been like being thrown out of this room and into the river.'

'Then the Americans came,' said Dong. 'You had to deliver the work they wanted. They made certain of that. There were no sinecures under the Americans. The work ethic was high. In the beginning, there was a lot of drive and discipline, though they did not always know what they were driving at. They were at heart good people. And I will say this for the Americans, they let you talk to them. But they isolated us even more. As the war came closer, we were the last to know anything. To keep our jobs, we had to keep away from other Vietnamese, who could be Viet Cong. So when the Americans left, we were lost.'

Dong spoke with a grimace. His voice was tinged with bitterness. His smile was the sign. It was the smile of an old man who saw his life ebbing away before his eyes.

The turn in the conversation made me apprehensive, and I went and sat near an open window, a watery Huda beer in my hand, and looked over to the other shore to a line of low concrete roofs of a market on the banks of the Perfume River, downstream from the Citadel. It was a crescent moon night. The misty rains of afternoon had stopped. The noise of the city hustling toward the close of day seemed furious and was matched by insects with shriller, more metallic sounds. An entire feral orchestra seeming to work itself up to a climax.

As evening approached the sun went into hiding. A line of black clouds appeared as suddenly as an invading army. The sun's last rays struck out for one final, lucid minute, when the tips of the trees and scrub stood out, hard and particular, against the sky. Presently, the city's hubbub was frayed by a murmur like the sound of the sea, the murmur growing into a far-off seething which came forward in invisible leaps. On the heels of those small breezes came the force of the wind, full, warm, and powerful.

In that dark, the city and riverbanks became spellbound in silence. Here and there some cicada or bird worked away, but they were isolated stones rippling the slick surface of that silence. The air was thick and gusts now blew the heady, sensual smells of that sprawling riverside market into the room.

Vietnamese markets produce a unique aromatic medley. I sniffed deeply, trying to dissect the smells. I could distinguish the reek of ancient fish and crayfish stalls from the exhalations of the river, and I could make out the musk smell of tar, a smell that came from the sampan village anchored across the river, where seine nets dipped in grease were hanging on poles to dry. With more difficulty I could distinguish the bamboo smell of wood fires from the stalls where eels and pork were cured over pot furnaces consuming scrap wood and sawdust. Tangled with these dominant smells were more subtle, recessive smells—the acrid stench of the local coffee and the urine stink of a nearby tannery. The smoky riverbank, the racket of fishmongers, the seaweedy smell, the sight of plenty, gave me a feeling of well-being and elation.

It did not last long.

There was something wrong with the legs of the woman who approached. Her body swung like partially filled sand-bags between crutches whose horseshoe-shaped supports cupped her forearms. Movement seemed tortuous, and gave her face the wasted, worn-down look of someone sentenced to perpetually struggle uphill. Penned into her body were the most unspeakable experiences of life, but also the alertness of a gracious warmth. Engaged in that over-abundantly beleaguered human face was nothing but resistance.

Screwing up her eyes, she said, smiling 'I am Loan, Dong's sister,' her painted mouth unfurling like a flag in a breeze. She spoke in a soft, exhausted manner, like someone saved from drowning. She had a slow smile, one reluctantly given. Her hair was dyed raven black, and there was a kind of mysticism in the rising gaze of her eyes. Her cheekbones were fine and high, close to the skin; hers was the debris of a once extraordinary beauty.

'My brother informs me that you are investigating the war,' she said formally. 'I was a doctor here all through the war. In the month after the country became one, they left me alone. But I was waiting for them. I was married then.'

Loan shrugged, preparing her indictment of recollections.

'They came for me as I was expecting. They took me to a village not far down the river. It was night when I arrived, and I could hear screaming. Girls screaming, women screaming. Those screams scarred my imagination. I wake at night and hear the same hideous screaming. In the shadow of the hut in which they had placed me I saw the face of another woman, cowering. I asked her who had been doing the screaming. "Those are nurses who cared for the Americans," I was told. "They are packing them onto trucks and moving them to the north."'

Dong's sister moved to a corner of the balcony, into the light. The yellowing plastic of artificial limbs shone through the brown and gold knitted silk of her *ao-dai*. Both her legs had been cut off at the knees. Perhaps the amputation had been necessary to save her life, but who knows, and I lacked the courage to ask.

'I was stunned when they let me come back here. Ten years later. I was a good doctor in Haiphong. I did anything they asked. Yet I always wanted to come home.'

And she did return. She had come to understand, as she never understood before, the absolute isolation of her position, of her family's position. In the Vietnam that now existed there was no one who was for them but themselves. No one in all the thousands of people who lived in Hué. It was a revelation. For the first time since childhood she felt absolutely free from fear. She had the sensation, even in her physical weakness, of liberty, as though she had been freed by the savagery of her past.

When the spirit experiences such moments, it trembles like a liquid brimming in a glass. I could see that she did not want to lose it. The muscles on her face were moving and tightening with immense self-control.

'So things have changed?'

She wanted to believe this was true. Then, with that particular sadness that suppresses tears, she said: 'The changes that will make life better are for my nephews and nieces, not for me.'

She laughed then, prolonging a happiness she did not appear to believe in. Laughter made her small skull look fragile. Within it was cradled a century's history. All the dead were there, their deeds and misdeeds converging with all the unanswerable questions, those things about which you can never be certain. Time always goes fast when a life nears its end, but Loan had approached the end so often that, speaking as she did, patiently and to the point, I had the feeling that time had dissolved for her. It was as though that active life as a conscientious medical practitioner, as a wife and sister, had been a long battle to reach a state of calm self-possession.

In people like Loan, Minh and Dong the human condition met its match. Each outlived dissatisfaction. And what remains after the passing of everything is the disciplined sadness of stoicism. This is how life cools, I thought. For decades it is hot, everything so intense, and then little by little the intensity fades, and then comes the cooling and the ashes.

As her laugh died there came from across the river another, more extraordinary, roaring laugh, which I first took to be a strange, amplified echo. It ended abruptly and then it came again. The sound was animal in its carnality. Not the husky, abrupt roar of a tiger, of which there were still a few dozen surviving in the wastes of the Central Highlands, though none were known to stray down into Hué, and that roar was not like any other animal noise I had ever known. It was not a still time of night, for cicadas were striking and there were the rattle notes of birds and the flutters of bats. That sound broke through it all; it was like the shout of a drunken man, maniacal and sudden and yet concerned with some private domestic matter. It was the roar of Lear in madness on the heath.

Dong and Minh now came over to us. Forlorn features seemed to have settled upon all of them. The discussions they had with me, so familiar within the confines of their home, appeared to mean everything and nothing to them. They seemed withdrawn. They knew that their only remaining cause was the family's solidarity, deeper than any ideology, their cult of independence and culture, their difference from other people.

Humane, enlightened, the two brothers and their sister seemed to be regarded with respect and awe by the more alert and perceptive of the younger generations of the family, recalled fondly as figures not only of the family's past, but of an excellent, defeated, and ultimately doomed way of life.

Cosmopolitan, decent, aristocratic Vietnam did not die of natural causes. It was silenced.

VI

Across the Plain of Jars

FOR THE JOURNEY west into the Central Highlands and Laos I left everything inessential at the Morin Hotel, carrying only a small overnight bag and two notebooks. There would be few chances to change clothes over the coming days, whether I succeeded in getting onto the Plain of Jars (so named because of the giant stone structures that punctuate the landscape) or not.

On leaving Hué I was resolved on two things—to explore the scene of some of the fiercest fighting of the Vietnam War, and to discover what remained of the old French coffee, tea, and rubber plantations that once dotted that mountainous landscape.

Laos, the Plain of Jars, was only a side issue, but because the Lao government had refused to grant me a visa to travel in the country I found my desire to see the plain taking possession of my schedule, and my mind.

To venture there I was to be driven across the Lao border, and hundreds of miles inland, in a rickety old truck. Dong had found a reliable guide for me in Vang—a half Lao, half Hmong tribesman who, as a lorry driver, made regular—probably illegal—runs between Laos and the highland cities, to Hué, even to Da Nang. I really did not want to delay any longer than necessary my arrival in Hanoi, but I was told that the drive into Laos, because of the terrain, would take at least three days, maybe four. The trip would absorb a week in all, there and back.

It was grey, misty—a fog made worse by windows grimed with oil and soot—when the bus I was on arrived in the village where

Dong had arranged for me to meet Vang. My fellow passengers, who barely moved on their threadbare seats, remained silent throughout the eleven hour journey; not a dozen words passed between them on the trip. For half the journey that old bus pitched about unsteadily on rutted roads and coasted down gentle inclines; but there were intervals when a grinding of the transmission could be heard, when the engine was engaged and the bus rocked as it chugged uphill.

Save for the odd solitary hut, there was little humanity to be seen, only former plantation fields gone over to jungle waste— rippling reeds, giant creepers, burned out and bombed out stone buildings, artifacts of an extinct civilization. Ruins were all that remained of what had once been one of the most prosperous regions of colonial Annam. It's hard to imagine now, I was later told by someone who could remember the great plantations of her childhood, that the *colon* villas in the area once dominated the landscape.

I took off my pack, sat down, and swilled the warm bottled water that I carried. A man and a woman who looked to be his wife watched attentively. The man disappeared but the woman continued to stare. She wasn't relaxed; she hadn't even put down her small bag. This was a woman who would have been hard to overlook anywhere. There was her extreme thinness and the mouse brown hair that curled in the dampness and stood out around her face. Most of all, there were the expensive clothes that seemed to portray, in their perceptible disrepair (a safety pin was visible in the hem of her linen skirt) some equivalent disrepair in her morale. Her eyes, staring fixedly, were blank, as though she had arrived at the practiced inner calm that therapists seek to provide. That reverie ended when a young Vietnamese boy offered to take her luggage. Her face instantly filled with alarm and, speaking not a word, she stood in an even more protective posture.

'I suppose you are an American,' the Frenchwoman said in English with a hint of disappointment.

The Frenchwoman, her name was Sylvie, told me that she had grown up on a plantation such as the one that once dominated this village, but that when she hired a car to revisit it she discovered that nothing now remained of her family's home. Not a stone of that fine house was standing, not even the monuments in the plantation graveyard were visible through the creepers. So she and her husband had decided to visit this villa, just to 'remember so that I could explain to my grandchildren what it was that we had.'

In the years since the preludes to Vietnam's wars had forced them to flee, her family's fortunes had fallen far and fast. Bankruptcy proceedings in a courtroom in Lyon decades ago made her father appear a hopeless and chronic defaulter, although through some miracle he avoided imprisonment for his debts. He spent most of his later years at his sister's country home in the Jura, shooting hare and other game in the mountains, occupying himself in aimless ways.

Sylvie could still remember her father rushing headlong through the large double-doors at the front of her aunt's home, enveloped in white plantation clothes, stalking to and fro like some strange giant, and shouting about the laziness of the plantation hands.

Ever since the death of her mother, her father had become absorbed in his own lost world; as a young girl, Sylvie was left in the care of the aunt and of hired nannies from the village. The humiliation was daily: the cheerless meals, the constant reminders of her family's dependence and insolvency.

What Sylvie's family possessed in the Central Highlands was a vast estate of over one thousand hectares; perhaps hundreds of Vietnamese worked its lands—in a 'slave economy' as she now recognized. She also recognized the 'extreme boredom' that claimed her parents' lives. They would have had next to no contact with others of their class and so that all they might do with their leisure time was to lay day-dreaming out of the windows of the villa at the green hills, a landscape where the only other living souls were hunched over in toil. Of her young girlhood Sylvie could remember most the days when small caravans of lorries of supplies would arrive and the vague dreams of liberation that came with them.

We were approaching the ruins of the plantation house through an expanse of marshland. To the right were shrubs and trees from what might once have been a garden or a park. There was no one about the place; no one to ask the way or to learn about the plantation's history. This villa, like so many others, had been reclaimed by the bush. Vietnamese peasants first came to squat in the house after the flight of the French, then to pillage, picking the villa clean of metal, wire, timber, bathtubs, sinks, and lavatory bowls, leaving only ground floor shells of stone and masonry.

During the American war the villa was decimated by five hundred pound bombs, its land peppered with anti-personnel mines which, decades later, still claimed a child's leg or an old woman's foot every once in a while. Today, much of the base of the villa remained standing, and it looked old, like a tropical, overgrown Tintern abbey.

Years ago things must have been different. For long periods there was little scope for the social display of the mounting wealth of such *colon* families, so the enormous profits were lavished on the villa and its outbuildings. All the things, said Sylvie, that a good *haute* bourgeois family transplanted from, say, Lyon or Lille, needed in order to sustain their social position and way of life were brought over from France by boat. Taken upland by the liveried steam train that ran from Da Nang to Hué, then by sampans upriver came furnishings, equipment and knick-knacks of every description, a grand piano, curtains and portières, Limousin tiles and bathroom fittings from Colmar, the boiler and pipes for the hothouses, cases of Alsatian hock and decent claret, lawn mowers and great boxes of crinolines. Now there was nothing, nobody, no dock master in peaked cap to direct the unloadings from the slender river boats, no servants, no coachmen, no house guests, no tutor for the children, no hunting parties. In those ruins an entire epoch could be imagined and seen to pass away.

In the colonial era immense rubber and tea plantations dominated the Central Highlands; the planter culture stretching east to the seaside hills at Da Nang and as far north as the Chinese border. One plantation not far from Hué alone contained thirty thousand hectares of slopes covered with tea; the lycée at Hué—where Ho Chi Minh was educated—would be emptied to help with its harvests. Rubber was the most profitable commodity, or it could be in the good years. The Port of Saigon had dozens of docks and fleets of fast schooners, ocean barges, and skiffs to ply the trade routes to a fast industrializing Japan.

Sylvie's family came into ownership of their plantation by accident. The heir to the estate's founder chose not to take up his inheritance and instead sold the entire property to a distant cousin. The Pacific War had broken out, with the Imperial Japanese Army on its murderous march to Nanking in China. In Europe, Anschluss between Austria and Nazi Germany was in the air. Economies were collapsing, panic was spreading, so the price was low. Etienne's father, who came from humble origins and who had worked his way up from a cadet to a senior officer in the infantry, and who had fallen in love with Annam during a tour of duty in the 1920s, was already forty-two when he purchased the property from that cousin. The other rubber and tea farmers in the region were the sons of speculators and Parisian banking and insurance families—there were some lowly aristocrats, second and third sons who had to be provided by their families with something, so long as that something did not have too high a price on it. The original plantation villa had been built by such a man, one trying to recreate his family's place near Tours on the cheap.

The comfort and extravagance of the villa was something rare in the three *pays* of Indochina. It was famed for its barely-to-be-noticed transitions from interior to exterior; those who visited the property were scarcely able to tell where natural jungle ended and the planned tropics began. There were wide white and panelled drawing rooms and an orangery for the cool dry season nights. A corridor might turn without notice into a stone cloister at whose end was a ferny grotto where fountains splashed.

Outside, a lawn, like the baize on a billiard table, once rolled down to the river. There were fresh bouquets of flowers in the morning, birds of paradise and peacocks fluttered on silken tapestries, lovebirds in the aviaries and cockatoos in the garden, arabesques in the carpets and the edged flower beds. The effect was an illusion of harmony and permanence.

For Sylvie, the most incomparable sight was the villa seen from the mountains above on a cool spring night, the gleaming radiance of the orangery illuminating the heart of darkness. Not Baudelaire, not even Rimbaud in one of his opium dreams could have conjured so magical a scene. Imagine climbing the campanile, she said, standing at the top of the tower and being brushed by the silent wing of a bird gliding by in the night. In the shimmering, snow-white glow of the orangery the flat blackness of the lawn looked like a calm sea.

Sylvie's melancholy grew as she walked and reminisced in that ruined villa, which might well have been the scene of her own buried life. She still lived in Vietnam, at least in her soul. Vietnam in her girlhood may have been poor and the *colon's* treatment of the Vietnamese cruel, but it was Sylvie who, in returning to France, had lost her way. Her father could never detach himself from the loss of the estate, the loss of his imperial life, and he had gone down with it. Over the years, Sylvie's resentments had turned to a kind of hysteria. Her past had vanished, leaving her exposed. As we spoke she sat quietly on a large stone, knees apart, and looked down at the ruined foundations of the villa, shaking her head slowly from side to side as though contemplating the depth of the imperial tragedy of France, of Europe, of the West here in Vietnam. All the while her husband stood mute at her side.

It was the final parting that she most remembered, the family camped on the dock in Cholon amidst bundles of their possessions, semiconscious from exhaustion and fear after the long thirty-six hour railway journey from Hué to Saigon. Elections brokered by the UN to reunify the country were underway: Ho Chi Minh looked the certain winner; there was no idea yet that the Americans would scuttle the elections and insist on the south remaining independent, of the decades of renewed war to follow.

So Sylvie's family fled, yesterday's colonizers in fear of Ho's looming colonization from the north. Their sole desire was to get away, to get away immediately, leaving almost everything—the house awash in flowers, the gardens, the car and plantation machinery. Why such desperate haste? There had been no mass slaughter of the white masters by the Viet Cong, she admitted. No villas had yet gone up in flames.

So what did trouble them? Was it the consciousness of the colonizer—hitherto asleep and concealed in a thousand ways—awakened by the approaching doom of the colonial way of life? That unclean conscience probably did not affect everyone, perhaps only a few. Many, like Sylvie, probably felt completely innocent.

So, on that dock, Sylvie learned the toughest lesson that life can teach—that it makes no sense. When that happens, happiness is never spontaneous again. It is artificial and brought at the price of an obstinate estrangement from yourself and your history.

Sylvie now extended her personal anxieties to France: she saw her country infested by waves of the wretched of the earth who would once more strip her of her culture and household, leaving people like her dispossessed. My look must have suggested that I thought she was being paranoid when she expressed such fears, but Sylvie—her voice calm and lucid, for she had the vast patience of the obsessed—insisted that the death of France was already underway. Every city in France, she said, was surrounded by rings of African, Arab, and Asian peasants with their poverty and carnality, their rage; they were waiting and preparing for their moment of triumph, 'when they would steal our possessions and throw us out into the rain.'

Sylvie looked down, like an animal eating in secret, her eyes shining within their gloom. In that position her cheeks drooped; and they aged her, adding to her air of melancholy. She began to speak of some great friends in Aix who now lived surrounded by Algerian immigrants: poor people, hateful people, unforgiving people, she thought those invaders to be. Her friends had owned their apartment for twenty-six years, a lifetime, they raised two children within it. Now their world was disappearing before their eyes; their life was being drowned out by alien sounds. They would have to move from their apartment; *they were being thrown out into the rain*. Who was there to help her friends? No one: no one had helped her father; no one would help them. So she voted for Jean-Marie Le Pen and his National Front at every election, but she didn't really believe in him or his movement. No help would come from anyone or anywhere.

It took time to pull Sylvie's story out, through her melancholy and frenzy. Her memories were like despair; they shrieked in hysteria more than Madame Mai with her brutalized years in the re-education camps, or Ut with his decades of desperate, stoic improvisations. Everything in Sylvie's life and in the life of her country since the loss of Vietnam seemed to her to have gone wrong.

Around us the once neat plantation lands now gone to bush stretched miles in every direction. As dusk approached the *colon's* world—brightly lit villa, the huts of the plantation workers—could be imagined in the gathering twilight. Loss of that world was like a calamity with which Sylvie could not ever come to terms. For Sylvie, memory formed a trapdoor into a bottomless past.

Though Vietnam and the idea of Vietnam remained dominant in Sylvie and probably her family, it was surprising how little of France remained in the minds of the Vietnamese people. Most people under thirty said they heard and knew next to nothing about the French from their parents or grandparents, and had learned only about the battles against France—Dien Bien Phu—while in school.

Dong had thought about the French a lot. He believed the French responsible for 'giving us the idea of a modern state. Before the French came we had an emperor, but no real government.' But he was the only person who expressed a sentiment like that. Another man said that the only history he had learned from his parents concerned Ho Chi Minh and, further back in time, the origins of the Viet people: they had wandered south from China, crossed the Red River into an 'empty' country, inhabited only by a wild race called the Chams, whom they drove away into the deep forests. For most people I met the past was blank; history began with their memories. That vacuum may have accounted for the disappearance of France, and also for the tolerance the Vietnamese felt toward Americans nowadays.

In the French colonial days, an old schoolteacher told me, school histories began 'with our ancestors, the Gauls.' Vietnamese history, as now written, restored Vietnam to the Vietnamese, but it was no less opaque: a roll call of politburo sessions and Ho's sayings, mentions of great battles. The victories over the French and Americans were foreordained. But with the events of national reunification history ended.

Vietnam's genuine complexities had been banished. In any case, facts in a book cannot give people a sense of history. Where little changes in the material life of a people, where the land and weather are so overwhelming, there are no answers to be found in the past— neither for Vietnam's needs, nor its bewilderments.

*

LAOS BEGINS as you approach the Vietnamese border along Route 7. The landscape is one of hidden villages suddenly come upon, like crocks of earthenware buried in the soil. Sodden in the monsoon rains of spring and summer, in the dry winter season this was a place of sunsets in hazes of dust, of short twilights where the sky, at the last moment of day, would go green over sharp violet mountains.

Sometimes the road was more of a sewage ditch than thoroughfare. The smells were awful; everything rotting; scum drying on the trunks of trees. I thought of some of the old, unused lanes around my family's country home, farm roads that were almost an impenetrable tangle of nettle, thistle and thorn between the revealed roots of overgrown trees, the smell of sodden, sour earth everywhere. That memory brought to mind the war games I used to play with my brothers as a child. War might now be futile and frightening; but back then it was full of fantasy. You dug trenches, built pontoons on small creeks, took part in imaginary patrols and skirmishes. There were one or two imaginary moments like that along the road to Laos, my taking sight at the cover of trees and following with imaginary potshots.

Contorted in the cab of Vang's lorry (every square inch, including the passenger area, was crammed with goods to trade), it was hard to sleep during the night that it would take to reach the Lao border, both for the smell of diesel fuel and because of Vang's snoring. So the next day, as we crossed into Laos, I dozily watched rags of silver cloud spinning across the sky, and a sea of blue-green scrub rising in terraces and white dust streaming off what appeared to be saltpans on the plain. During that first day in Laos the only disturbance for many hours was an old Soviet Mig 9 fighter plane flying over Phu Kheng, the mountain of courage, where at the height of the Vietnam War in a supposedly neutral country American-backed Hmong tribesmen had held down seven divisions of North Vietnamese regulars and Pathet Lao guerrillas in some of the most blood-curdling battles of the Indochinese wars.

I could not ask Vang too many questions. His plans, whatever they were, for getting me in and out of Laos without a visa worried me. But experience has taught me that there are times when it is inappropriate to ask questions. If you queried, if you expressed a reservation, it meant that you didn't trust; you were sceptical; you were afraid. I had told Vang that I wanted to make this trip. *Make up your mind—are you ready for anything or not? There is no time. It is too late for indecision, for hesitation, for alternatives.*

Vang conveyed those impatient questions through his shrugs and appearance. There was a kind of lustre to him, like something made of wood, durable and burnished. He was completely instinctive. Some men are destined always to go first, to lead the way. Vang was one of them. Whatever there is to know, they learn it before others. Their existence gives others strength and drives them onward. So, I decided: Vang was a man who would get me where I wanted to go. That was written on him. It was the promise of his nature.

Dust and yellow earth replaced green as the Plain of Jars began. Grass became wiry. Palm trees marked the roads. Few other great trees could be seen, and the roads were barely distinguishable from the burnt over landscape. The plain was steppe, not bush, a steppe variegated only by wilderness, and the still-visible pocks and craters of America's carpet bombing against North Vietnamese troops and supplies, for the plain had been used as a staging area for movements up and down the Ho Chi Minh Trail. Some of the pale hills were pocked with deep green patches of scrub: here and there peasants cultivated a lower slope. Few houses or villages were to be seen.

At noon Vang's lorry crossed a bridge over a dry stream and stopped outside a bar, a crowded, dark, lean-to like structure, what South Africans would call a *shabeen*. Wheezing, rusting, the hulk of a Lao bus pulled up just after us and a woman got off with what looked to be her son. She must have taken up two seats with her bulk. She masticated betel juice and wore jangly gold earrings and a Chicago Bulls baseball cap pinned over her hair. A look of abstract horror passed over the boy's face as the woman manoeuvred herself and their parcels into the street.

Permanent houses in that settlement were of cinder block with iron stove pipes and a tangle of electric wires above. Sagging, fanning out in places, the roofs of those dwellings were of corrugated iron, rusted dark red. Where the concrete and brick houses gave way, the shacks of real peasants began. These were patched out of palm, bamboo, and all sorts of bomb fragments and shrapnel scavenged from the plain. So much contorted metal was strewn about: it was like a wilderness exhibition of those intimidating modernist sculptures you find blighting windy plazas in great cities like New York, think of 'Tilted Arc' by Richard Serra. A single man was walking up the street, an old khaki military cap pulled low over his face. He was carrying a sack and walking into white dust-clouds, out into the country. Some boys sheltering in a doorway were tormenting a cat. From one hut came the noise of a radio and sizzling oil. An emaciated arm appeared and tossed a dog a bone. The dog pounced, then skulked off.

Many people here were Hmong tribesmen, Vang told me. During the Vietnam War they were incredibly fierce and brave allies for the Americans. Under the command of the Hmong's General Vang Pau, they painted their bodies and flayed prisoners of war alive. One legend that circulated among the Viet Cong and Pathet Lao said that the Hmong sucked at the hearts of the dead. Indeed, Vang told me that once, in a cave, the Hmong had fixed to the head of a captured Pathet Lao a cage in which a large rat had been imprisoned. As the rat starved, it ate into the officer's flesh and brains.

'Education' for their boys consisted of running, climbing, insolence, and sexual athletics, though the breaking of the marriage bond among Hmongs was forbidden and second marriages by Hmong widows or widowers were frowned upon. The wedding nights of widows are marked by mockery—the beating of cans, noisemaking until sunrise. Such 'night noise' occurs in many peasant countries. Throughout Laos the Hmong were thought of as insular, obstinate, reserved, and glum—pedestrian and energetic fatalists. Their villages were clean, dour places. For over a century the Hmong had frightened through sheer bloody-mindedness anyone who encroached upon their lands—French, Vietnamese—out of their wits. At the end of the war in 1975 the Hmong felt betrayed and abandoned by the Americans. Throughout the 1980s many left Laos for the United States, the only place that would take them in. Of the thousands of Hmong who remained, scattered out of their tribal areas by order of the Pathet Lao communist government, most appeared to be tough, and would be a lot tougher if they gave up drink. They were either farmers on the family/community system in which property belonged to the family, and the head of the family council decided on his successor among his children. Or they were peasant sharecroppers—and the success or failure of that system depended on the liberal and reasonable spirit in which it was worked.

Outside the village were little irrigated plots of maize and rice, and orchards of bananas and papaya. Along the line of a dry stream were dwarf willow-like trees, blowing about and showing silvery undersides. Displaced Hmong tribesmen had been cutting branches and there were fresh white cuts and the mellow smell of sap.

We drove upward, slower than before, to a little stone lodge on a high burned spur above the plain. Vang seemed to swear to the cluster of children who ran toward his lorry. He got out of the cab and poked about in the back, like some skeleton in a graveyard prodding among the graves. In daylight, Vang's clothes sagged on his body like a flag around its pole. The lines and creases on his emaciated face repeated the fantastic dreariness of his clothes. His dirty brown eyes bulged out of their hollows with the brilliance of many fevers. He shaved irregularly, and at the side of his head thick grey hair was bushed over his ears; otherwise, his head was streaked with lines of sallow baldness.

Vang's wife greeted me with a slight bow and without eye contact. She was a very short, withered, raven-haired woman with a high breastbone like that of a plucked fowl. She examined me with the nervous defiance of a child, as though at first she did not want me to come into her home. This soon gave way to the happiness she felt at her husband's return. Quickly, she tried to explain in her simple English that she remained in her home, above and alone, while her husband went on his driving safaris for weeks at a stretch. She would see no one during his absences, no one except farmers driving their long horned cows across the plain, or monks in their orange saffron robes crossing the pass on their ceaseless journeys of beggary from one Lao province to another.

In the past, their separations had been longer. When the war ended Vang spent three years in a Vietnamese 're-education' camp. On his release, the Lao government refused permission for him to return home. He was so determined to visit his family that in that first year of freedom he did so twice, in utter secrecy. But money affairs cropped up. It became necessary to go home openly. The manner proceeded in the usual Indochinese way. First, his wife's relatives used what 'influence' they could muster, working through relatives of relatives, and through the elders in her home village, who were members of the Pathet Lao. He was told to come.

This return home required courage, for at that time there were thousands of political prisoners in Laos; but in addition to courage Vang had the insurmountable Hmong conscience. He fought with the Americans, he told the Pathet Lao authorities, because his conscience told him to do so; not necessarily for Hmong autonomy, but simply because it was the duty of a Hmong man to obey his tribal elders. Such a conscience must have maddened and annoyed the Pathet Lao who had done the opposite, they had made their country subservient to the Vietnamese, but, for all the revengefulness and intolerance of the immediate post-war years, the Lao authorities appeared to recognize the man in their enemy, and allowed Vang to come home.

The house of Vang's family was in the highest silences of Laos, remote in mud in the rainy season, languishing under a sun of fire in the dry winters. Below it you looked out and down upon the Plain of Jars, a panorama of rock and mountain distinguished by its collection of giant jars or kettles—most around two metres in size—made out of stone and scattered helter-skelter everywhere. You might as well be looking at the rock islands of Arizona and New Mexico. Many legends were attached to them, but the most believable story is that they were giant funeral urns; the largest for aristocrats, smaller ones for their minions.

As Vang and his wife were reunited with each other indoors, I climbed into that barren range, those hushed peaks scarred and bent in silent opposition to wind and sun and cold. In the air there was the acrid tang of what smelled like wild lavender, and the sticky heat of resinous trees. There was neither wind nor sound, and the tops of the passes seemed to be a threshold onto some ultimate solitude. Here, not so many miles from the teeming landscape of Vietnam, nature had a vast, stupendous space on which to play, and no restraint. There were miles where the soil looked like stripes of red lead or ochre, distances of sulphur and tin, the sharp colours of incineration, as if great areas of the Plain of Jars had been raked out of a furnace, which of course, during the American war, it had been.

Far away and below were the jars that gave the plain its name. You could spend a lifetime looking at those bizarre stone jugs—their strange colouring, especially the colouring of iron, blue steel, violet and ochreous ores, metallic purples and burned vegetable pigments which came upon them as twilight gathered. Like the statues of

Easter Island or the monoliths of Stonehenge, those monuments frightened by their scale and by their suggestion of a mad, heroic age. How many peasants were worked to death to make and carry such gargantuan artifacts—some were said to weigh as much as three cars—to the plain? But they also humanized the place, for without them the plain seemed a landscape abandoned to monsoon rains and the fires of the sun. The colours of the jars I examined were of a rusted knife, a bruised body and bleached bone. Only little red flowers which the Hmong called *baa* (and which Vang's wife used in a soup, like basil) brightened the ground surrounding them. Here was a place where nature had died, where it left behind as a legacy only its spectre, geology.

More sinister still was the Hmong Resettlement Village, to the west of the regional capital of Phonsovanh and reached after a long drive. It appeared to have been deliberately located under the flight paths of Lao fighter planes on their patrols, in case the Hmong started causing the government trouble once more. The place had the mummified culture of a Navajo village in the American southwest: the women with wind-beaten complexions, long heads, box-like bodies, strained shoulders and frightful high spirits, all conscious of their family connections and responsibilities. The men were their opposites: shrewd, lazy, talkative, and dressed in the shabbiest hand-me-down Western-style clothes you could imagine. The gross vulgarity of their gestures was disarming. They were easily angered, and raged against the government's forcible relocation of them to that place, where they have not even been allowed to build traditional Hmong houses, with stilts and cooking rooms off to the side.

About two kilometres from the top of one of the passes was the stone lodge of Vang's family, which stood just barely off the road. Vang and his wife had three children and some goats and chickens. Their two little girls gurgled strange complaining sounds in Lao as their elder brother busied himself about the lorry. It was so unusual for anyone to stop at their house that the children kept interrupting their chores to watch me with curiosity and pride, though without coming near. The Hmong did not encircle and molest strangers in their midst in the way that other Indochinese children did with their plaintive cries of 'Where you from?' A restful and smiling indifference were their protection from beggary. Like the rest of their nation, they regarded foreigners as fantastic, abnormal and absurd—people of the wrong size, the wrong religion, and of intolerable ideas. Envy and covetousness did not exist in the Hmong. Instead, they seemed shocked by the sight of wealth, and perhaps wondered at what corruptions and debasements had to be endured in order to get it. Outsiders, they seemed to think, came from a kind of spiritual slum.

Coming back outdoors, Vang and his wife began to fuss, bringing out a set of stainless steel knives and forks, in addition to green plastic chopsticks and a cloth towel, which she folded precisely like a napkin; each was placed on a table underneath a rusting protrusion—it may have been the tailfin of an American warplane—that served as an awning over the front door of their lodge. She seemed to pity me for my journey, but on her lips all the time were words that, somehow and for some reason, she could not fashion into speech.

'Ughh..arrre you—you—with a wife?' she asked, the dainty light of curiosity in her eyes. Her daughters giggled as she spoke to me, and she scolded them harshly in Lao.

'No, I'm not married.'

'Not ever?' Her voice tinkled like a cowbell.

'Never.'

'It must be his life,' Vang intruded. 'You think it is terrible that I travel for three and four weeks and I only go a few hundred kilometres. He travels from the other half of the world.'

She looked at me with a baffled sadness and shook her head, as if she could not understand anything about such a wandering life.

'My husband and I...' she started. 'No, no, no.'

She rose suddenly and returned indoors and made me some tea, singing in Lao to herself, at times speaking aloud. She brought some slices of mango and dried meat, and as I ate them she watched me wistfully, her head nodding to one side and then to the other, gathering words and on the point of speaking them, and then remaining silent.

Standing at the edge of Vang's property, the night sky seemed to drop down all the way to my feet. There was a warm smell to the land and its pungent scrub, the trilling of insects as numerous as the large stars, which came down so low over the plain that it seemed as if you might put out your hand to touch them.

In the morning that sensation of a besieging nature was the same. You awoke to feel that the bush had encroached a measurable distance closer during the night. Every smell seemed nearer and more pungent than the day before. Millions of new stalks had grown, millions of new insect larvae hatched.

That encroachment also seemed to have been physically transplanted onto the people. There was a small crowd gathered late in the evening as we planned to leave before dawn; they were amiable, grinning, leaf-chewing people who came out of the shadows to watch Vang prepare the lorry. The skin of the men was like bark, or a rind of dark fruit. You felt that the bush first drew them into the shadows and then worked upon their lives. Something would begin to burn in their inner darkness.

Vang laid out a clean mat for me to sleep on that night. Everyone in the family slept on the floor. Even at home, Vang was a restless, thundering sleeper. His children flung themselves down on stacks of straw at the side of their mother. The wooden door was closed. Through the chill night the hut snored, roaring like a den of lions.

*

BEFORE returning to Hué, tracing a huge arc to the south, a necessary trip if I was to catch the train to Hanoi, Vang stopped at the Vietnamese border village of Na Lat, situated at the foot of a long, easy slope; a wisp of vapour hung above the cone of a mountain looming nearby; sometimes that cone appeared lost in cloud. Na Lat's rich wet soil, ploughed deep by water buffalo, was black, volcanic. Mud-walled rice fields came right up to the village.

Entering a village like Na Lat was to enter an enchanted world where everything—food, houses, tools, rituals, reverences—had evolved over the centuries and had reached a kind of perfection. Everything fitted together like pieces in a jigsaw puzzle. All the houses, whether of concrete or walls of woven bamboo, stood in shade; every tree had its use. Many kinds of bamboo were visible, some thick and dark, almost black, some slender and yellow with streaks of green that seemed to have been dripped by an overloaded brush. This sort of bamboo was made into beds, furniture, walls, ceilings, sleeping mats. Rice was what ruled Na Lat in the same way that it ruled almost every village of Vietnam. Rice was food and the cause of all labour; it marked the seasons. Even today, in old, traditional houses you sometimes found a small room at the back—a shrine room for the goddess of rice.

An old woman (but you really cannot estimate with any degree of certainty the ages of the poor in Vietnam; she may not have been much past forty-five) with a pinched face and dry hair like that of a shrunken head, brought tea and a pot of stringy chicken and sticky rice for me to eat with my fingers. After serving, she waited nearby, striking with a stick at pot-bellied pigs and a few chickens that came rooting in the dust about my boots. Although I am a country person, those animals made me nervous: bantam pigs with their snubbed snouts seemed like the primeval ancestors of the fat white porkers I knew as a boy. The rooster had a hideous Dali head and mauve surrealist flaps of skin that he tossed aside to expose his beak or eyes. That cock-bird was perched like a vulture on a hut above my head, blowing out his tail, a dingy flea market fan with some of its bones broken. It hissed with balked pride and hate like an evil, old eunuch. I wondered how many parasites swarmed under the motley layers of its black feathers. Domestic animals always appear to reflect the prosperity of their owners—gentlemen farmers possess plump, complacent and easy-on-the-eye fowl and pigs; those burrowing and ravenous tapirs and down-at-the-heel cocks could belong only to people living on the rim of subsistence.

Na Lat presented a picture of the pain of old Vietnam, but I also noticed that it contained much that was new. The school and post office spoke of the present: ochre-coloured one-storey buildings with wide, stone-floored verandas in front of them. There was even a small restaurant with a sign saying 'Karaoke' on the door. Improved agriculture, and agricultural trade with the rest of Southeast Asia, brought money to the village. A hum of motorcycles was never far away, and a red-tiled roof down a narrow lane announced a brand new home. The government had brought electricity to the village eight years before. Now half the village was connected to overhead wires; one or two huts glowed at night with the sterile blue light of television screens. But the connection charge was high: two hundred and fifty thousand dong (twenty six dollars), a month's average wage in a city like Hué.

Electricity really wasn't for the poor. The party cadres hadn't, after all, strung electrical wires across the mountains just to light the villages, though Lenin had once defined communism as 'the dictatorship of the proletariat plus electrification of the country.' Their primary purpose was to develop the economy and that meant agriculture; without electricity, irrigation schemes would fail. Electricity mattered mainly to people with land to work. In many houses oil lamps remained in daily use. Most huts in the village remained without electricity, and village life as a whole still assumed its rhythms from the steady beats of the tropical day. Twelve hours of darkness followed twelve hours of light; people rose before dawn and retired after dusk. Every day, as from time immemorial, darkness fell on the village like a kind of stultification.

Having been left to themselves for so long, villages were incredibly impoverished, but simple goods were trickling in, albeit superfluous goods that answered no real need. Electric lights, motorcycles, karaoke machines: no one in the village had the wealth to possess them all. What arrived was half for show, demonstrations by the few and the connected of their social position. In that communist country, as everywhere, development was touching people unequally. This new wealth, widened the gap between the landed and the landless. The party men, with that new wealth now controlled the village's life more totally than traditional elders had ever done; they had become a law unbound by tradition or anything else.

Some of the bloodiest battles of the 'American War' were fought in the Central Highlands and so the Viet Cong moved into villages like Na Lat. Its village headman was in the Viet Minh during the 1950s, and was a Viet Cong commander in the 1960s and 1970s; one of eight billeted in the village.

I asked: 'Were you well organized?' The headman laughed at my question. 'What do you think?' It had been a time of chaos; and it was hard nowadays, as it is in most places in times of peace, to think of war in such a soft setting: such small and fragile villages, such vulnerable fields, requiring such perpetual care.

Fragility was deceptive: in Indochina it was the village, not the clan, that lay at society's heart. 'The laws of the emperor are less than the customs of the villages,' ran a famous Vietnamese adage. So tenacious was the village's hold on the Vietnamese imagination that, after the American retreat, Ho's communists tempered their ideology with pragmatism and so rarely subverted the role of the village in daily life.

By welding together small and otherwise self-sufficient families to meet the demands of the rice culture, the village evolved into an efficient unit of local government, and in the 15th century, when the Chinese court abandoned the village mandarinate, retiring the lowest order of its officials, villages became quasi-autonomous units. Throughout the era of Vietnam's modern wars, the shells of settlements in the central highlands—often half-destroyed by battle—exhibited the loyalties that villages must have claimed in the traditional landscape. Standing like small fortresses in the centre of rice fields, villages like Na Lat were closed off from the world by bamboo hedges. In the imperial days, when the local mandarin rode out from the stone ramparts of his citadel he travelled alone, more an ambassador from Hué's royal court than overseer of his domain. He possessed only the authority to negotiate with the village council on the amount of taxes to be paid or the number of army recruits pressed into the empire's service. If negotiations broke down, the mandarin had no resort but to call in imperial troops who would set the hedges of the village ablaze.

Nearly self-sufficient, villages required from government only the planning of dykes and external defence. Councils of notables conducted village external affairs, organizing religious and social life, managing village administration and outside relations. These councils were patterned hierarchically, after the Confucian order, yet remained plastic enough to adjust economic as well as Confucian relations between families. To keep petty disputes out of the hands of the mandarins, over the centuries the councils evolved an informal sort of common law to regulate the brittle network of family relations upon which lay the reality of the land and its production of rice. In times of war or revolution, villages shut like oysters from the disorder of the outer world.

In their self-sufficiency, villages injected subtle powers of resistance into the peasantry. High bamboo walls shut out strangers better than any jungle redoubt. During the Indochinese wars, when guerrillas slipped into a village, they became invisible, and were aided by a ready-made system of logistics and supply. From confrontations with the armies of imperial China, to combat with the French Expeditionary Corps and the US Army centuries later, guerrillas carried out a scorched earth policy with the consent of village councils. Underground and grassroots: the resistant village was the essential source of Vietnamese, Lao, and Cambodian identity.

It was in Highland villages that the fiercest fighting of the Vietnam War took place. Jumping out of helicopters into a Viet Cong controlled village, those young soldiers probably saw nothing but danger. Searching, frantic, they would likely find only old men, women, children, collections of wooden tools, altars bearing scrolls of Chinese characters, paths leading nowhere—the economy, geography, and architecture of an alien world. Searching for booby traps or a cache of arms, they might find only bamboo matting over a root cellar, huge stone jars of rice in musty black air. Did the stone jars contain a season's supply of rice for a family or a week's supply of rice for a Viet Cong platoon? Only with experience would they begin to dig in the root cellars, peer into the wells, trace the faint paths out of the village, search the landscape as soldiers of the emperor had once searched the villages. Only then might they find the entrance to a maze of tunnels, to the labyrinth that was the Viet Cong's first line of defence. At such moments, the earth must have appeared as a thin crust over a hostile rabbit warren of subterranean rooms and bunkers, some running for miles, from one village to another, or to secret places in the jungle. Bespoke for the Vietnamese, such mazes were too small for Americans to enter, too long to follow and destroy.

Only with the aid of an informer or POW could storerooms be found with their sacks of rice, bolts of black cloth, salted fish and fish sauce, small machines made of scrap metal, Chinese herbal medicines and stolen American pharmaceuticals, textbooks and printing presses, landmines and high explosives, surgical instruments and surgeon's rooms.

In the old ideographic language of Vietnam, the word *xa*, which both the French and Americans translated as 'village', was derived from three Chinese characters meaning 'land,' 'people,' and 'sacred.' Here was Vietnam's holy trinity; the three ideas inseparable. When any man or woman abandoned the land, moving beyond the bamboo hedges, they abandoned their souls, committing their spirit to the earth with the bones of their ancestors. More than mere superstition, that belief made sacred the idea that it was the land which formed a complete picture of Vietnamese life: all human relations—social, political, economic—appearing visibly within it, were inscribed on a map of each soul. To forsake the land was to lose everything your spirit required; to be a stranger on the land was to have nothing and to be nothing.

'The world is what it is,' V. S. Naipaul begins his great novel of post-colonial Africa, *A Bend in the River*, 'those who have nothing, who allow themselves to become nothing, have no place in it.'

VII

The Turtle Pagoda

NEAR DAWN, after a night of winding toward godforsaken junctions and coiling back to the main rail line, the slow, dusty, bumping caravan reached Hanoi on time, much to my surprise.

Throughout the night we travelled in the strong smell of the earth and its herbs, the scented smell of charcoal smoke, sweet human sweat, cooking oil, and urine. Along the tracks was a landscape where bamboo gave way to palm trees, their lower brown fronds often brushing the roofs of the carriages. Many tall banana trees along the tracks appeared to be dead or dying; a few trunks and white bare branches stuck out above the green bush. Lower vegetation was at times tattered, not cut back, and sometimes opened every now and then onto what looked like grassy African savannah land, but here appearing blasted and macabre in the evening mists.

The night scene at each stop was unvarying. The station would lie a mile or so from the centre of town, a frazzled old brake jerking the train to a halt before it. The night porter, who'd been spitting and coughing up and down the hallway half the night, went around banging and shouting at the car doors, jangling their latches, waking the wretched passengers whether they wanted to get up or not. A searchlight swept the station yard as the train stopped; huge moths ghostly white in its beam. The station was usually at the end of town where wilderness began: bamboo, thick grass spilling over rice paddies, the earth when a beam of light would hit it showing red and black and grey. Sometimes jungle seemed to be promised, but the bush never grew very high, never became forest: here was a peopled wilderness.

No matter the hour, traders invariably materialized out of that green nothingness. Up and around both sides of the tracks they came, like the pincers of an encircling army. Peasant women bearing blue plastic bags of food—bananas, sticky rice, mangoes, fried shrimp pancakes—shoved them up toward the windows of the sleeping cars. Other traders thrust large black beetles skewered on sticks at you, or the charred little hulks of cats ready-smoked, *boucané*. Freshly killed cats, the tips of their tails slit, tied around the neck, and trussed up together like gamebirds, were also displayed for sale. Cat was a Vietnamese delicacy, and a cat that fetched 40,000 dong (three dollars) in Hanoi could be had along the rail line for a third of that price.

The man and wife with whom I was sharing the sleeping car signalled to ask if I wanted to try a few of the beetles, or maybe a leg and thigh of cat. The couple smiled and rubbed their stomachs as if saying 'Yummy.' Half asleep, I tried to shake my head emphatically 'no,' but did not have the heart to disappoint them. So I nibbled at one of the beetles and nodded approvingly. Then I accepted some green vine leaves, bitter and stinging to the tongue, the green mash drying on it and leaving no spittle, only a film of white foam. Cat was where I drew the line, and so to avoid their cheery, appalling cat munchings, I roused myself and wandered down the narrow passageway. On the floor of the last compartment a pretty young porter wearing a peculiar white calico-like gown was fast asleep on a bedding of palm fronds. The four bunks within were claimed by male porters. Vietnamese sleeping arrangements were always cramped. Looking out into the station at one of the stops, I saw an iron bedstead in the ticket office. Three men were sound asleep on it, one in blue and white striped pyjamas. They were snoring their way contentedly through the only moment of their working lives that mattered a jot; the arrival of the Hanoi train.

Even at the ungodly hour of the train's arrival, the Hanoi station bustled. Old women, when not slicing betel nuts and reddening the floor with their spittle, were preparing little kiosks and stalls along the pocked and shadowed walls for a day's trading. Most of the people in the station hall looked glum and grubby; they moved slowly, a different race of people altogether, it seemed, from the feisty Vietnamese of Saigon.

How many ordinary things—pipes, trolleys, door handles—were broken or missing? In Saigon, some replacement would have been improvised. Here, if something was broken, no effort was made to fix it. Weeds grew high out of rusting track beds; decaying coaches and wagons rotted in their sidings. Woodwork exposed was woodwork destroyed in that humid climate. Vietnam National Railways, a heroic colonial era effort in construction and maintenance, was half-ruined by American bombing during the war. In the Hanoi station, that material ruin endured, but not merely because the war had been so devastating. No, the wasting seemed deliberate, like the souring of all spheres of life that the Soviets practised to sinister perfection and then exported to Vietnam as they did throughout their old empire.

Army troops were embarking for Haiphong. They made little noise, small men moving in platoons, without horseplay. Such uniformed soldiers were rarely seen in the south (and when visible seemed as garrulous and smiling as anyone else you met), but here they strutted in a quiet ecstasy of self-importance. Two officers stopped and demanded my passport. Their eyes were like warm, lazy flies, impersonally examining me. One drew closer. He impressed his magnitude in the communist scheme of things on me by a smile whose purpose was to make me uneasy—the smile of power acting benignly. The soldiers looked at the passport, they read, mostly they stared at the photograph: was it me? Holding my passport before his face, the taller of the two looked at it, then at me, back and forth. Something was bothering him. He motioned that I remove my glasses, then looked again at the photograph. His concentration was immense; his mind was working feverishly. I knew what all that effort was about: he was looking for enemies, and an enemy would try and trick you with clever documents. No enemy would get the better of him. The soldier's mind worked, pondered, his eyes staring to and fro at my passport and my face before he handed the blue book back and signalled for me to leave.

One last indignity remained: to get out of the station you had to pass the massed ranks of inferior officers who checked your train ticket before allowing you to find a taxi and leave: after all, you might have tried to travel free. These men and women were dour, officious devils who had the melancholy of people who endured the monotony of life lived without any ideas, and certainly with no joys, to distract their minds and not very much in their stomachs either. They looked as if they were thinking of some other world.

Things weren't much better at my hotel, where a small crowd was hanging around at the door in the pre-dawn darkness. Young men from that street were trying to extort money from visitors for carrying luggage a few feet from the taxi to the entrance. A porter at the door tried to keep the young men back, but that protection was offered to the hotel, not arriving guests. Understanding this, five or six of those boys fell upon me the minute I got out of my cab. Their shouts and hectic arms created a kind of feeding frenzy. The boys were small and unhealthily thin, and wore polyester jogging clothes that exposed their frailty in bone and muscle.

*

MY FIRST DAY in Hanoi was spent accompanied—followed, watched, take your pick, it was hard to pin down his job—by Tran, a functionary of the ministry of finance, which had been alerted to my presence by a man from Vietcom Bank whom I had met in Saigon. Small, with big ears, a flat wide nose, and distrustful pale brown eyes, Tran was a man of silence. Even though his English and French were merely serviceable, no more than that, they were enough to secure his job as an 'expert in external affairs.' Over the course of half-a-day he muttered only a few place names, and when I asked him additional questions, he said : 'I don't really like talking.' So my first tours of the city were spent in an ushered silence.

In appearance and atmosphere, Hanoi was much more European than Saigon, Hué, and Da Nang. Businessmen who settled in Vietnam preferred to live in Hanoi. One reason, it had a cooler climate—for the first time in weeks I could risk the sun and go outdoors without a hat. Along the Ho Hoa Kiem Lake in the evening the air was as cool as if beneath a great blue branching tree. Cries from street hawkers and buskers were still heard, and on a lakeside bench an old man with a standing scale offered to weigh you, but the night brought less expected sights: you could see young people, strolling gently in groups or in couples around the lake shore. These courtships were demure, chaste really. It was as if the people hadn't the need for intimacy, their nerves were quieter, the marriage bed was their goal. Men and women seemed happy just being together in the dark, bound by old rules and customs which both knew, accepted, and respected; there was no fear, no anticipating nerves; what passed between those men and women was gentleness, the most delicate hint of sexuality—a hand on a hand, an arm along the back, the faintest of physical contact and the heightening of the imagination.

It was not a place for the young alone. Groups of older men strolled together, their wives trailing behind, in slow, chattering, stately walkabouts. There were stands selling cheap ice cream and fried bananas. Every one seemed happy, even the very emaciated cyclo men, those bicycle rickshaw drivers who assault you from everywhere, whose bones stuck out of their coats and breeches like jagged flint. At an outside café near the lakeshore you could buy strong Vietnamese coffee sweetened with condensed milk, aromatic green tea, or a warm, brown Hanoi beer.

The lakeside was crowded at night because many of the people lived their days in incredibly small spaces. From those tight living spaces, every evening they came out fresh and clean and brisk. Whole families, not slum-dwellers, lived in one room; they might live in that room for generations. I thought of them as a kind of urban peasantry. Years before the father or grandfather had left their villages and now the family could not return: in some cases the village might no longer exist, destroyed by bombing or replaced by some of the collective farms that the North Vietnamese tried to build, aping the *kolkhozes* of their fallen Soviet patrons.

Tran had grown up in a family like that. He became a member of the communist party when he was young, climbing up through its Komsomol ranks. Now, in his late forties, he was a man of authority. He had his own little office in his ministry's annexe building on Thuong Kiet street, with a waiting room filled with straight-backed chairs for people with petitions and their needs. But he had lived for the first thirty years of his life in the one room where he had been born, in the Quan Ba Dinh district near Hanoi's huge west lake. Tran now lived in the top flat of a tall block among other party and state officials. Within walking distance was the tenement with the one room that had been his home for more than half his life.

It was hard to figure out where to go or what to do. There were some bars, but Tran said they were Vietnamese and not really 'for' me. We went past a water puppet theatre—'only amateurs are performing, you won't see the best and you don't want to get splashed. They love soaking foreigners,' said Tran, so we didn't go in.

When I asked to stop this aimless walking, Tran protested firmly. 'How can we? No, we will see more.' Then he fell silent again, and we walked on. Whenever I began to drift behind or linger over a sight, Tran became edgy. His jangled nerves agitated mine, and I began to be edgy, too. There was no way to make a comfortable connection with him.

Going back to the hotel I saw a young girl, no more than fourteen, burning little chits of ersatz paper money in a small pile at a curb. Dead matches stood in random rows like beetle tracks. Crowds of strolling people passed her by without noticing. In a trance, her large black eyes stared at the flames, only her left arm moved as she shifted the embers and stirred the fire. 'It's a ritual for the dead,' said Tran. 'Remember the funeral procession you saw this morning? Our children mark death in this way.' The girl's stare was unbroken, fascinated, almost unconscious, something beyond place and beyond time.

The funeral Tran mentioned was something to remember. Thùoc Bac and the other streets near the Camellia Hotel were narrow and tangled like string. Here, domestic Hanoi was warm in its tints, its stone faces ranging from sparrow-brown to pink and raw crimson. The tall Haussmann windows, the pilastered doorways, the fine fanlights over some of the front doors retained, despite wear, tear, and neglect, a Gallic family dignity unspoiled by extravagance or pomp. Of course, much of the area was ragged and dilapidated, but there had been a really powerful drive at re-housing in the northern part of the neighbourhood, near the Dông Xuân market. Neither the planning nor the building attracted. Little civic imagination appeared to be at work in Hanoi.

The sun had not yet taken a firm hold on the sky when I rose early that morning; Tran had not even arrived to babysit me. Few people stirred in the streets. Sometimes from a doorway there came a sickly stench of burning oil. A woman lit a charcoal fire in a big stove standing outside her door. Passers-by stopped to watch or to eat the long strips of cane fried in oil that she was preparing. Those strips were cut into coils like large earthworms, and were served over a bowl of steamed rice.

A funeral cortege, a strange vehicle like a green milk cart, appeared. Bumping through the narrow streets, crowds were summoned, seemingly by the tinkling of a bell. Men and women stood to the side as the small lorry with its coffin protruding from the back passed by. Behind it marched men in black with white strips of linen knotted around their foreheads. They were engaged in a kind of sing-song chant: a dirge song of the earth. The mumbled chants snored under the wide eaves of the small buildings. No voices spoke more eloquently of the ashes and earth than those urban male voices. The sheer sadness of those monotonous low dirges was intolerable and heart wrenching. Is there a more terrifying sight than a procession of mournful young men?

Women came at the rear of the procession, though some of the elderly—grandmothers and great aunts perhaps—were packed into the back of the lorry, hunched on a bench alongside the coffin. From the narrow, pocked balconies above, only women were watching. Taking up the rear were the first Buddhist monks I had seen in Hanoi. In old photographs of the city you were struck by the sheer number of monks, huge or frail, amiable or sullen, in bright or burnt orange saffron robes. Nowadays, no doubt because the wats and pagodas were tactfully keeping their great numbers out of sight, there were very few on the street.

The procession stopped under a stone arch near a small Buddhist temple. The crowd of men were in black trousers and white shirts, no one followed as the procession passed, leaving a strange hollow in the usually crowded street. The lorry marched, mourners marched, the priestless procession moved on, motley stragglers gathered behind it. The coffin was borne out of Hanoi towards the man's home village at a rapid pace. The crowd almost ran through the crowded city, descending toward the Red River past an altar cloth of acacia trees, silent sentries like extinguished candles. Swept along, as if by a current, I followed, the sound of the mourners swelling like the starting up of aeroplane engines. In a smoke of white dust the crowd advanced over featureless roads across a steel bridge to the far side of the river where, after more marching, it eventually petered out. In a small cemetery, men in white cassock-like smocks similar to those of Catholic seminarians or altar boys, waited amidst small marble and concrete tombs. It was a compact burial ground, like a miniature fort.

That funeral introduced me to the Vietnamese preoccupation with death. No other race in Asia has that obsession—and with good reason, given the country's history. Popular signs of the cult were as noticeable as the more sumptuous ones, like Ho's mausoleum in the centre of Hanoi, a clone of Lenin's refrigerated resting place in Red Square, its kitsch modernism topped incongruously by a traditional Taoist arch. Houses, big and small, were sombrely decorated for periods of mourning, not for a mere funeral day alone; balconies and doorways hung with cloths and sashes. Death was a family gala.

In that cult, no doubt, was some of the old imperial Vietnamese love of pomp and spectacle. In Vietnamese poetry, I was told later by Pham Tiên Duât, perhaps the country's most acclaimed poet, the theme of death was treated again and again by every writer. That preoccupation was common in Catholic art, and Vietnam after all was ruled as a de facto Catholic country for most of a century. But Catholic artists elsewhere do not have so exclusive a passion. *The Sorrow of War* by Bao Ninh, the one Vietnamese novel to unflinchingly portray, from the North Vietnamese view, the terror and madness of the American war, owed its dramatic success not only to its lurid and carnal realism, but to the sense of life as a ceaseless, heroic life-and-death struggle, to that sense of life being corroded at the height of commitment by mortal or moral weakness. In how many ways, Bao Ninh reflected, can human beings be shown meeting their death?

Monsoon rains forced me to stay in my hotel that evening. The chill in the air inhibited thought, so I turned on the small television in my room and surfed the local channels: most of what was being shown was the usual Sovietized claptrap. Then I came upon a film of a woman being beaten and raped. The men attacking her were repulsive—leering, grinning, half-crazed. It was only after you saw their violence that you saw who the men were: they wore the uniform of the Army of the Republic of Vietnam. One soldier even had an American army medal prominently displayed on his chest. Finishing their attacks, they skulked off, after casually pulling up their trousers and ignoring the woman, like a pack of hyenas, sated and finished with their scraps.

The woman recovered herself slowly—then, an epiphany. She ran and ran, through dark streets, past undifferentiated and indifferent people. In a secret house she found what she was seeking. The Viet Cong commander consoled and comforted. No frown, no clenched fist, no rebuke for her having consorted with the soldiers in the first place. He was her protector, bending slightly as they talked, happier to serve her than she appeared to be in seeking his aid. Revenge, he whispered, would one day come. Then the screen blackened. The story was finished. After a generation of economic reform and an opening to the world, the old revolutionary hatreds were still being stoked, the old Marxist mantras recited anew, rosaries of broken promises.

The news programme that followed shattered this spell. By personal order of Prime Minister Phan Van Khai, three dozen restaurants in Hanoi that served cat meat were ordered shut. A wave of catnappings was sweeping the city and the countryside as well; they had to be stopped. People's Committees across the country were ordered by the politburo itself to be vigilant against restaurants still serving 'little tiger' meals. My landlady, Madame Dang, watched the report, grinning. Her gums were puffy, her teeth in danger of uprooting. 'This will leave the rats free to eat our crops,' she said, spitting betel juice into a tea cup.

*

PHAM TIÊN Duât always repeated my questions before answering. He was a poet, a man careful with words. Although he now held a bureaucrat's job, deputy director of the Union of Vietnamese Writers, he came across as a real writer all the same, humane and reflective.

Writers in Vietnam had only a few strategies open to them in dealing with the communist system. They could support the authorities, they could go into opposition, or they could discover a small sanctuary for themselves—the more distant from politics the better. Nature was such a sanctuary. In a country in which people had limited access to television and photography, Pham's verse, which he read over the radio weekly, had no equal. His descriptions of nature were a kind of escape for millions, a peaceful retreat. Pham's language, I was told, was rich and magnificent. The party wanted everything to be without character, without distinction, grey, but in Pham's writing Vietnam was colourful, wonderfully alive. 'Poetry allowed us to recall our real language when we could not hear it anywhere else.'

Pham never wrote about the achievements of the government or the heroism of the war. He didn't really seem to notice them. The war, against the French, against the Americans, Pham conceded was necessary. Yet it now seemed past and dead, a waste. It was not that he was anti-political or even apolitical; he could accept the communist party's failures but not its dishonesty about those failures, and this isolated him within the writers' union. Pham was obsessed with restoring to the public mind the eternal beauty of his country, and the crystalline language that was being lost each day. For war not only corrodes the senses, it corrodes the tongue with jargon and vulgarity. His talk now was of the new volume of poetry—the verse in that cycle was primarily autobiographical—that he was writing and with which he was having trouble.

Men often know what their destiny is, and it seemed that Pham both knew and was reconciled to his fate. He was of about fifty, thin, tall, and slightly bent. When he spoke about poetry he rolled his big faded eyes, as if he had reserved the honour and interest of discussing his most private excitements with you alone: that he was admitting you to his innermost secret. Otherwise, he had an endlessly careworn expression.

'Vietnamese is a very beautiful language; its beauty survived many things, the Chinese, the French, it even survived intact the change from an Oriental symbol based alphabet to western script. Still, it is hard to translate, but part of the reason for that is its charm. For example, if a man is addressing his wife there are so very many ways that he can do it. He might say "You," but that is considered rude. Or he might call her "Little sister," and she will chime in "Brother" in return. The most beautiful is when a man calls his wife "Myself"—"How is Myself?" he will say to her. And there are others. He might call her "Mother," and she will call him "Father."'

Mother, father, I said to myself silently: it sounded like one of those American TV marriages from the 1950s: 'Ozzie and Harriet' or the parents in 'Leave it to Beaver.'

'That formal tongue was hard to keep during the war. We were living in rubble, patching our skins, the government not really able to look after us well. Suffering and poverty were everywhere. Whatever laughter emerged was mindless; the sort that comes when people feel a great tragedy in the air and the world becomes ghostly.'

'Every writer, of course, served the war effort. Some more than others; those that did the most did well, but when the war ended, what they wrote was devalued, just like our currency. A few of us preferred our language to the few things you could find to buy and eat. Language became the only reality for me, the only one that mattered. Many tongues were coarsened by the war, as their lives were coarsened. That coarsening was protective, but when language fails to reproduce all of reality, a deadening of the soul results. Language is our witness to ourselves.'

My meeting with Pham was accidental. I had received an invitation to the Writer's Union, its headquarter in a dark villa on Nguyen Binh Chieu in the northeast of Hanoi.

In his dark blue suit the union's director, Huu Thinh, acted like a prince of that decrepit institution. Seated when I arrived, seated he remained, inhaling self-esteem, a Rothman's cigarette pinched between the thumb and forefinger of his small right hand. Thinh had the practiced insolence of one who achieves power through observation and mimicry. The cheeks of his small head were chubby, smoothed by age like worn coins. He looked collected, brisk, and dangerous. A black voice, richly hoarse, came from the full lips of that small man.

A junior member of the politburo, Thinh let me know straight away that his time was precious, he could spare little of it for me; he was off to see his comrades on the central committee to plea for higher salaries for the union's members. So Thinh was one of the men who administered Vietnamese culture, whose job was to bring the aims of literature into line with the aims of society, to make literature less inefficient from a social point of view. You wrote, if you could ever do so here, into the teeth of this. His deputy, Mr. Pham, would be happy to see to whatever it was that I required.

Just going to the Writer's Union—with its bureaucratic, faux black lacquer furniture and cork bulletin board of appointment schedules—you received the clearest sense of how much intellectual life in Vietnam had been eclipsed over the years. The literary world was alive only with talk of subsidies and political scandal, and I cannot do more than crudely suggest the obvious reason: censorship. Informally I gathered that many writers no longer found state oversight of all they wrote to be as odious as they once did, because Vietnam was politically tired out. In another sense, that intellectual sterility appeared due to a swing in the pendulum: the war as a subject had exhausted itself, but like Eastern Europe's dissidents and artists after the fall of communism, Vietnam's writers had not yet found a theme with which to replace it. A large number of the country's best poets and writers had been driven into silence by the insistent, deadening focus on the war; their remaining muzzle nowadays was only a matter of routine, not policy. They were probably officially free to publish anything that was not obviously political without molestation. Few dared chance it. Older writers with whom I spoke were not only out of touch with what was going on in their country, but were also incurably divided, quarrelling the fanatical quarrels of the powerless. Most wished to forget the war and the secret, murderous post-war tribunals. The business of surviving the terrible times during the war and the re-education periods after the war, of keeping their heads above water, of getting enough for their families to eat, had, it seemed, permanently bewildered and exhausted them.

Pham was of that shadowed generation. He didn't reject history, he internalized it; he simply took it for what it was: a hideous national upheaval that multiplied the levels of individual grief. In this, Pham was a born democrat, as all good poets are: they cater to the entire nation, and employ its language. If he was different from his public—and his books sold, there was no income in it, but they sold—it was that his language and ethics were not really subject to historical adjustment and manipulation. He was that lone and perhaps foolish figure whose fate it was to love something with all his being.

He was a man of northern North Vietnam, where Catholic and French influences were less than in the south of the country. The society in which he was born was extremely insular, yet Pham was a man of cultivated and cosmopolitan interests. This was the heart of the trouble he was having with his poetry.

I thought of the troubles that Ut and Huu and Dong and Madame Mai had in maintaining a pattern to the events of their lives, their progressions from aristocracy and meritocracy to pariahs and back again to adventurers in the new economy. That difficulty in integrating the parts of your life into a whole was also part of the problem for Pham. But Pham's dislocations were not abrupt; he had simply lost touch with the ideas and the forces that had animated so much of his life; and he found that to write without a feeling for what and where he had come from was to reduce his poetry to little more than a sequence of events. That was why he had thought about putting away his writing. He had gone back to his high school, his first jobs at a newspaper in Hanoi, to try and recapture some of his past; and the little he had recovered had come like an illumination.

This was what came out of our first meeting. It was necessarily short; he had to introduce me to all the assembled writers, with their writer's questions: is it true western writers get paid in advance for books they have not yet written? And they can get thousands of dollars? Millions of dollars? Is that true? Do people get paid by the word? And people live only by writing? With each question, envy and innocence filled the air like smoke. At the end of the meeting, Pham invited me to his home. 'I will meet you at your hotel on Wednesday at six in the evening,' he said.

I didn't think of Pham as someone whose life had been utterly shaped, ineradicably distorted, by the regime under which he lived. The impression of him that I acquired after our first brief meeting was of a man who had achieved a separate peace, a restful, reassuring calm.

That Wednesday Pham was prompt, arriving at five minutes before six, and seemed pleased that I was in the lobby waiting for him. I told him that I hoped I had not interfered with his work—the writing of his poetry. His negative shake of the head was as gentle as I could have expected.

We walked out onto Thùoc Bac, Pham moving with the authority of a man known to everyone. Men were lounging before a drinks stall lit by a fluorescent tube. A pushcart passed, a man knocking a piece of bamboo against the side of the cart. Those carts and stalls, though an intricate part of Hanoi street life, were absent from the areas where there were modern hotels in which western businessmen stayed.

Pham's apartment was in a French house, not really an old villa but something low with sash windows and a tiled roof. It had a brown painted door with a brass handle that was lovingly polished. The rooms were whitewashed but possessed little furniture, save for a large chandelier. French colonists came to Hanoi with few possessions, but clung to their ornate chandeliers. There were also a few modern sculptures and many Vietnamese ink drawings.

We went to the back of the house. Pham said, as if testing his English, 'this is my garden.' It was small and years ago had been skilfully planned. Pham had kept up with the pruning. The blossoming cheery tree in the middle of the garden was pollarded. The gate at the back of the garden was bamboo. We sat there. 'My wife will join us,' he said.

Darkness was falling; a light appeared on the veranda, and against this light, her face in shadow, there appeared a tall slender woman in a linen trouser suit. She hesitated on the veranda, providing water to a small white bird in a cage. After whispering softly to the bird, Hoa approached, losing some mystery as she emerged from the shadows into the light of the garden. She came barefoot, with certainty and style. There was boldness in the line of her body. It was solid and warm and the breasts beneath her blouse were small and lifted. Everything was hidden, yet nothing was concealed. I could see her dark nipples. I was staring and knew it, trying to isolate elements of her sexuality, but it was like memorizing the reflections of a diamond. The slightest movement, and an entirely different brilliance appeared. Of course, it was her face that I searched most, her gestures, her expressions.

For a moment, she seemed strangely grave. Pham lowered his eyes and she spoke to him in Vietnamese; he was briefly without breath to answer. She was not smiling; there was a glint of anger about her dark brows and the garden lamps brought out small shadows to her lips. The candour of her body had something in it that was lovely but frightening.

After Pham introduced us, Hoa spoke in a quieter, more musical voice; but the body came between the words—solid, firm, and peremptory, and underlined everything she said with resignation and sadness. Hoa then lightly touched my arm in the way some women have of reaching out to strangers unconsciously and then drawing back as if realizing the gesture's sexual freight. She moved away then, to pour tea, passing me a plate with small bowls of sweets, puddings of a brilliant orange colour made from beans.

I asked about the sweets, 'What are these?'

Hoa said, in barely accented English, 'They are made from beans. You will like them. My mother makes them.'

Pham said, 'I was being interrogated about our language. If we speak differently because of the war, because of unification.'

'Interrogated?' Hoa laughed.

Interrogations were on Pham's mind. A general who had written a letter complaining that the pace of reform was too slow was about to be arrested. Two days before its suppression, everyone in Hanoi was speaking about the letter. At the union today, when Pham had mentioned it, the Director had turned his back on him.

'Is it serious?'

'It has never happened before, so who can know? It is their way to make him wait for the arrest, "sweating him out," isn't that what you Americans say? They will detain him in a day or so. They will interrogate him, probably in a friendly way.' Pham hesitated. 'No, friendly is not the right word. Correct. He is one of them, so they will treat him in a correct way. And if he recants, it will be like nothing ever happened.' He paused. 'All that lying. Our ocean of lies. Translating truth into lies. Translating one lie into another lie. The competence people display in their lying! The *skill!* Carefully sizing up a situation, and then with a calm voice and straight face, delivering the required productive lie.'

Hoa sat on a bench across from her husband, laughing at the untidiness of the garden. 'We didn't have any garden when we were in Chicago,' she said. She pronounced the word 'Chicago' with pride. Pham had been a poet in residence at the University of Chicago for one term years ago. He remembered Saul Bellow and his beautiful diction; Alan Bloom with his prissy, prickly conversation. Although Hoa worked in a French-supported centre to promote traditional Vietnamese handicrafts, and so had frequent contacts with people from the West, her memories of that time in America, of her time in the world outside Vietnam, enchanted her still. She produced three photographic albums of their Chicago year: the two of them in an apartment window overlooking the Loop, at Wrigley Field, outside the Fine Arts Museum, wading at one of the beaches along Lake Michigan. The photographs didn't tell much about their life in America. They helped me understand only one aspect of their reality: they showed that Pham and Hoa were no longer fully *of* Vietnam, that both felt that the world they now inhabited was no longer fully theirs. In Hanoi, they were isolated.

So the conversation drifted, not about poetry and language, or even politics, but about the past: Vietnam's past. Was it possible for the Vietnamese to really leave the past behind? So many people seemed so forgiving of America; so many young people were completely unaware of what the war really was.

'The Vietnamese past was a tragic tree that continued to cast its long shadow,' he said. The past prevented the Americans from coming back and investing for twenty years; even now, with diplomatic relations, very few Americans came. The past prevented reconciliation with China. 'There is a joke that everyone tells. The Chinese could drown us all without war, just by lining their population along the border and ordering everyone to pee. Were it not for the past', he continued, 'an accommodation could be reached with Cambodia. There was always the past.'

In our conversation we could not reach a conclusion about anything or find an answer to any question. It was stimulating all the same because a curious vividness was given to everything Pham said by the imperfection of his English. Faults of accentuation, misplaced words, gave his conversation a suggestion of penetration and meaning. There was also an irresistible quality of innocence, of enticement and friendliness. 'Our war,' he said as he escorted me to the door, 'was fought to bring about independence and a country of peasants and workers. We achieved that. But something more.

Something worse. We got a culture of peasants and workers. Crude, primitive, simple-minded, a culture that reeks of virtue. The terrible temptation of idealism! We must master our idealism and virtue and vices. Aesthetic mastery, otherwise we are worthless as writers, worthless and ludicrous.'

*

HANOI WAS two cities at once: an Asian rabbit warren, and a spacious colonial capital ventilated by wide boulevards shaded by ancient trees. In both parts, the city had witnessed a pattern of development endemic throughout the Third World: rapid, unnatural growth in the capital city was paid for by the neglect and further impoverishment of the surrounding countryside, that neglect creating a monstrous disproportion between the capital and the rest of the country.

Cool breezes off Hanoi's three interior lakes blew through the streets. The sense of a careless, reflective life, of innate rather than forced or crowded elegance, was constant in the old, central colonial quarters of the city. Part of this was luck. The arrival of communism was a disaster for the Vietnamese economy, and for millions of its people, but a salvation for Hanoi. For with it (until recently) urban development came to a halt. The city froze as if it were in mute bewilderment before the impending Sovietized age, seemingly unwilling to attend to it. The tradition of 19th century European empire building was to go for the grandiose. That century was the age of the construction of vast imperial conglomerations like New Delhi and Shanghai. Hanoi escaped this for political reasons. The only really grand public buildings are the railway station and the delightful beaux-arts opera house. Otherwise, the chief monuments were provincial French. Seeing the central city, it was no surprise that Paul Claudel, an old Asia hand in the French diplomatic service, was said to have experienced a poetic rebirth after taking long walks along the brimming, windy Ho Hoa Kiem lake. But Hanoi's spaciousness was not splendid in the Haussmann fashion of Paris; it was dozy, provincial, and encouraged idleness.

Hanoi was a city built not of brick but of a yellow stone that seemed to make it float; its church steeples were simple and war-like and the towers of its official buildings were harsh, though in the evenings softened by the orange glare of the sun. If you imagined Hanoi's skyline until recently, before foreign investors came and their glass towers arrived, you saw an implacably religious city, everywhere you looked might be the steeple of a pagoda or Catholic church. But this spiritual belligerence was not like that of the helmeted skylines of eastern Germany that convey the spirit of religious wars; Vietnamese anger, even its ideological rages, was always domestic. It suggested a family quarrel going on from generation to generation. Austerity, plainness, obduracy were the words that came to mind before those prosaic houses of worship that were so indifferent to decoration.

That glimpse at Hanoi's skyline came at a dinner hosted by a department secretary in the finance ministry and his young wife. The apartment block was one of those in which flats were distributed by the party according to lists—the keys were personally handed to the chosen by the district secretary. The criterion of allocation was simple—the closest family members of the central committee received the best apartments, after them came cousins and officials in the state ministries. The view from their modern tower was of a low broad mound of heavy red roofs, one above the other like a pile of earthenware, with only white slips of wall and reflections of glass showing here and there. An oriental town for the oriental noises, in which light came from a distance to harden and darken, the sun at dusk becoming a flame, the city a wilderness that the flame seemed to be consuming.

My hostess blinked as I studied the view from the plate glass windows of her drawing room. She was anxious to convey how much Hanoi, her home city, had changed in the six years in which she had been married. 'Back then, people would relieve themselves anywhere—in the street, in the lake—at any hour,' she said with a giggling, unrecognized self-loathing. Her husband chimed in: the people were fast; they adjusted in an instant to the times; they all knew in their bones what was permitted and tried to find a balance between what they could get away with and what they knew was necessary. Their revulsion toward their own country, with its roots in the artificial caste superiority of the Communist Party hierarchy, was equal to a foreigner's hidden fear. The combination was not new in

Vietnam; it had occurred countless times during the French and American occupations, those marriages based on self-hatred and self-love, and Vietnam was always the victim.

My host, besides working in the ministry of finance had another thing going for him: his wife was the daughter of a former politburo member and remained well-connected. Now this man, whose official salary was a pittance, probably not more than sixty dollars per month, had arranged along the walls batteries of electronic equipment, television sets and VCRs, cd players, amplifiers, speakers, shelves of American movie videos and compact discs. And the table was set with all kinds of food, fresh fruits, caviar, Rhone wines, nuts, cheese. He sat at the head of the table, smiling broadly in his dark Christian Dior suit with the cardboard shop tags still sewn onto the outer sleeve, electronic equipment twinkling at him from all directions with their little red eyes.

In a way, the couple lived outside Vietnam. Their flat floated above the city, and was in a building where only foreigners and the 'lucky' Vietnamese who might marry them lived. Patrolled by party officials, members of the elect moved about the city in Land Rovers, Mercedes, BMWs and Jeep Cherokees, stopping at markets and street events like visitors from afar.

*

STREET SMART, street tough Hong (Rose) glared at me with a look that I would not soon get over. She was waiting at the corner of Ho Hoan Kiem Lake beneath a black-pronged tree dipped in a vivid spring paint of buds. She fell behind me, nattering without pause. When at last I turned and asked why she was nagging me, tugging at my elbow, I saw that she was a walking human shop: on a tray were postcards, books, maps of Hanoi, stamps, coins, old Vietnamese and Red Army medals, and cheap knock-off copies of Graham Greene's 'The Quiet American.' Vivacious and talkative, only a few years behind the times in her American slang, Hong's hair was black and cut in a fringe above her skittish, brown, hollow eyes. She was plainly so used to living on the edge of survival that her nerves appeared frayed to near breaking.

Day in and day out for the first four days of my stay in Hanoi she accosted me as I walked along the lakeshore. Of course, I had encountered gangs of such kids elsewhere in Vietnam, none of them spic-and-span, and more than a few constantly scratching, making me apprehensive. So I did not expect Hanoi to be different. Here, indeed, those urchin-hucksters did seem miserable in the usual ways of poverty, which they appeared to accept without indignation. But there was something more than that: they were spiritless. Of course, none of them—they all had a smattering of English; Hong's English was excellent and she even had a touch of Japanese and French—wanted to answer prying questions. Still, more than a few did, probably because they were afraid something might happen to them if they did not. After all, who knew what magic, what connections, these foreigners might use? All seemed to suspect that my questions were somehow connected to the government. Sensing their unease, I began to feel that I was preying on the unfortunate.

Hong's jauntiness stood out. Her high cheekbones and flattened nose gave an alert, sceptical expression to her face; she looked as if she did not believe a word that anyone said to her. She did not seem very healthy, but rather had that splendid hardiness you find in a city sparrow.

There were colonies of such street kids everywhere in Hanoi, children who came from villages to the city to go to high school but who wound up dropping out and sending money back home to their parents, supporting their families instead of their families supporting them. Peasants in their thousands tried to leave the land to live in cities like Hanoi, and children like Hong were a part of that tide. The population of big cities had enormously increased over the last decades of peace, which delighted communist party chauvinists, but the means of supporting that new huge population had not grown with it. Not far from Hanoi I saw a village from which seven-tenths of the population had taken flight. The roofs of its empty houses had fallen in. Nowadays, outside all Vietnam's cities and big towns there were slums of temporary shacks, built of scrap wood and flattened tin. As in Bombay and Calcutta, at night the streets were full of sleepers.

Canute-like, the government tried to stem that swarming in. Not long after Ho Chi Minh's death, the party instituted the most infamous Leninist tool of population control, the Soviet system of household registration, known in Vietnam as the *Hac Khau;* moreover, the local party committee of your birthplace maintained a personal dossier that tracked your every movement and change of address. Sometimes the government sent in the army to level the shantytowns, but they soon sprang up again. The idea of such home-lessness and beggary appalled the party, particularly as the beggars pestered tourists, who would see in the beggary of a few the beggary of all. To the party, the poor were more than a nuisance; they were a disgrace. By abandoning their assigned roles in their villages, they lost their claim on the state. During my stay there was ample talk in Hanoi of rounding up all the beggars, of impounding them, expelling them. There was also talk of declaring the city closed, of forcibly keeping out new arrivals. When you heard such conversations among the Vietnamese elite, you felt as if you were in a city under siege.

Kids from the same villages tended to stick together. They rented rooms jointly, the worst flats in the shabbiest tenements across the Red River Bridge. Six or seven often shared one room, and they sometimes could and did move on the spur of the moment. Six to eight storeys high, the buildings themselves were the urban equivalents of plantation barracks, the equals in late 20th century Hanoi to early industrial England's back-to-back workers' terraces. Vietnamese families ramify, and there might be eight people living in one room, so the arrangements of people like Hong were not very different from those of other people. Even the corners of rooms could be rented out, as in Dostoevski's Saint Petersburg, with people sleeping in shifts. Those tenement rooms were really a base, the single room opening onto a central corridor, and the back of which were lavatories and 'facilities.' Life in such places was lived in the open, in the areas between the tenement blocks, on the streets.

Hong lived on the fifth floor, at the back, in one of those dreadful towers; the building was like something built in Siberia during the Brezhnev era. It was so shoddily put together, so crooked, so lopsided, and so squalid that it should have been torn down before it was ever handed over for people to live in. Kids like Hong had nothing at all to do with the people who lived on the same streets, and in the same tenements as them, and were unwelcome at night outside in front of the building where they roomed, those streets where mothers nursed their babies in public. So the kids became aloof, outcasts, playing cards and telling stories to each other about the tourists they may or may not have 'stiffed' that day.

Many, if not all of the parents of those street kids, were illiterate, so you wondered where their tropism towards learning came from. At a high school near the Vietcom Bank on Hang Bai Street I asked a teacher about them. She said that she had never heard of any who actually returned to school after they quit. 'Their parents demand all their money, all their time. *Give! Give to me!* They can practically hear the shouts from the village. So, even if they save enough money to pay for school, families back home want everything for themselves. I am not saying that they don't deserve it, maybe they do.' When I asked if any of these kids become criminals, a pained look came over the teacher's face. I'd struck a nerve. 'The parents can trick them out of their lives without really trying. If I did not see it every day, I would not believe it.' Some of those children, she said sadly, became gifted grifters and salesmen, the most vulnerable or the pretty ones became prostitutes. Parents would sometimes even encourage that.

It turned out that Hong had begun to think about marriage. It wouldn't be easy for her because men would suspect that she might have turned to prostitution to support herself. There were other men, she could always attract them, she knew that much about herself. But she thought it would be nice if she could marry and finish school— she drew the word out, *schoooool*—and that would be her victory over all she had endured.

Did she have any fun, ever?

It was the wrong question, at least not a good one. She became grave, silent. Something had been breached.

When, after a few moments of silence Hong spoke some more, I noticed that she was using words that she had heard me use. Like 'content.' When we spoke about marriage, about her having fun, I must have used the word. Later it came back to me. And her use of the word made an impression, not only for its mimicry, but because she used the word in a way that she intended, as a way to convey something that her English vocabulary, and probably not her Vietnamese one, either, had ever contemplated. She was talking about how everything in Hanoi was becoming a matter of buying and selling; she even knew that she could sell herself. That was not how she remembered her life before Hanoi: at her parents' home in her village there was a garden with orchids and even some fruit. Both were at times for sale, but they were not grown for that reason. They were intended to allow her parents to be 'content.' Perhaps she had not fully worked out the meaning, the idea, behind the word yet, but she believed in it all the same.

Walking back to my hotel, across the Red River Bridge and into the heart of Hanoi, past the brightly lit Turtle Pagoda on an island in the middle of Ho Hoan Kiem Lake, I spied the usual young lovers. Many of the facades of the lakeside buildings seemed black. Was it grime or the smoke of wartime disaster that had stained them? Hanoi seemed grainy in the evening light in which everything, every human deformity and cheap enterprise, was for a brief moment pure.

Then a young man tried to steal a German tourist's purse. Her shouts for help roused men from every direction who subdued the thief and bustled him into the little police substation just down the lakeshore. As I watched, an old gentlemen moved to my side. 'It's terrible,' he said in perfect English, 'the things the young do for money. I've seen Paris, I've seen Moscow, Beijing too and I know the world. But our young today! The things I now see.' His speech finished, the old man walked off into the darkness. So many turns of fate had confronted that old man, I thought. I was impressed by the idea of all that he had witnessed; his life must have been an immense journey and it led only to this seemingly final disappointment. It seemed as if the real world was being discovered by those made innocent by ideology.

VIII

Days of the Dead

CAMBODIA opened instantly: the break with Vietnam was tangible. No one, however, just 'happens to go' to Phnom Penh. It is a stop on the road to nowhere, and to live there is to live in antimatter. So, choosing Cambodia's capital city as a travel destination implied premeditation. You needed a definite purpose in order to go there, though that purpose would almost certainly be suspect or ill-conceived.

Buddhists believe that nirvana is a state of unbounded happiness, when all that is most desired, awaited, and longed for becomes yours. Entering Phnom Penh's Pochentong airport I felt only a vacuum of human promise. Queuing to be cleared through customs, I received a brief course in Khmer impossibility. No one spoke. Not the men loitering everywhere, rubbing indifferent faces and the night out of their eyes; not the slim female customs agents combing and petting their flat black hair with their hands. A stink of disinfectant fused with urine assaulted, a stench redolent of the late and unlamented Union of Soviet Socialist Republics. Beyond the exterior plate glass walls dust swirled and people moved robotically under a sun of brass.

High on a wall, information boards clicked news of flights delayed and abandoned. So many flights seemed disrupted that it appeared as if some natural disaster or national emergency was taking place. From time to time you heard the roar of a plane taking off, but these were planes that many people in the departure lounge were waiting to board: at that moment, however, different flight numbers with different destinations had been attached to them. Royal Cambodge Airways never had enough aircraft, and over the past month, or so I was told, a number of planes had been withdrawn from service. International flights had recently been established—to Singapore, to Bangkok, even to Tokyo. Planes booked for a domestic flight were sometimes commandeered to meet the demands of the new overseas routes. So domestic service was in daily chaos. Air travel, however, remained a necessary part of the country's administration; every day much of the government was, at any moment, marooned in Pochentong or at provincial airports, as if by an act of bewitchment.

I watched a group of officials waiting for a flight, walled off behind glass and talking desultorily to five Americans in madras shirts and golf course attire. Three of the Americans had only just arrived; they huddled together, relying upon each other. These were not tourists or businessmen; they looked, instead, like the sort of Americans that Washington sends out quietly on special assignments, the sort who head special consultancies and cultivate special relationships within that fluid world where collecting information is indistinguishable from using information, that world where diplomatic, commercial, and private interests merge in a global pool of exchanged favours.

Everyone appeared in a state of impervious heaviness, faces shut down by solemnity, faces on strike against life. These were the Khmers as I imagined them to be under Pol Pot's Khmer Rouge— used, broken people with anxious tales of harassment and flight, of fantastic endurance and pitiful collapse, their voices tremulous with rancour and vibrating with pain, a choral society proclaiming vehemently, 'Do you believe it? Can you imagine it?' even as they affirmed by a thousand acoustical fluctuations of tempo, tone, inflection, and pitch, 'Yet this is exactly what happened!' Such things can happen—such things happened to me, to him, to her, to you, to us. In Cambodia, I would soon learn, stories are not mere stories; they are what people have instead of a life. You become your stories because you are not permitted to be anything else. Here storytelling is a form of resistance against oblivion.

Waiting, watching, it was not long before you met returning

exiles. Not many, a single middle-aged woman standing here, an entire family standing there. Small bands of survivors. Easy to spot. They were better dressed than local Khmers, but the nervous pushing bustle of other well-groomed visitors, German, Japanese, and Thai businessmen, was not in them. Neither was the .quick-minded fortitude of the Vietnamese visible, their speed in isolating and abstracting problems, at detecting and deferring to—and sometimes overcoming—sources of power. Those returning exiles appeared blinkered, detached from everything alive or dead. They had the primary protective instinct of the successful refugee; they never looked back. Or almost never. Years before, they turned their backs on the only world that they knew. *Who could blame them?* Now all life was a blur of opposition. Their indifference appeared like a kind of ascetic religion. They were aware of nothing but their individual selves; the consuming nature of their self-absorption now a zealous mechanism for defeating all awareness of others.

Despite their stillness, their solemnity, they seemed people of excess—excessive in silence, excessive in reserve, excessive in suspicion. They had learned to concentrate, to the exclusion of past and future, in a prolonged amnesiac fugue. They knew from cruel experience how all man's hopes end: they end in nothing. For decades Cambodia was a mass producer of such exiles. Sunk in their diaspora into material ambition or apathy, fatalism, intrigue, or quarrels, those returning exiles—carrying little more than overnight bags—were not like those mouthy Vietnamese-American computer nerds I had seen on the prowl in Saigon in search of docile, divorce-averse wives. Instead, those Khmers seemed to think of themselves as that almost extinct breed of American, the old Puritans of New England, the elect of God. Which, indeed, they were in many ways: they had survived when millions of others had not.

In this kingdom of exile and expatriation, even the country's beloved ruling monarch, King Norodom Sihanouk, did not live in his riverside palace in Phnom Penh but resided in lavish exile in state guesthouses in Pyongyang and Beijing. When a king cannot bear his kingdom for more than a few days at a time, you realize that you have entered a country scarcely able to tolerate its own people.

Keeping your distance was the logic of the place. Immigration was finessed through a picket of automatic weapons. By whose authority the weapons were brandished (Royal Cambodian Army, or National Police, or Customs Police, or Cambodian People's Party militia, or any one of a proliferation of shadowy and overlapping forces) was anyone's guess. In any event, eye contact with the men carrying the weapons was to be avoided. Documents were scrutinized, up and down and back again, by people who probably could not make head nor tail of the language in which they were printed.

In Vietnam, I had seen two classes of people: those who had power and those who did not. Two classes were also visible in Pochentong: you saw thin, crumpled-up peasants, lean and noble looking people; you also saw the fantastic divide between them and the bland, unlined faces of the fat, whose chins sagged like melons under their jawbones, men whose small eyes had the innocence, the surprise, the resignation and the malice of people privileged to be obese in a land of hunger and poverty. So, Cambodia, like Vietnam, appeared to be a country split down the middle: but here the divide was between those who ate well and those who did not.

Cambodia invariably brought me down to such fundamentals; he eats well; she does not; she lives; he does not. Lucky and unlucky: the familiar words of Khmer life displayed a primitive dichotomy between good and evil.

Thlauk was the Khmer embassy official who had issued my Khmer visa in Hanoi. As she was going to Phnom Penh on the same flight I was taking, she had promised to wait and take me into the city after I cleared customs. Originally, when I met her at the Khmer embassy in Hanoi to purchase a visa, my intention was to fly back to Saigon and take a boat up the Mekong to Phnom Penh. Shaking her head and vetoing this plan, Thlauk issued her own travel advisory. There were many reports of piracy on the river, she told me. Don't even think about doing that. Besides, her country's politics had turned violent once more. Better to go straight to the capital, check into a good hotel—'You can afford one, can't you?' she asked—and get a sense of the place before venturing into the countryside.

Thlauk was free with her time and open with her advice because her diplomatic posting was ending. She had been reassigned from Hanoi to the Khmer embassy in Germany. In the ride into town she began to lay down rules about Cambodia, telling me all the things that I should and should not do. 'You'll learn the things to look out for soon enough, the details on which to concentrate. But I will give you a start.' In myriad forms, her warnings became ones I would hear time and time again. Don't walk the streets after dark; don't use a motorcycle taxi, only a car; never go to nightclubs. If stopped by thugs or the police, keep your mouth shut; do everything they ask. Never go near Tuklo, the hooker shantytown just up the road from the new, concrete Japan-Cambodia Friendship Bridge that spanned the Bassac river. Avoid venturing into any building occupied by an opposition political party, or being anywhere near political gatherings. Political dirty tricks here consisted of tossing hand grenades into rallies. More of these warnings came as we shared a taxi to the Intercontinental Hotel on Mao Tse-tung Boulevard. I felt like a patient hearing details about the operation I was to undergo. I would have liked to have ignored them, but the city we were passing through on the way to the hotel incited unease: one-walled enclave after another, districts surrounded by no-man's lands of utter desolation. As the taxi pulled up at the guard post before the Intercontinental, I turned to ask if there was anyone she would recommend that I meet in order to get started in trying to understand the place. Thlauk, who had been in a robust mood, grabbed my hand to say good-bye. 'I don't need to help you with that,' she said, staring dully out the window. 'Not at all. In Phnom Penh, you are surrounded by eye witnesses.'

*

THE MORNING light was brilliant and flat, the sort of dry season day when whiteness eats at your bones and you feel a metallic emptiness in your belly. A motorcycle driver recommended by Thlauk was waiting outside the hotel. Sa Ron was a thin nervous boy with a drained sort of face; his eyes, set back into his skull, watered with the wind.

Weaving through the morning traffic, we soon turned onto a white gravel road that led to Tuol Seng, once Phnom Penh's premier *lycée* but now both a national museum and a memorial. The few dozen tourists visiting the city at any one time, and most official delegations from abroad—diplomatic, commercial—were inevitably deposited at the former jail for a visit. Many touched the cell walls where so many Khmers had been incarcerated and murdered, as if it were a shrine. Most jails in Cambodia were old and brutal monuments to colonial rule. Tuol Seng, the unintended prison, with its bullet pocked modern concrete, was the most infamous.

Drivers who took western tourists to visit Tuol Seng were fulsome in their descriptions of the brutality of Khmer Rouge oppression; Asian visitors, particularly those from China, received more guarded tales. Sa, a young man who lost most of his family in the killing fields, and who said he had no faith in the future, was disgusted by the urge of foreigners to visit the place. In this, Sa was like most other Khmers; many had a horror of events from the Pol Pot era being commemorated. They were haunted by the notion that so much bad karma could be imprisoned within a museum's walls. Once started, Sa's reminiscence about his family tumbled out so fast and furious that it seemed a chaotic delirium of which I could grasp little. No orderly stream of memory arranged his thoughts; his mind seemed to have rushed back into childhood as if he had been caught in a burning ball and hurled there, his spirit shrivelled to the dimensions of a child's small frenzy of life. Tuol Seng, he said, was a monument to all the lies and betrayals of Khmer history. Better to pull it down. Destroy it. Move on.

At the entrance to the palm-lined schoolyard, disturbingly gentle for what I knew lay within, two Khmer girls in dirty floral dresses were selling tickets. A policeman—short and dripping sweat—monitored the transactions from beneath a flowering frangipani tree, cocking his head every now and then to check out a small hive of activity within the barbed wire enclosure. In the centre of the schoolyard stood a small, one-room building with barred windows. A group of older men and women were gathered outside of it, clutching numbers, waiting for their papers to be checked and a Polaroid taken. They were being processed for voter registration and needed an official stamp and photograph before they could be certified as eligible to vote in elections to be held later in the year.

The officer swiped the papers from one old man and mumbled a few words that the man repeated. When the guard finished, he reached for the papers of the woman next in line to repeat the ritual.

The old woman cringed and ripped the papers from his grasp.

'Come on, dearie,' the officer appeared to say with the soothing, humouring-the-mad manner of a London bobby.

'Oh come on,' the man, probably her husband, appeared to wheedle her. But the old woman only shook her head 'No' and locked her hands behind her back. The old man now gently uncurled his wife's fingers and tugged the papers loose.

The officer pronounced the oath, the old woman echoing the words after him as if she were about to choke. The officer smiled, nodded 'OK' and then stamped some form on which the woman now scrawled her signature. On the wall behind were photographs of King Sihanouk and Queen Monineath. The old woman sucked her thumb and stared, bug-eyed, at the Queen's diamond tiara.

'Now what?' the officer seemed to ask, a growing impatience evident on his face.

The old man nudged his wife out of the way, shaking his head, 'Nothing.' The two ambled inside for their photographs. They returned in a few moments, walking past a flagstaff without a flag and across the burnt lawn. It had rained a little during the night and they splashed through one or two remaining puddles until they reached a group of young boys booting a football against one of the former schoolhouse's walls.

For three years, beginning in 1976, Tuol Seng served as the main torture centre of the Khmer Rouge in Phnom Penh. Twenty thousand men, women, and children were 'processed' within it—beaten and brutalized until they 'confessed' to being enemies of 'the ankor' (the party), photographed with identity numbers hanging around their necks, finally killed in ways that would make your hair stand on end. In keeping with the Luddite spirit of the Khmer Rouge and their loathing of capitalist modernity, the preferred instruments of execution were axes, hammers, and bands with fixed blades that were fastened to the throat to slit it.

There was also a kind of small, rudimentary gallows where men and women once hung like braces of pheasants. Some years ago I saw photographs of Tuol Seng's victims at an exhibition at the Museum of Modern Art in New York—horrific suffering reduced to an aesthetic. Nowadays, in Phnom Penh, those yellowing photographs were posted like giant sheets of stamps on the walls of the old interrogation rooms. The eyes in those photographs were black and concentrated; men and women, old and young, staring into the nothingness that awaited them. Tuol Seng's other classrooms-turned-dungeons, rotted by damp, were plastered with photographs of mutilated corpses taken from the institution's meticulous files. In one was a model-map of Cambodia composed of skulls.

Tuol Seng meant certain death for those who entered it: treason was always the charge, and death was 'righteously' imposed after confession. Outside the first row of cells hung a sign from the old days. The sign listed ten 'security' commandments:

1. You must answer accordingly to my questions. Don't turn them away.

2. Don't try to hide the facts by making pretexts this and that. You are strictly prohibited to contest me.

3. Don't be a fool for you are chap who dare to thwart the revolution.

4. You must immediately answer my questions without wasting (sic) time to reflect.

5. Don't tell me either about your immoralities or the essence of the revolution.

6. While getting lashes or electrification you must not cry at all.

7. Do nothing, sit still and wait for my orders. If there is no order, keep quiet. When I ask you to do something, you must do it right away without protesting.

8. Don't make pretexts about Kampuchea Krom in order to hide your jaw of traitor.

9. If you don't follow all the rules, you shall get many, many lashes of electric wire.

10. If you disobey any point of my regulations you must get either ten lashes or five shocks of electric discharge.

Not long after the Vietnamese invaded Cambodia to oust the Khmer Rouge, Tuol Seng was converted into a museum modelled on the Nazi concentration camp museums in Eastern Europe and renamed the 'Genocide Museum.' But Pol Pot's killing fields do not really fit the internationally accepted legal definition of genocide, which the UN defines as 'acts committed with intent to destroy, in whole or in part, a national, ethnical, racial, or religious group.' Although Cambodian citizens of Vietnamese extraction and members of the country's minority tribes were singled out for Khmer Rouge persecution, the root crime of Pol Pot's regime was the systematic mass murder of ordinary Cambodians by the Cambodian state. As in Stalin's USSR and Mao's China, slaughter was committed in the name of Communism, and to say that it was not genocide does not diminish the horror. If anything, killing your own people may be more unfathomable than the us-versus-them murder of 'others.'

Nearly all those killed at Tuol Seng were Khmer Rouge members, operatives, or sympathizers. Within a year of seizing power, the Sorbonne graduates (Pol Pot, Ieng Sary, Khieu Samphan, and many other senior Khmer Rouge leaders had all attended university in Paris) who commanded the Khmer Rouge effectively annihilated most of their country's urban and educated classes. Paper money was abolished; the entire population reduced to slavery as forced labourers, without schools and without medical facilities. Yet Pol Pot remained wary. Revolution, he believed, had to be a continuous dialectical struggle with counter-revolution. But as he searched for counter-revolutionary enemies in a land laid waste of opposition, his paranoia became unbounded. Like Goya's painting of Saturn devouring his children, the Khmer Rouge began to cannibalize themselves. The rough numbers of those loyal to the regime killed within Tuol Seng sketch the curve of Pol Pot's savagery: two hundred 'enemies' processed in 1975; two thousand two hundred and sixty in 1976; more than six thousand in 1977; ten thousand in 1978. If the Khmer Rouge can be said to have had a guiding principle it was this: *purge or be purged.*

'None of my relations were killed here,' said Sa, with certain pride, 'they were killed somewhere else.' That brief glimpse into Sa's family history, in the middle of this death house, was revealing, for it touched on the unquenched desired for justice: those killed in Tuol Seng, his tone implied, were somehow culpable. Those killed elsewhere were not.

As we walked toward Sa's motorcycle every sound seemed to have fled. Dark fragrances washed down from trees huddled near the prison wall like lost children. The sky was dazzling, a primeval glow. As if summoning itself for the first or last time, the sky became a piercing blue. In that undiluted light the concrete buildings paled, seeming to dissolve.

Then, as would happen again and again in Cambodia, the absurd struck. We were preparing to leave when another visitor entered the school's former playground. He loudly paid for his ticket—if he was going to be charged, he wanted a guidebook, or at least a guide, he barked—and wandered toward us, a well-dressed, cheerful, vigorous looking man. He was, I supposed, in his early fifties; he was probably a prosperous businessman, but he looked more like a robust, opinionated, old-fashioned bartender on his day off. He was American, perhaps Canadian.

'I hope I'm not bothering you,' he said. 'I was going back to my hotel and then remembered that this place was supposed to be nearby, so I. decided to drop in. God, they are letting it rot,' he muttered, kicking at the burnt turf. 'What a mess! What a pity! It's awful. They should keep it up, spic and span. Maybe even add a video centre. One day maybe even one of those virtual reality devices so that you can get a sense of what the Khmer Rouge time was really like. If they cared for the place, if they did a little planning and made some investments, people would come. I've been to Auschwitz, Treblinka, and Buchenwald. There are facilities you can use at all of them. Even the Russians are getting the hang of it. I hear that they now have organized tours to the gulag, Perm 22, Kolyma. Here? Just look at this place;' he kicked another divot in the mottled grass. 'There is nothing. I'm telling you, this is a lost opportunity.'

Snack bars and videos and loos for tourists: that was how the history of human sorrow was to be commemorated.

*

A CERTAIN tendency toward dressing up, or disguising a situation, may have been inevitable in Phnom Penh, because Cambodia's unimproved situation was such that to consider it as given, was to come face to face with moral extinction. Which was precisely what Youk Chhang did each day.

The office of the Documentation Centre of Cambodia that Youk directed was set behind a tall black wrought iron gate in a low rent district of concrete bunker-type houses on Sihanouk Boulevard, not far from the Bassac river. The Centre, commonly known as the Genocide Project, was housed on the building's upper floors; someone had to come down into the courtyard to let you in. Once approved by the doorman, who visually frisked me through a peephole in the gate, I was escorted to the Project's office through a garage. No trophy Land Rover, Toyota, or Mercedes four wheel drive clogged the driveway, as they did at the compounds of most NGOs in Phnom Penh. Only a battered white Nissan and some aging Suzuki motorcycles were to be seen. Steps to the office were narrow and slightly twisted; the lights were low.

Seated at his black desk, Youk was going through the morning letters, faxes, and emails. Like a gambler looking at his cards, he glanced and threw some letters, unopened, into a trash bin. No telephone stood on his desk; it was like he did not trust that instrument for his purposes. After a few moments Youk looked up and addressed me by my last name. At first it seemed like scorn. Later I realized it was his style.

Youk was constructed like a heron—a lean, taut, and blade-faced six-footer. He had the look of someone without a choice. His story had been made up beforehand. To tear himself from things on behalf of his cause—that's all there is for him to do. And it wasn't just his physique that was a filament of steel; his character, too, was tool-like and contoured like the polished silhouette of an airline fuselage.

Youk had what a former colleague of mine, a Glaswegian Scot, called a 'watch-eye': pale for a Khmer and slightly bulging. Those eyes were the most striking feature in a face of absolute composure. Out on the street, he was as anonymous as any Khmer. In his face, if you looked carefully, were flashes of patience and strength and the ethic of those schooled to accomplish impossible things. He was one of those men, like Atticus Finch in *To Kill a Mockingbird*, which all societies require but rarely find: the sort of men and women made to do our dirtiest work.

Behind Youk's desk was a photograph from 1986 of Pol Pot holding his daughter like any loving dad. Above that photo was one of Youk with his own nine-year old daughter. Youk noticed my interest in that juxtaposition of photographs: 'I'm not sure that anyone gets the irony. Not here.' Then, more wistfully, 'how could a father do what he did, what he was still doing at the time the photograph was taken?'

The sympathy I felt was for Youk's singleness of thought and, given the fears within the government about his Project (how many of Hun Sen's people, let alone Hun Sen, had bloody hands from their roles in the Pol Pot era?) what must have been an unbounded capacity for loneliness. A necessary loneliness. Within government circles he was famous, or nearly so. Because little was known by them about his background and real motives, Youk was perceived as a threat. He was CIA; he was working for the Chinese; no, the Vietnamese, who sought to keep Cambodia out of the orbit of China, were his real masters. You heard all sorts of things. Slanderous, paranoid stories could be picked up in any ministry, like confused shots fired in the dark. Attacks on Youk or the Project that reached the newspapers, published among the sports scores and crimes, were cut out, collected, and filed away by the Project's staff. Youk pretended to scorn those clippings. He kept them despite himself; he didn't fight back with his own tabloid broadsides. What he had done, what he would do, could all be explained by the documents, he said, and those would be revealed in the great criminal trials of the Khmer Rouge that he dreamed would one day take place. To engage in tit-for-tat fights, something might be lost that way. Struggles of the greatest value, he knew, were conducted alone.

As all of Youk's moral principles had assumed the fixity of the laws of gravity, he appeared also to know and observe little. His was an existence completely focussed, and one of the last fanatics of a religion, the religion of truth, that seemed to have been killed off across Indochina. Within the Genocide Project he found his life.

The Khmer research assistants in the Project's office watched Youk as computer screens glittered. You could hear the velvet din of microchips, that thin, threadlike murmur. Some of the Project's staff were working on satellite photographs to trace the existence of killing fields. From outer space, laser photography could determine if tracts of earth had ever been disturbed and if the soil content was different—holding or withholding more or less heat—from the soils around it. When identified and located, those sites could be excavated in search of bodies or skeletal remains. On a smaller scale of massacre, that technology was tested after the Bosnian war in places like Srebrenica. Now, an entire country was being x-rayed from orbit.

Others among the staff of twenty five were examining over 350,000 pages of documents—oral histories of survivors and perpetrators, profiles of Khmer Rouge cadres, ministerial orders, supply requests, dispatches, maps, photographs, letters, copies of the songs sung by Pol Pot's army as they marched their fellow citizens into the fields and to their deaths, the personal diaries and letters of young guerrillas. 'How are you?' one 15 year-old boy wrote to his father in 1978. 'How is my village? How is my cow?' Despite their loathing of modernity, it seems, the Khmer Rouge were modern in one thing: their love of paperwork and bureaucracy. They were as painstaking in documenting their slaughters as the Nazis. 'When I showed Ieng Sary some death orders with his signature on them,' said Youk, 'I thought he would go into convulsions. He had forgotten his Parisian training, that urge to keep the files perfect and up-to-date.'

The staff was like a revolutionary cell. For the cause you gave everything. They were leading a visionary existence. One day they would walk up wide steps to tremendous applause.

Girls working on survey maps, and young men scanning documents into computer files for future use by an international war crimes tribunal, came up to Youk with their questions, or to describe the progress of their assignments, their thick lips parted in expectation. He would lower his eyes to their papers, his eyelids quivering as he frowned or smiled against the artificial light. Sweat stood on the coarse skin of his face as one girl described the diary entries of a Khmer Rouge officer. Such moments made Youk's face look like that of a naked boy, fearful and desperate.

The banality of evil: up to now I had thought Hannah Arendt's most famous maxim as nothing more than a bit of too-clever-by-half journalistic phrase-making, something that could not possibly capture the horror of Eichmann caged within bulletproof glass during his Jerusalem trial. The documents that Youk had collected, however, cardboard box after cardboard box, told me that I was wrong. So much despair, so much pain, so many tears were represented in those bland pages. The fate of the Khmers: mindless persecution and mayhem. All of it was recorded in Youk's documents. Each page represented someone praying for endurance, someone begging for his or her life. I could sense under Youk's determination to decipher and disseminate all of this the gnawing of a deep personal agony. It eclipsed everything, distorting and recasting his whole vision of the world.

True scholarship should always outlast the scholar. Insights, learning, maybe even comfort: they are transmitted across time and tongue by meticulous documentation. Youk spoke of his work in that way, like one of the Irish monks caring for all the known world's learning in the midst of the dark ages. But Youk's dark ages were also his own life story. He had lived in the killing fields but had escaped; his family did not. It was one of those experiences that cuts a life in two. He found himself in a refugee camp afterwards, then in Dallas, Texas. That American education, however, did not create distance; when he completed law school those green fields and paddies called him back. His life was in that ground.

Those fields had been a furnace for Youk. The demands unending, the pleasures—yes the pleasures—cruel. Goya knew them; Thucydides; Isaac Babel too. One morning there are normal household smells, your mother cooking, laundry being washed in a rain barrel at the back, and at the next a sudden arrest and hasty sentencing. The Khmer Rouge knew the family was a nest of intellectuals, or worse. People were being killed back then for the crime of wearing eye-glasses. So all of you got marched to join others who were also without hope, marched to wild districts, handed shovels and told to dig. It was a dam you were supposed to be digging, but also your grave, and in silence, the silence of which you would soon be part. In your grip was the spade's smooth wooden handle, and the first shovelful of earth seemed like one of the most precious moments of life. If only it could be made to last. In those years, nothing lasted; your family was buried in shallow paddies with anonymous others, flies feasting on their faces. Somehow you escaped.

Seated there, recalling everything, Youk tried to physically seize these things again. The expression on his face said it all: after all the research, the introspection, there was still no reason that Youk could grasp for what had happened to him, to his family, to his country.

*

IT WAS YOUK Chhang who arranged for me to meet Entero Chey, a leading Phnom Penh lawyer and entrepreneur, and a partner in a San Francisco law firm. Chey was enthusiastic when I called: 'Yes, come and meet the rest of us.'

The 'rest of us' was a group of Cambodian writers and intellectuals who were meeting that night for one of their irregular dinner gatherings. The *Lidee Khmer* (League of Cambodian Intellectuals) had taken some time to get going, as there were not only debates about who should and should not be allowed to join, but also about where to hold their *café litteraire*. Organized by a group of Khmers who had returned from professorships at the University of San Francisco and the mathematics faculty at Strasbourg, there seemed to be no single location in Phnom Penh that could or could not have been deemed out-of-bounds by at least one or more of the would-be participants. Eventually, an outdoor restaurant across the Japan/Cambodia Friendship Bridge was chosen, down a lonely stretch of river and set on pylons overlooking rice paddies.

When I arrived a dozen people were seated under a covered terrace that looked over the Bassac river. Vigilant faces, unrecallable names. The light was cool, filtered through ferns and flowering jalapani, around each bulb was a little cloud of river insects. There were old wicker rockers and a map of the city and a wooden table with a typewriter, a can of *Planter's Mixed Nuts*, assorted local newspapers and dog-eared, fortnight old editions of the *International Herald Tribune* and *L'Express*. In the shadows beyond the bar was a battered refrigerator from which the club's members fetched bottles of red-labelled Angkor beer. We sat in the sedative half-light behind a table littered with broken pistachio shells, drinking cold beer and talking in a desultory way about *la condition Khmer*. A lime-throated bird warbled above; a colony of toads skipped across the floorboards. Gradually, the beauty of the place had an anaesthetic effect on me, temporarily deadening that receptivity to the sinister that afflicts almost everyone in Cambodia.

The host that night was one of Chey's fellow members of the bar, a crippled lawyer. Phnom Penh was full of anxious, idle lawyers;

hundreds of students take law at the university. He clasped his hands as if in prayer and bowed, the traditional Khmer greeting, then his fingers gripped my arm and he fixed me with an intense stare. On his face were weariness and the haze of ordeal. He gave me a sticky aperitif of his own manufacture and sat me in a chair. A man of forty-something, he had read a great deal, chiefly poetry and the novels of Camus and Sartre: he loathed both Frenchmen for their 'realism.'

'There must be a great romantic revival, and not just here but everywhere,' he said in an exalted, pretty way. 'After Pol Pot, the world has only the possibilities of becoming romantic or of becoming nothing. Pessimism, I believe, is going. There is joy. Everywhere you look,' he said. 'In the heart,' and he plucked at his breast. 'In the spirit,' he said, boring a delicate finger into his ribs. 'In the mind,' he said, pinching his eyebrows together with four fingers.

'After twenty five years of horror?' asked Pen Samarith, the editor of Phnom Penh's major daily *Rasmea Kampuchea.*

'Because of those horrors,' the lawyer continued. 'I will give you an example. In Pol Pot's time I was arrested and put to work in ditch. It was like being condemned to death; you got out of the ditch when you died. I saw my friends, some of the best people in Kampuchea, taken off to be beaten to death. I went last year back to the place where we worked in that hole. I went down into the spot where I used to be. It wasn't horrible. It was indescribable. "Here", I said, "is where I crouched at night. Here so-and-so died beside me, and from here many were taken out and seen no more." And you know what? I was happy. I was not sad, I was not filled with guilt. I wasn't happy because I alone had survived, but because I lived it all over again. I felt ecstasy. That is what our country is still feeling now, ecstasy at having lived through terrible times—exultation, a heroic feeling that one has been chosen, that a people have been chosen to endure everything. We Kampucheans *are* a chosen people. It is romantic. It is poetic. It is strange. It is not real and yet it is real.'

Prek, who advised the liberal opposition leader Sam Rainsy, had been, unlike the lawyer, an early supporter of the Khmer Rouge. Yet he said much the same thing about the Pol Pot years: the horrors were unspeakable, but 'the sensation, the excitement in the emptying of the city, of building a whole world again, was pleasing.'

Until he, too, joined the death march. That exodus to the fields was more than a displacement in space and time. 'It was the beginning of our dehumanization: those who reached the fields where they would work and die—if they had not died along the road—were stripped of everything that is human. Your surname: gone, useless, worse than useless. You didn't know where you were; you didn't know what the Angkor would do with you. Your language was taken, for you did not want to give yourself away by how you spoke; no one spoke to you. You were a tool, an oxen in the field; you were a thing; you were nothing.'

The number of phantasmagoric stories I heard seemed endless. And it wasn't just the Pol Pot era that stunned. There were innumerable strange situations today. Where else in the world could a man and his wife travel to a village—Duk Meas, a hamlet in Kampot Province was the place—in order to find young girls for their string of Phnom Penh brothels, with no disguise that this was their business? The couple would pay parents $100 for a girl of ten or eleven; if they cared to sell three daughters at once they could be paid with a used Honda motorcycle. The girls were tied together by rope and paraded through the village as the couple collected more girls.

Where else but in Cambodia would a distinguished surgeon, trained in Paris, return home to renounce his profession and the world, repent not only of his past life but of his knowledge and go about, as a novice monk, prescribing herbs for the sick, refusing money, and living in squalor? Cambodia after Pol Pot produced an enormous number of solitaries; the pagodas by no means absorb all the country's disjointed souls, the unwanted and uprooted. There was a tale about two old ladies shut up in a big house along Sisowath Quay. They had moved into the house during the days when the Khmer Rouge had emptied the city. They were the daughters of a royal clerk and of a family that claimed ancient distinction and wealth. Alone in the empty city, these two ladies found their fortunes worthless; no one could be paid to get them water from the river as there was no running water in all Phnom Penh. At night, they would go out late so as not to be seen, getting the water themselves from the Tonle Sap. This was the only time they left the house. But the

women were old and terrified they might be seen. Fear shut them in.
They died of thirst.

That night I listened to dozens of tales of endurance, of family
and personal pride, and this story of the two old ladies, like that of
the bordello owners and the lawyer, did not sound untrue.

Only one person, the vice-rector of the Royal Phnom Penh
University, arrived late that evening. Of the seventy-six professors at
the university at the time of Pol Pot's march into Phnom Penh, only
two survived the Khmer Rouge years. He was one. Always intransi-
gent. When a group of Khmer generals under the leadership of Lon
Nol, acting on orders from the Nixon administration—or so most
people believe—overthrew King Sihanouk, this man calmly
squatted in the street before the US embassy and set himself ablaze
in protest.

He described the scene. He was a young man then, sitting cross-
legged and straight-backed on that empty street, gracefully seated in
front of the crowd who gathered to witness the event as though to
observe a religious ritual. He upended a large plastic canister,
pouring the kerosene over himself, drenching the asphalt around
him. Then he struck the match. A nimbus of flames came roiling out
of him. The flames seemed to be shooting forward into the air from
within him, not just from his mouth, but in an instantaneous eruption
from his scalp and face and chest and lap and legs and feet. Because
he remained upright, giving no indication that he could feel himself
ablaze, let alone cry out, the US Marines guarding the embassy at
first thought it looked like a circus stunt, as though what was being
consumed in flame was not the scholar but the air, the scholar setting
the air on fire while no harm befell him. His was the posture of
someone leading an entirely other life at that moment, one
untouched by what was happening to him in view of the entire
world. No screaming, no writhing, just calm in the eye of the
inferno.

News photographers snapped; news cameras rolled; the Marines
in their dress blue uniforms reacted, throwing him to the ground;
beating out the flames. By some miracle he survived, spent two
years in an American hospital, skin graft after skin graft painfully
applied, only to be sentenced, five years later, to a Khmer Rouge

work camp. One day he was left out to die by the camp commandant, buried up to his neck in mud, abandoned for fire ants to devour. Some tribesmen, however, came out from the forest before dawn and dug him up with their hands. He survived the next two years with them.

In that riverside café, he contributed little to the conversation, though he followed the discussions closely. Slender, olive-hewed, the first thing I noticed about him was not the mottled, bite and flame scarred skin on his small hands and the taut lesions peeking through between the opened collar of his shirt. No, what I noticed was his quiet manner of sitting, his absolute stillness. A whole philosophy was in it—his legs natural, his wrists and hands even more at ease. For some time after the Vietnamese invasion he had been placed in a madhouse, supposedly for his own good. Seeing him, I guessed that probably all that he had required in that place was an out-of-the-bedlam corner in which to squat in thought. Watching him sit aloof in that shadowy café, I imagined him doing the calculus in his head; providing answers to unsolved equations. What was unimaginable was that such a gently abstracted man should be capable of dousing himself, in silence, with gasoline and setting himself on fire, or that he could remain silent for hours on end as insects gnawed his grafted flesh.

Like him, I listened carefully to the conversations—utterly attentive and mute. I did not want to speak carelessly, knowing what so many of them had suffered. 'For God's sake,' my friend and colleague Andrzej Rapaczynski advised me when I went to Poland for the first time after communism's fall, 'don't get carried away by what people tell you!' I remembered that warning, yet it was not long before I began to feel that I had been dropped into a shoreless sea.

From the start of the gathering, the conversation fogging the air was instantly serious—'tormented' is perhaps a better word. Small talk was not something you heard often in Phnom Penh. Those people, however, were not much given to the usual mandarin pursuits of solutions and abstractions: though intellectuals, their lives were grounded in the specific—like all survivors, they had acquired the art of the practical. Besides, how much can ever be resolved in looking for clarity? Cambodia allowed for no smooth or glib alternatives. Every choice seemed full of difficulty and heartbreak. Here were some sentences spoken that night: 'It is not possible to speak of intellectual life in Cambodia. Everyday we lose more. We are regressing constantly. Intellectual life is drying up. You are looking at the intellectual life of Cambodia; here in this room. We are the only survivors. Some of the others are out of the country, in Paris, in London, in Los Angeles. Others are not writing or thinking because they are involved in political action. Some still disappear. Teaching remains very dangerous; if a student misinterprets what a teacher says, then the teacher may be detained. The best teachers from the old days are in exile too. Or they are dead. There is no one after us, no young ones. It is all over, don't you realize?'

Such despairing discussions were not strange to me. Intelligent, informed people throughout Eastern Europe often used an 'endgame' vocabulary. Nevertheless, intelligent discussions, black prophecies were not *always* idle chatter. What was erroneous about them was that people invariably inject their own intelligence into what they discuss. Later, when historians look back, they reveal that what really happened was mostly devoid of anything like intelligence. History and politics and their impact on culture are not at all like the notions developed by intelligent, informed people. Tolstoi made this clear in the opening pages of *War and Peace*. In Anna Schérer's salon, elegant guests discuss *the* scandal of Napoleon and the Duc d'Enghien, and Prince Andrei says that, after all, there was a great difference between Napoleon the Emperor and Napoleon the private person. You had *raisons d'état* and you had private crimes. What was perpetuated (even in a outdoor café along the Bassac river) in all civilised discussion was the ritual of civilised discussion, of civilization itself. In Phnom Penh that night, such a ritual was a kind of triumph.

Strip the conversation of mandarin flourishes, however, and what remained was talk about survival. Throughout all my days in Indochina, that tropism toward the primal was the hardest thing to grasp. You sat for tea, a beer, or dinner with charming people, and would suddenly realise that the person to your left had lost a father, mother, grandparents, and three cousins in the first year of the Pol Pot regime; that in the street outside, coolly sweet with night flowers and dark green under lamps tacked to poles, many other families had lost children and parents and friends. On a soft night, in the domestic or social ceremonies of filled glasses and overflowing ashtrays, thoughts of an unappeasable hatred, of an absolute and unremitting enemy—evil remains the better but more unfashionable word—were hard to grasp as *real*. It was only slowly, over time, that you began to understand that there was one fact of *Khmer* life that could not be taken for granted by anyone: the right to live. How long, I wondered, would it be before any of the people seated around me would even begin to take that right as natural once again?

No sooner had I asked myself that question than my mind turned one hundred and eighty degrees. A few of the people seemed curiously lethargic about their current freedoms, and I began to wonder if the credit of communism, of revolution, still ran strong with any of them. How many, I asked myself, might have once exulted—in private or in public—at the slow death of the American-backed Lon Nol regime between 1973 and 1975 and the first appearances in Phnom Penh of the Khmer Rouge?

In one of his journals, Baudelaire suggested that life was a hospital in which each patient believed that recovery would come only if he or she was moved to another bed. Visiting Phnom Penh, you could not help but become an amateur, involuntary student of Baudelaire's morbidity. You learned from shopkeepers, cab drivers, market women, and street hustlers alike that 'revolutionary' ideas (bed-changing ideas), which were nowadays banal and thoroughly discredited across the continent of their birth, had deeply penetrated, and perhaps still remained—burrowed and buried, yet very much alive—within all levels of Khmer society.

Anticipating the coming victory of communism in 1975, the procrustean bed that cures all evil, many Khmer intellectuals—was it because so many had gone to university in Paris?—readied themselves opportunistically, even enthusiastically, for careers in the new regime. Baudelaire spoke in *Mon Coeur Mis à Nu* of his wild excitement during the Revolution of 1848, of a 'desire for revenge' and sensual 'pleasure in destruction.' Some of the people in that riverside café may also have yearned for the thrilling atmosphere of the Inquisition, the *auto de fé*, which a successful communist revolution invariably initiates. Little did Phnom Penh's chattering classes know back then what Pol Pot had in mind for them! Since the fall of the Khmer Rouge, Cambodia's leaders had decades in which to teach the Khmer people the facts of communism everywhere. Instead, Hun Sen's regime denounced the crimes of the Khmer Rouge without denigrating the ideas that animated those crimes. Hun Sen, to justify his repressive measures, told one impertinent interviewer that freedom was less important that equality, security, and the welfare of the peasants. In helping to interpret such muddle, political theorists appear to be less useful than mythologists and demonologists.

*

ALMOST HALF a century after France gave Cambodia its independence, the grandeur of the French-built city could still be seen in a ghostly way at night, when the crowds of the day retreated. That French-built city could still be glimpsed, because little had been added since independence. Energy and investment had poured into Asia for decades but Phnom Penh had been bypassed and seemed, instead, to be living off its entrails.

Certain buildings in Phnom Penh seemed not to have received a touch of paint in fifty years. On some walls and pillars old posters and glue had formed a tattered kind of papier-mâché crust. Scrape away the crust and you might pull away the stucco. The majority of buildings looked between fifty and one hundred years old. Many were long and narrow, with large open windows at the front, and long low porches across the second storeys. Some were big and rambling, with wings and cupolas and pillars with front and side balconies. Some wooden buildings remained on every street, unlike in Saigon, good teak and mahogany had gone into them, as well as good carpentry. Despite the current poverty of many owners, some effort was being made to keep them up. Yet all but a few looked dilapidated. Roofs sagged, pillars were missing from porches, many rotten beams had been replaced with corrugated steel strips or by new boards that didn't match in size and quality. The eeriest thing was that a city of one million retained an empty look, as if, decades after Pol Pot had evacuated the city, Phnom Penh's citizens were ready at a moment's notice to run off to somewhere safe.

The city's famous old hotels—the Grande Hotel, where André

Malraux awaited trial for his thefts from the temples of Angkor in 1923, for example—were closed, in advanced decay, and Khmers now squatted in rooms once off-limits to them. Decay within; decay without: Phnom Penh retained the feel of a colonial city just at the moment of independence, when after a long underground struggle peasant armies invade the capital and camp where they will.

Invade, camp, squat: they are the right words. In 1976, the city had been emptied by force, the entire population frog-marched into the countryside. When the Vietnamese invaded two years later, Khmers trickled back and camped in the empty buildings. As the Khmer Rouge armies were pushed westward toward Thailand, refugees from the forced evacuation of the city and peasants from the countryside arrived in Phnom Penh, clogging large areas in and around the city. Since then the population of the capital had trebled, but the housing stock had barely increased.

By day, there was no room on the streets or in the large sun burnt parks. Few places offered shade. The two air-conditioned buses that once ran from the city's Soviet-built Central Market had to be discontinued because people would pay the one thousand riel fare (about twenty cents) and never get off. You could drive slowly along a dug-up road and through the crowds to the Naga casino club, and there the city's elite could go jet-skiing on the Bassac river all the way down to where it flows into the Mekong. Once back, the kerosene and diesel and petroleum fumes would undo the little good you may have done yourself. People said that when the French ruled the city's streets were washed every day. France built the city and stamped its mark on it. That time was now regarded as Phnom Penh's golden age.

A city with more than one million people, with almost no public transport, with few industries, Phnom Penh seemed to exist nowadays only because the French had built it. So many jobs appeared shadowy and political, part of an artificial administration for an artificial economy living off global handouts. At night the enduring life of the country—the peasantry of the fields and paddies—appeared in the heart of Phnom Penh, as the armed guards outside ministries and private homes (their jobs were also shadow jobs; they protected nothing) barricaded their territory by using whatever industrial junk was at hand. They lit fires on broken pavements, cooking messy little curries, and then slept. When the city was hot, the gutters smelled wretchedly; in the rains the streets flooded. And the unregulated, undead city was spreading: meandering black rivulets of filth in unpaved alleys, the water shimmering with mosquito larvae, children wandering everywhere, multitudes of little stalls and, in the free spaces between buildings, plantings of cane and maize, transplanted remnants of rural life.

As in other parts of the world where the rich return from work by starting their cars by remote control in fear that a bomb has been planted, there is in Phnom Penh—both among its political elite, its new rich, and within the expatriate community of diplomats and workers for charities like the Red Cross, Medicins sans Frontières, CARE, the Norway fund, UNICEF, Oxfam—an intense immersion in the intricacies of personal security. You can't miss this obsession. Security installations in certain neighbourhoods—in the NGO district around 304th street, for example, or the villas of the government elite on Sihanouk Boulevard could have been trans- planted whole from the *kleptocracy* dacha villages that ring Moscow. Even modest houses, businesses, and hotels posted on their walls detailed information about the building's external and internal perimeter defences. In a city where home televisions remain rare, there was a brisk business in household motion monitors and closed- circuit television surveillance systems.

As for the buildings themselves, you could call their style of architecture 'paranoid postmodernism.' Ornamental grilles on homes and offices alike tended to have a defensive intent, giving such dwellings the appearance, not of places in which people lived and worked, but of redoubts in which they hid. The city gave the impression of being under siege.

Which was precisely what Phnom Penh had been for decades. The general assumption of the need for extra legal means of protection dominated the marketing of the expensive new villas popping up around the city. One Singapore firm in Phnom Penh spe- cializing in home and office security claimed that it could install bullet proof glass capable of withstanding a round of AK47 rifle fire, that old Soviet standard being the weapon of choice (because it was so readily available) among the city's thieves and ill-disciplined troops. The city's most popular club, located on the road past

Pochentong Airport, was a shooting range where the elite and their children could refine their skills on any imaginable weapon: small arms and AK47s, hand grenades, bazookas, even Soviet-made tanks. Everywhere such weaponry made the 'Pol Pot time' (for that was how everyone referred to the Khmer Rouge years, as if they formed an era outside the normal course of history) appear almost visible, something just beyond reach.

Once, on a shady lane behind the royal palace, while walking to the Globe Restaurant on Sisowath Quay along the river, I recall reaching for a notebook and hearing the clinking of metal on metal ringing up and down the street as safety catches were removed. On the whole, few people walked around in those areas; pools of bougainvillea blossoms lay undisturbed on the sidewalks. Most houses around the royal palace and in the NGO district were more recent than those in other parts of Phnom Penh, less idiosyncratic and probably 'smarter,' but the lone memorable features were their walls: walls that reflected generation upon generation of violence; the original stone, an additional two or three feet of brick with decorative iron spikes, often gaudily painted gold on top. There was even the rare wall with a small watchtower and gun port.

There were also a large number of public works projects that would not exist save for overseas funding: new water pipes being installed along Monivong Boulevard courtesy of the Japanese government, Chinese teams repairing a bottled water purification plant. These were unusual. Almost everywhere you looked in Phnom Penh you could see abandoned projects; unmoving cranes suspended above the tops of unfinished buildings gave the impression of a desperate, foresaken, busyness. The feel of Phnom Penh was that of an African capital a month or two before or after a coup. Only a kind of tropical entropy, apathy, and volatile poverty prevailed, with grand schemes defeated well before they could even begin to be realized.

To be alone in such a city, I thought, to be improvident or penniless within it, was to feel darkness on every side.

IX

Village of the Damned

IN TAKEO province to the south of Phnom Penh, at the entrance to the village of Angtasom, next to a billboard boosting Tiger Beer and another fading advertisement promoting Pepsi, was a small poster depicting a large pink condom and warning of the dangers of Aids. Beneath the condom, daubed neatly in English, the words 'Massage $1' were painted, an arrow pointing down the road to an open-air market straddling the centre of town.

Spying this, Sa nudged me; I was showing my true colours at last. His dark eyes twinkled—*you are like the others*. But I disappointed him. We had not come to sample the local whores. Youk had suggested I visit one of Angtasom's village elders, a man named Ta Karoby ('Ta' meaning grandfather) who was the village headman throughout the Khmer Rouge years. 'He probably ordered half the town killed,' Youk had said. 'And, just at the moment of death, he would hack out their livers and eat them raw...stealing their life force, that's what Ta thought he was doing. Now, he lives quietly among the children of the people he killed.'

'No one bothers him? No reprisals?' I asked.

'None at all,' said Youk . 'You see, all of his orders came from within 'the system.' Those boys who robbed you, Angtasom's people would execute them without a second thought. Street criminals break with the order of life. But Karoby, he was just doing what was expected of him. How can anyone question that?'

'Is this why Pol Pot's henchmen go unpunished, why no one is clamouring for trials?'

'Nazi camp bosses used to say that they were only following orders; the Khmer Rouge elite think that they were only giving orders.'

'Will Karoby talk, I mean say anything?'

'If he'll talk to you,' Youk said, 'you'll learn something. If he won't, he'll let you know right away. No time wasted.'

We drove into the busy market hoping to find someone to help us decipher the directions provided by Youk. It soon became obvious that Karoby was some minor celebrity in Angtasom, as many of the market stall owners recognized his name the moment Sa asked about him. Within minutes, we were on our way, down a dirt track toward a scatter of rusting tin roofs half hidden beneath drooping palm fronds. In a side-less bamboo hut at the edge of one cluster, teenaged boys and young men were shooting pool; beneath the heavy wooden table a mottled, pot-bellied pig lay asleep, snorting little swirls of dust. The players were standing around, talking in hoarse voices. The felt on the table was worn, like the sleeves of an old suit. Still, the soft click of the balls was like a concert. Despite the hustler struts of those boys, the snoring creature below the table did not stir.

We parked the motorcycle below a pair of young palms and alongside a windowless metal box that was, Sa noted, the icehouse for the village. A brown songbird trilled in the branches above it. Harlequin goats grazed in a field of bone-white grass. They appeared motionless, rooted like stones. Behind the cluster of huts, set down in a clearing of red dirt scraped bare for fear of snakes and soldier ants, there were about a dozen concave cylinders of corrugated iron, with generations of families lying and squatting in the shade among heaps of bundles and jerry cans. Papers and bits of plastic were flying in the breeze, and everywhere there was the drifting smell of shit.

A small nude boy, spying me as he played in the dust, shouted, and within seconds we were mobbed by naked and half-naked children clamouring at our hands and legs with a soft insistence. Flies fed from the caked corners of more than a few of their eyes. I squeezed a few outstretched hands. Some of their gazes were melting: brown, timid, sometimes canny.

Sa spoke to the eldest child. Grabbing my upper arm, Sa said 'follow me,' and pushed his way through their fumbling touches and blank eagerness. One boy ran ahead. If he intended to warn or wake Ta Karoby, he needn't have bothered. *There he was.* There *it* was. Ta Karoby had heaved himself to his feet and was moving toward us, the boy following, kicking at stones.

Ta Karoby was barefoot and impish-looking, with greying facial hair and one eye clouded by disease—Trachoma? Bilharzia? He wore a black Nike cap atop soft, fine white hair like the fluff of a dandelion and one of those red and white bandanas, knotted at the neck, made infamous by the Khmer Rouge. Emaciated, he hitched his trousers with every step. Under Pol Pot, Ta Karoby was strong enough to crack open skulls with one blow of a shovel. Now he seemed as benign as an old goatherd. Rather look after a goat nowadays then cut someone open and devour his liver. You need to be in your prime for that. Ta Karoby had sowed his oats and settled down. Could barely remember the hell he raised.

So how could *this* pathetic ruin be *that* killer? But combining the role of arthritic gimp with mass murderer is not hard. After all, the Nazis proved that fusing radically divergent lives was more than a psychopath's prerogative. That Ta Karoby was good at leading his dull village life made him even more loathsome. The mystery was not that Karoby the executioner and cannibal became an amiable, shuffling village fixture, but that people who once watched as he murdered husbands, wives, sons, and daughters were now able to pursue anything like a normal life—that so many villagers in Angtasom managed to lead run-of-the-mill lives after Ta Karoby and the Khmer Rouge, *that's* what was unbelievable.

Karoby looked clean through Sa, waggled a finger at me, and sniggered. I felt myself at the centre of a great emptiness. Sa spoke to Karoby in Khmer. The old man listened like a superior child, his jaws moving faintly up and down as though he were an animal tasting the last of its cud. Then he ducked and retired back behind the tarpaulin.

'That's it? He won't speak to me?'

Shooing the children, Sa turned to me. 'Anyone who wants to see him,' Sa said with a smirk, 'has to pay fifteen dollars.'

'What for?'

Sa spoke to Karoby through the tarpaulin, and the old man pondered with a furious concentration. 'If you want to hear his story, you have to pay. Other white people before you have paid him. So must you,' said Sa. The old man scowled, preened, and clicked his fingers as I paid the money. The curiosity in his eyes made my skin itch.

After the Khmer Rouge were driven out of Phnom Penh by the Vietnamese, had he ever felt threatened, I asked. Karoby had turned Angtasom into a cemetery, his neighbours into inhuman creatures devouring rats and each other. He'd organized it all—mothers who ate the gizzards of dead birds, fathers burying their living daughters in pits. The crying. The shrieking. Everywhere the dead. Later, during those early weeks of Vietnamese occupation, many survivors took their revenge on the killers amongst them, hacking them to death, stoning them, burying them alive. Killing the children of the killers, too. So, had Karoby thought about fleeing?

Sa translated slowly. Because the local dialect was different from that used in Phnom Penh, Sa had some difficulty. Karoby looked a little disturbed and incredulous; his speech thick and crumbling. His expression said it all: *Remorse? Go fuck your remorse!* No, he was never afraid, he never left Angtasom. He stopped speaking, seeming to smile sardonically at the thought of pursuit by people in the village. Keeping the past at bay was no problem. He was at home all the time, he continued. No one came for him. No one said anything.

Karoby looked, for a brief instant, ashamed when he saw my horror; that is, his mind was ashamed, but Karoby lived by instinct and instinct is unrepentant. He lived the life that he had lived, Karoby said. He would go on living it. Here. There was no mortification of the flesh in that sentence of loneliness—if sentence it was—which he pronounced on himself. Whatever self-torture he felt was in the ineffable sensations of the spirit.

Did he feel any guilt at all for what he had done, I asked.

Standing bird-legged, Karoby looked perplexed, as if he didn't understand the question. So Sa repeated it. But there was no impulse to self-punishment. People punish themselves because they feel guilty, but Karoby was having none of that. Just the opposite was at work. My questions about guilt were making Karoby angry. He began to speak disparagingly about the people in the village. Sa was having difficulty translating what he said, conveying Karoby's barely disguised rage and contempt. Still, I think I got the gist of it:

you wrong a man once then you wrong him again as a revenge for making you feel guilty. In making you feel guilty, your victim wrongs you. So you are justified in wronging him a second time. Morality held no pride of place in the matter. Revenge was inevitable and necessary.

One guilt cancelled another, or so Karoby seemed to think. All his murders, the cannibalism, had been wiped out by the shame that people imposed upon him; by the bad karma that people claimed he would carry through eternity. To demand a sense of sorrow from Karoby was against all his tradition and his reason. Guilt, even if aided by deeper guilts about human nature, was nothing against the tradition of karma.

And responsibility? Did he feel a sense of responsibility if he did not feel guilt? The smiling laziness went out of Karoby's voice. He was an unwitting accomplice, nothing more, he said, his voice small and strained and practiced.

Did he really feel free in Angtasom? I asked. He did not know, said Karoby. He daily became used to his freedom, for he had been a subject of the Khmer Rouge just as much as anyone; he feared for his life in those years, too. All Karoby's life was composed for such a vigilant journey. He knew that his movements must be calculated still, his meetings with others in the village planned and staged. But he had little interest in the village and its life. The young children, the old, the health of the crops did not arouse a response in him— except, as he said, there were too many people around.

In his heart, he disliked his fellow villagers. They were too numerous, monotonous, like so many fleas on a dog. Did he miss his power over them? He often thought of what he would do if he still ran the village, he said, eyes glistening: power still enslaved him.

Guilt and responsibility had not closed in upon Ta Karoby. The village was like a confusing, shapeless product of his bemused intro-spection. It was still his.

So Buddhism salved and ameliorated. 'Why don't you take your justice and leave it in the West,' one village elder told Youk years before, after one of the young researchers for the Genocide Project discovered that Karoby was living in Angtasom unmolested. Karma meant that all lives were composites; the idea of a good life meant a composite of lifetimes of good karma. People lived with all their lives all at once: all their good, all their evil. If a murderer such as Ta Karoby was accepted in the village it was not because justice did not matter, it was because justice was self-imposed. Ta Karoby would carry his bad karma with him through eternity.

*

AT ONE that afternoon, buses arrived in the market to pick up people returning to outlying villages. These departures seemed more like a family gathering than something set to a schedule. Like those peasants, we needed to depart if we intended to reach the port of Sihanoukville before night.

The road south was two-laned but empty of traffic. Here and there, small villages squatted. Bees hummed around hives. Runt bananas ripened to the colour of a pale sun. Clouds of something like thistledown drifted across the view and in one field stood two white cranes and a lone ox, all bone-thin, etiolated. Near the side of the road I saw a dead goat, the mother standing alongside it, motionless, leaning slightly. The goat seemed shrunken, as if melting into the earth. Here was a pastoral scene sculpted by Giacometti.

Everything white, everything empty. But an hour past Angtasom, the road to Sihanoukville passed through a landscape richer than any I had seen in Indochina; soil brimming with life, bananas, rice paddies, palm trees, maize, the remnants of old plantations. Tall reedy grass grew below the palm and coconut groves; long-horned cattle found pasture in that shade. Everything seemed to be turning in a great, incorruptible cycle, too ancient to vary but in which life was measured out in a shopkeeper's precise portions.

Heat that in Phnom Penh and Angtasom had been impossible became more pleasant. Water and sun encouraged vegetation that sheltered and cooled; lush green covered the grey clay earth where, every now and then, it had been exposed by roadworks. Khmer villages were never far away; stilted huts with their steep pitched roofs and low woven palm-thatch walls were set in little gardens. Such houses rotted within five years and were abandoned. Every once in a while you came across little streets of houses from the colonial period or from a Malay or Chinese settlement from before the French era: two-storey shop-houses of stone with corrugated iron roofs, the shops set back a bit from the road, the roadside shop window sheltered by an overhang from the house above. The dates—painted on the reconstructed shop-houses, or in raised concrete numerals—showed recent rehabilitation; many were from the 1950s and 1960s; the French had developed the colony late.

In the centre of Sihanoukville was a Roman Catholic church; nearby was the entrance to the ruined shell of a French colonial barracks. Elsewhere, however, history, like the tourist economy of that faded resort, had dissolved in the heat. So I killed most of the afternoon on a pier, sitting in the sun and watching the ocean. The shore at low tide was wide and flat; sewers poured into it. Muddied sand was pitted with the holes of small crabs. A cargo ship packed with huge logs lay at anchor in the harbour. Three barges, each with a bare-backed, saronged Khmer at the tiller, were moving out from what may have been a canal—really an open sewer, the water a sickly, slick grey—toward it. Although Cambodia seemed an abandoned place, those teak logs showed that Cambodia remained a part of that wider world: it remained a land to be plundered.

There was commonly a bizarre side to the sense of violation which you felt everywhere in Cambodia, and in the rampant destruction of statues—historical and religious—the Khmer Rouge ran true to form. The most notorious stone victim was Buddha. Everywhere in the country you encountered headless images of him, courtesy of the Khmer Rouge. Other casualties included King Norodom I, the monarch whom the French catapulted onto the long forsaken throne of the Angkorian kings to assist the colonial governors through collaboration in ruling the country; he was also the father of the present king. A lazy, amiable, and harmless sovereign, an Indochinese version of Egypt's King Farouk, King Norodom spent much of his life in nightclubs in Paris and Nice, drinking absinthe and listening to ragtime. In Sihanoukville the pedestal for an equestrian statue to King Norodom now stood empty. Bronze plaques beside the plinth had been broken away, except for an upper fringe of what looked like banana leaves; flood lamps that once illuminated the bronzed monarch were smashed, the wiring apparatus pulled out and rusted. When the statue was blown up in 1975, the head was blown out into the sea. 'Oh, we are a haunted place,' Sa exhaled mildly, as if reproving a disappointing child. 'To survive here, even the dead must be on the winning side.'

Now, more than twenty-five years after that defenestration, in another time of political rupture, the statue was to be repaired. Like the wats under reconstruction throughout Phnom Penh, a special effort was being made to rediscover and restore old Cambodia. A fifty-year old statue, a five-hundred-year-old Buddhist temple: in them the so-called real Cambodia would, it was supposed, live again. Khmer civilization was eternal; the mass murders and defilements were, it was supposed, but instants in time.

On my first and only full night within the city, Sihanoukville provided one of those evenings that conspire for happiness, when everything goes right. A taut, clear wind stretched across the darkness. Stars were scattered from horizon to horizon like the night fires of an army camp.

Night crowds, wraithlike figures drifting without purpose, collected near the beach to promenade in the warm fresh air; little braziers burned along a fresh tarmac road, and bells clanged in the Catholic church tower far off. A Catherine wheel whirled on the beach. Rockets hissed into the sky to burst into flippant, trivial stars. A wat was holding a prayer service and I saw a miniature monk bowing and scraping in a pool of light, his orange toga fluttering. The sound of the bell and the rockets and the crowd faded as the evening wore on, leaving only the scents of unknown flowers drifting on the night breezes. This, I felt, was how tropical life should be lived—joyfully, lazily, with fireworks and rice cakes, domestically.

Happiness and contentment, however, never last long in Cambodia and the next morning, I knew, those good feelings would be gone—I was returning to Phnom Penh.

*

BACK IN Phnom Penh, the bar in the Globe restaurant was a short semi-circle, accommodating no more than two dozen elbows. It stood in front of you as you entered from Sisowath Quay, which overlooked the Bassac River. That broad, palm-lined avenue was under reconstruction, with imported paving stones and plantings. Two weeks earlier, Hun Sen sent one of his goon squads to occupy a casino just down the quay from the Globe. Its French owner was arrested; the casino was now Hun Sen's property. Determined to make the thing profitable, Hun Sen dispatched an army of workers, who were trying to make the neighbourhood more attractive by rebuilding the once elegant riverside promenade. Workers marched up and down the riverbank with shovels and picks, led by a weary elephant hauling heavy stones; it could have been a campaign of Hannibal.

To the right as you entered the Globe were half-a-dozen dining tables set below spinning overhead fans. One or two of the chairs were rickety; when a fat man sat they would squeak like new shoes. But the pub's patrons believed in sitting down; if there were vacant chairs at the tables, no one ever stood around the bar. A second-storey dining room looked out over King Sihanouk's palace and the royal pavilion where the King would watch the annual dragon boat race that celebrated the day when the river reverses course because of the heavy upland rains. (Once, a boat manned by a crew of ex-pat NGO workers sank in the choppy waters of the Bassac in front of the King. Protests, handwritten by Sihanouk himself, were delivered to all the major European embassies. A great insult to the throne had taken place: the near-drowning men had neglected to doff their caps to the King.) In this room there were more formal dining tables. The food in the Globe was mostly Vietnamese, but there were also barbecue nights of bangers and mash, and steaks and fries for ex-pats.

The restaurant was open all day but a crowd didn't show until late afternoon. A few of the regulars preferred the Globe to their homes. Duncan, the bar's owner, called these the 'steadies,' they kept the place solvent in times of political unrest when, save for Australian backpackers, the tourist trade evaporated. The ex-pat community here seemed a kind of orphanage, wary in its appearance, warier still in its demands. Word travelled swiftly here, but in place of friendship there was something else which may or may not have been more valuable: the comradeship of shared suffering.

Comradeship was displayed in the familiar, in efforts to recapture what was left behind back home. One night, it was a spirited game of charades among the Brits, the Aussies, the Yanks like me; but as the game wound down, and people prepared to leave to meet their self-imposed curfew in that Wild East city, everyone was still full of vitality. It was, like so much else in Phnom Penh, a borrowed, artificial vitality. In the morning, it was gone.

*

THE DEAD, or pieces of the dead, turned up everywhere in the city, everyday, and were as taken for granted by people as the body count in slasher movies like *Halloween* and *Scream*. The presence of a body was suggested by the proximity of vultures, who first attacked soft tissues like the eyes, exposed genitals, and tongue. A knot of motionless children on the streets, heads bowed or craning, might also suggest the presence of a body. You had to watch carefully though, for the hints could be fleeting. One minute some children in school uniforms would be rigid in their witness circle, and the next a little bell would ping and they would abandon a body lying in the grass to run and form a line.

Bodies turned up in driveways, in empty building lots, in garbage thrown into sewage canals. Every day *Rasmea Kampuchea* and the *Cambodia Post* were filled with cautionary tales. A father hacked to death by 'unknown' men. The body of the country's most famous soap opera actress, her lover a senior minister, found dismembered in her bed. A British diplomat supposedly got into trouble by searching a body before the police arrived. 'Somebody dies, it's better not to have your business card in his pocket,' Duncan quipped. Such stories were always presented in a practised, matter-of-fact way. Their absence of inquiry, of what editors call human interest, stunned through sheer banality. The fact of a murder would be reported, but that was all. Such blandness failed to obscure what was taken for granted throughout Phnom Penh: that forces loyal to Hun Sen's government did most of the killing.

A few newspapers, all were censored in various unofficial ways—a pair of armed men loitering outside usually did the job nicely and reliably—did manage to report rumours about government involvement in killings by carrying stories in which they deplored the spreading of rumours, or, as one newspaper put it, 'the propagation of falsehoods detrimental to public security.' In order to deplore the falsehoods, it was first necessary to detail them, which was the real trick.

Random violence, however, extorted the most fear. Here, any routine situation could turn to terror; any errand go horribly wrong. Among Phnom Penh's expatriates there was endemic apprehension in even the most benign activity—a stop at the Russian Market on Mao Tse Tung Boulevard to pick up a piece of pottery for visiting friends, a quick detour into, say, the Land Rover dealer on Sangkat Boeung Keng for an oil change. Any stop, anywhere, might turn into the scene of a robbery or a police ambush, or both. Once, while I was riding on the back of Sa's motorcycle down Monivong Boulevard, we were detained by a police roadblock. A crowd was gathered outside the Diamond Market, a specialty western grocery store where nostalgic tastes for Skippy's Peanut Butter or Marmite could be indulged. A shoot-out had taken place. Two robbers and four bystanders were killed. Bodies—two were covered in boiled noodles—were removed in an open lorry, shop windows shuttered, the pavement flushed with buckets and a hose. A woman keeled over in the street, moaning. A man with an injured leg was helped away. Five or six crows—hungry and anxious and dirty as buzzards—were rooting in the gutter, hunting for human scraps. The quick shadows of vultures swept overhead. Soldiers laid barbed wire around the crime scene. When the wire caught their clothes, they swatted at it. Flies were everywhere.

I recall being told by a patron at the Globe that one night in the Intercontinental, days after Hun Sen's coup, there was so much gunfire that she took the mattress and box spring off her bed and shoved them against her window. Another patron said that he kept three bulletproof vests purchased in Paris in his car. Before going home at night he slipped one on. Managers of Japanese companies in Phnom Penh were, I was informed, replaced every several months; their home addresses and telephone numbers kept secret from Khmer employees. French companies were said to bury the firm's real manager in a subservient number two or number three post. American embassy officials were driven in armoured and unmarked vans (no imperial bald eagle, no seal, no Cadillac with diplomatic plates) by carefully vetted and highly dependent Khmer drivers and Khmer guards because, or so Duncan said, 'if someone gets blown away, obviously the State Department would prefer it done by a local security guy. Then there won't be headlines screaming "American Guns Down Cambodian Citizen".' These local security men were famous for carrying automatic weapons on their laps. In such a climate the fact of merely being in Phnom Penh came to seem a sort of prison sentence of indeterminate length. You were held, as it were, at His Majesty's pleasure.

That the texture of life in Phnom Penh was essentially untranslatable became clear to me later that night. A game of charades at the Globe broke up a little after 9 pm. Sa was waiting outside for the fifteen minute ride back through the heart of the city, on major roads, to my hotel on Mao Tse Tung Boulevard. It was a mellow night and I did not sense the potential for anything remarkable.

But, just as any morning in Cambodia could turn lurid, any moment could seemingly turn final. Half-a-mile from the hotel Sa's motorcycle was overtaken by another bike on which two men were riding. Unnoticed, a second motorcycle pulled up directly behind ours. Sa and I were joking, not paying attention to the street. As Sa slowed something crashed into my left hip and I flew into the gutter. Before I knew what was happening, a rifle was placed against my temple. 'One hudrett dawrahh,' came the demand. I did not move. 'One hudrett dawrahh' came the order again. Sa said, 'You all right. Roll over. Give money. Do it.' I sat up, reaching for my wallet, the rifle still pointed at my head. None of the four robbers met my eyes. I began to open my wallet when one of the robbers jumped off his bike and snatched it from me. The gunman was seated on the back of the motorcycle, hunched like a man muffled in fever. His chin was nestled into his chest yet he had a look almost of exaltation, his gaze was directed down, his hair shaking in the slight wind. The barrel of the gun glinted. Sa asked the men in Khmer if I could get up. They smiled enigmatically, staring and pointing the rifle and gunning their motors. Abruptly, they hopped back on their motorcycles and sped away.

Stunned, feeling the pumping of my heart, I sat stiff on the road for a few moments, watching the world through a veil of helplessness. I looked around at the buildings, at the traffic whizzing past, everything going in and out of sight. My ears were a sea of dulled sounds; my chest felt empty; my hands weightless.

After an interval of hallucination, in another moment the robbery seemed to have no reality at all, only the physical pain. You got accustomed over weeks of travel in Laos and Cambodia to the idea of perhaps dying in the most bizarre way or in the strangest surroundings. In times like that you found that you had acquired, in so little time, a dreadful adaptability.

Sa moved about aimlessly, stopping and going, wandering in failure like a sleepwalker. He cursed the hijackers, his mouth fixed in a stiff, hysterical smile; but he was most appalled by his own guilt in failing to anticipate what was happening. He was eaten by shame and horror at himself. He had a feeling of responsibility for me, responsibility in a limited way for someone other than himself, and no Khmer likes such feelings. Responsibility was like an amputated limb that most Khmers had learned to live without. Maddened by his inability to do anything, Sa paced up and down, his eyes as brilliant as motionless lamps. I scrutinized him, suspecting him of betrayal. A small crowd of Khmers started drifting over, in silence. A big Khmer girl with a happy, sensual face offered me a sip from her bottle of beer. I declined, but her act of kindness had a tonic and soothing effect.

In a few minutes a military police cruiser pulled up and began to question Sa. I sat in silence. The police, at first, remained aloof from me but I was aware that I was somehow important to them, a proof of their power. I began to lose track of how long I was there; time appeared to have stopped. I wanted to leave; if I was going to be questioned, to make a report, I didn't want to do it in the middle of Mao Tse Tung Boulevard surrounded by a gaping crowd. Besides, I knew that the police would demand money for whatever they might or might not do, and I no longer had any cash.

A chill passed through me. Power, particularly when given to the powerless is a serious matter: when you meet up with such newly minted power, such as those Khmer policemen (they may have been Khmer Rouge guerrillas once, who knew?), a smile is worse than rude; it demonstrates a lack of respect. Avoiding eye contact with the police, I motioned to Sa and then got back on the motorcycle. One of the officers brusquely ordered me off, an expression of innocence on his face. I felt swept along by a current. The police tried to hustle Sa into their cruiser but, seeing my agitation, they did not. A kind of impasse developed. It seemed clear that if we did try to leave, the situation might deteriorate. It also seemed clear that if we didn't leave the situation would deteriorate. I examined the scrapes on my arms and the tear in my trousers. Everyone was standing in silence. Sa and I looked at each other and then climbed onto his bike. He switched on the motor and navigated around the police cruiser cleanly. Nothing more happened. What had happened, however, had been a common enough in Cambodia. First you are violated in one way or another, then you must endure a pointless confrontation with an aimless authority.

All those nice people at the Globe with their hopes and plans for reconstruction: some with clinics and mental health schemes; a Frenchwoman named Delphine with her shadow puppet theatre. Throughout my stay in Phnom Penh I heard plan after plan to address Cambodia's chaos. None of those solutions, however, addressed the Khmer vocation for terror. Call that my travel advisory.

I remained in Phnom Penh for three days more, outwardly cheerful but apprehensive about journeying inland. On the night before my departure I lay awake listening to music drift up from a party at the hotel's terrace swimming pool. I heard the cd player blare 'The Macarena' (for the fifth time, at least) at two in the morning. When the party ended and light streamed in through the blinds, I stirred myself from sleeplessness. Sa was waiting for me on the street in front of the hotel (Khmer motorcyclists were not allowed up the hotel's curved drive). After travelling less than half-a-mile I was seized by the conviction that we were not taking the most direct route to the quay where the boats to Siem Reap docked. Paranoia was in full swing. I wondered if Sa had set me up for the robbery; I turned my head repeatedly, convinced that we were being followed. That after another mile, it became clear that Sa was taking the correct route failed to reassure me: once on the quay I stood in the shade without moving.

*

THE QUAY swarmed with people and bushels of luggage. Buying

a ticket in the shipping office I had the uneasy feeling that I was thought a fool—or ignorant; the Khmers seemed to be talking about me among themselves with pity and amusement, chiefly amusement. I boarded without looking back on the city.

In a far corner of the deck a native doctor was examining a young child. He put a matchstick under one of her eyelids, turning it inside out in a hideous way. Next to her a little boy of about four, wearing an oversized sweatshirt, cried and coughed; a tubercular hack that cut through the din. Everywhere the deck was in uproar. The only quiet man was a young officer leaning against a bulwark with his rifle between his knees. He gazed with disdain, as though thinking that he would like the boat to sink and rid the world of its pestilential cargo. The pupils of his brown eyes were steady under his lids like a hunter tracking a bird in flight. Now and then he turned his head and spat into the water with official dignity. He looked an arrogant young man, a scorner of other races; a dogged one, too, for he smirked with contempt as he looked at me. A brute mysticism was evident in the steadiness of his gaze. He appeared to be that type of harsh young man who had outgrown idealism and replaced it with authority. I watched him at the gangway, sniping at his fellow Khmers, once using his foot on a woman as she struggled with her cloth bundles and cardboard boxes tied with rope.

Rusty, battered, needing paint, the ship was alive with a rousing barnyard life: tethered goats packed tight among the passengers, crated chickens lashed to the bow. An old *cabine de luxe* from the colonial days was a storeroom for buckets and rags. Light bulbs were missing from the fixtures on deck. The iron of the gunwale burned at the touch; tar sizzled in the seams. The ferry-steamer was overloaded with passengers, but this was more than a passenger ship; it was also a floating market. Whenever a village appeared onshore, trading sampans would paddle out to the steamer. Skilfully oared, these sampans lingered alongside as village crafts—mortars carved out of tree trunks, basins of cocoanuts—were bartered, loaded and unloaded.

The absence of men among the village traders made me realize something that I had seen but not acknowledged: in Vietnam and in Cambodia there seemed a surplus of women, for the wars and Pol Pot's regime had slaughtered millions of their men. It was then that

I recalled one of the first impressions I had on moving to England to go to Cambridge in the early 1980s as a student: all those forlorn looking ladies in places like St. Albans and Ely and Bury St. Edmunds. They were the forgotten girls of England's finest hour grown old, their boyfriends or husbands lost in Egypt or Crete or Singapore or Normandy, doomed to go alone, first with their parents and then by themselves, down the lane to the village church, girls whose hopes had long vanished. They had been robbed of their lives, and the elderly Indochinese women, those Khmer trading women with their brisk, dormant faces, I guessed, were just like them.

I searched the boat for an empty bench but the best I could find was one near the engine room with a bag hanging from one corner, indicating that at least one passenger had already staked his claim. There was a fusillade of banging, of grinding shudders, as the engine cranked over below. I enjoyed the swish-pump-clottering sounds of the boat's disembarking, and brooded a bit that nowadays there were no great adventures of the sea to be experienced. No *Lord Jim* or *Heart of Darkness,* no *Billy Budd.*

Struggling with my doubts and looking over maps, I became aware that I was being watched from the stern. A team of student missionaries had boarded at the last minute. They were sallow children from the pine barrens of East Texas and northeast Mississippi who had been priming young Khmers to know Jesus as their personal saviour as the team leader who settled on the bench next to me explained. A few members of the group removed their boots and were massaging their feet and bandaging blisters and sores. Two of the men slung hammocks from poles near the stern and were trying to sleep, hanging like bats.

Henry, their leader, was twenty-eight or thirty, no older than that. I took a good look at him. His cheeks were red—ruddy, not burnt by the sun; his eyes, behind steel-rimmed glasses, were clear and innocent. A Bic pen stuck out from his shirt pocket; from his trouser pocket a paperback, portable New Testament protruded. One day he would probably make a fine minister in some obscure Oklahoma town, or so I supposed. Already he saw himself back home in the Southwest, mingling in his sermons little Khmer epiphanies alongside quotations from self-help bestsellers.

His assistant was frightening. He sat across from us, holding his head in his hands like a mourner. Barely twenty-one, I thought, his was an intolerant innocence. Fresh-faced, he had the cold white smile of a television evangelist. Intermittently on the voyage, whenever he became dissatisfied, his roots would show in his gauntness: a wild-eyed farmer. I guessed that he was probably *the* religious fanatic of the group, having travelled half-way around the world to inform the Khmers, of all people, about man's wickedness.

The two evangelicals probably felt a special affinity in delivering their messages to the Khmers. Both knew the lay of landscapes such as this: the vast skies of the American south and west with their shafts of light, the nothing towns below the Manson-Nixon line with railroad tracks running through them and Pentecostal churches, dejected countryside with muddy little lakes and fading cabins amid cottonwoods and pines, Bible country, the air pure with poverty and revival meeting broadcasts.

Going upriver, through a landscape so familiar to them, filled me with dread. Discussions about religion and disease always seem to me to be worse than futile, but this was the stock-in-trade of road show evangelists. The glorious self-indulgence of describing in minute detail all your symptoms of the flesh or soul! People enjoy their religions as they enjoy their diseases, but they should keep them to themselves. I am about as interested in knowing about someone's faith as I am in hearing about his or her digestion.

Members of that fundamentalist flock gathered near the stern, one girl strummed a guitar and the other boys and girls sang along; they seemed determined to meet 1969 head-on. They played softly, standing in a little group as if talking to each other with no one else around. As they played, their shepherd was buttonholing as many passengers as he could, speaking what sounded like Khmer with a Southern twang. He seemed immensely inquisitive, noting whatever they told him in a tiny yellow spiral notebook with a drawing of the cross of the crucifixion on the cover. The group leader seemed to leap a little with joy with each meeting, talking endlessly, excitable as a circus dwarf. His assistant sometimes joined him, both enraptured by their passion for converting souls. One day, probably, the leader would give talks about his missionary work in church halls around the US when he got home. The fact that a foreigner was addressing them brought excitement to a number of unescorted

Khmer women. No Khmer, however, resented him: he was so pink and gentle. Besides, he also wore that protective local talisman: a badge from Hun Sen's Cambodian People's Party on his shirt.

No sooner was the boat out in the middle of the river than the assistant began passing out questionnaires to other members of the group. They were being asked about their experiences up to that point, and I watched a few of them painstakingly printing out their responses: *opportunity to bring to others the words of Christ, the joy of feeling the love and commitment of Christ, the most rewarding part of this experience, the most painful part.* Like devoted high school students, their concentration was so total that I hesitated to bother them. Instead, I tried to speak to the leader. Before he could answer, his young curate whirled on me as if spinning in his own self-contained little solar system. 'Do you really want to know what is most disheartening, what is heartbreaking? It is seeing people leave the crusade as empty as they came. To see these lost souls still lost, it breaks your heart,' he said, clutching his hands to his chest as though dragging a soul out of himself.

'And the most rewarding?'

'The most rewarding thing is to renew my commitment to bringing the Good News of Jesus as personal saviour to people who would never have heard it.'

To avoid being drawn deeper into this discussion, I nodded, turned, and walked about the deck. Two women lay sick on a yellow and green palm mat. An elderly Khmer was clinging with tendril-like fingers to the side of the cabin. A folding table was opened at the stern, and food was handed up through a hatch in the deck from the engine room—bowls of sticky rice and a plate of anonymous fish scraps from which the eyeballs stood out mournfully. My thirst was greater than hunger, but there was no mineral water, soda, or beer for sale, just a shocking kind of tea and the dubious water in a tin filter above the kitchen area. I couldn't face it, and rashly made my way down to the only *cabine*: a horrible cupboard just off the engine room with no ventilation and, no surprise, the stench of countless weeks and voyages. Diseased river water dripping from the tap looked unfiltered; the stained and leaking washbasin, a lime green gecko winking from its drain, was pulled out from the wall. Chrome plated towel rails were empty. Holes in the floor had been mended, like the holes in a sampan, with what looked to be river mud. The lavatory cistern flushed interminably. Its odour finished me; for most of what remained of the voyage I lay rigid on a bench on the starboard side.

A shout from above brought me hurrying back on deck. Explosions could be heard along the shore. Darkened forests began to light up, first in one place and then another, like a city coming to life at dawn. Soon a long stretch of shoreline was flashing. Black, silent shell bursts appeared, some showing an unexpected red core. The armies of Hun Sen and Prince Ranariddh, the son of the king, were firing mortars at each other.

'If you don't mind my asking, why are you taking this boat?' the evangelist asked me.

'I am following the route that the French writer André Malraux followed in the early 1920s when he went to steal from the temple at Banteay Srei.'

'I hope you don't have that same idea in mind. Hun Sen's government shoots people who loot.'

*

ON APPROACHING Siem Reap the river boat, as was the usual procedure, could not clear the channel into the dock and so passengers were ordered to climb down into smaller wooden crafts for the journey to shore through a forest of reeds. The small transit boats, really little more than dugouts propelled by lawnmower engines, snaked through narrow channels and then tied up to a mud bank crowned by a wall of wooden and palm-thatched *favelas*. Soldiers stood in the shade of a lone laburnum tree and watched us edge in against the shore. Rowing boats with missing planks rotted in that mud and were the colour of the mud; floating offshore on the brackish water were sampans moored between upright poles.

A plank twenty feet long bridged the mud river to a beach of black sludge where a crowd of naked children were waiting to try and wrest bags from the boat's passengers. Gulls, crows, and starving cats picked at little mounds of refuse. Shreds of clouds blew overhead like smoke. Disembarking, I began to slide down the bank until a Khmer fisherman took my arm and propelled me upward

through the muck. Atop the bank I was stopped by a policeman—
perhaps he was a soldier, who can be sure? He shook my bag
violently, listening. The scene was like landing at the foot of a
medieval castle: a plank bridge over a moat of ooze, the watching,
narrow-eyed, peasant wall of suspicion.

I marched down a lane to where taxis were waiting. Save for the
favelas, nothing was to be seen but a truckload of fish festering in
the sun, a dusty palm-drink stall, portraits of King Sihanouk (the
vulgarity of the reproductions made him appear flabby and greedy,
hideously regal), and a wooden barber's chair. Pairs of vultures
squatted on roofs near a spot where fishermen were shovelling their
catch—small silvery minnow-like things—into a waiting dump
truck. The only sounds were the cries of those fishermen, and a
rhythmic thudding on the roofs, like dusty carpets being beaten.
Those rumblings came from the aroused vultures, clapping their
moulting wings.

Here was a place besieged by scavengers—pirates along the
Tonle Sap shoreline, vultures in the streets.

X

An Outpost of Progress

NOT FAR FROM Siem Reap was the railway to Battambang. In the station, timetable frames swivelled empty and glassless. In the adjacent yard, past an open, unguarded door, was a true relic from a bygone age: a 1937 steam locomotive, one of the first used on Khmer railways. It stood amidst overgrown weeds; it was small, built for narrow gauge, and looked quaint with its tall coal-black funnel, and open cab. Yet somehow, it appeared whole. No one seemed to care about that locomotive, and perhaps it had survived for so long because it, like so much else in Cambodia, was junk.

The train I would take was about forty years old, made in France with a twin-diesel engine and green wheels. In the First Class compartment, the painted class designation appears to have survived the Pol Pot era, food had worked into the upholstery and filled the carriage with what smelled like last week's picnic. Second Class cars were clean and bright with slatted seats, the paint peeling, and a cast iron stove in the back near the exit door where a man was boiling an orange enamel maté kettle. Two Australian hikers sat among a heap of backpacks. They were arrogant, disdainful, and openly mocked the Khmer passengers, a huddled group of peasants. An old lady was talking to her favourite cat. She seemed normal enough until she turned her head and I saw a black-haired doll-sized face working out from under a flower-print shawl so thin you could see through it. The woman's thick hair and shrunken skull gave the impression of one of those Incan shrivelled heads from Peru, only this living relic had large listless and nearly heartless brown eyes.

With whistles and a jerk the train got started. Outside the station a rubbish heap lay stinking under a notice forbidding dumping. Crows bounded off the track as we passed, their feathers venting little clouds of smoke. A football game went on beside the line; half the teams just lazed on the grass. The old track cut across thornscrub and headed for a green line where a river came down and spread into a reedy lagoon. A flock of cranes took off, flashing orange and striping the water white as their legs lifted clear. In the distance mountains were blue, flickering in the heat haze. An army convoy smeared a dust-cloud along the horizon.

Not long into that journey the soldier walked over to the peasants and started a quarrel. He was slightly drunk, and his abuse amused the Australians, who encouraged him in his mockery. I sat back to watch this history of Cambodia in miniature. The peasants absorbed the insults for almost an hour before one of their men stood, exploded, and pointed the soldier back to his seat. Four other peasant men stood behind their leader. Bowing slightly, the soldier returned to his seat to sulk.

Along the rail line wilderness was enveloping a land where there had once been vast disturbances. Scrubland and savannah was burying, not only an ancient countryside husbanded for ages, but also the camps and fields where so many Khmers had been murdered in Pol Pot's Years One, Two, and Three. Peasant settlements were strung out along the tracks.

The soldier came to his station and stumbled off the train, clutching his small kit bag. Round the shacks of his village scraps of aluminium paper glinted in the watery sun. A woman came up from behind a shrub to help the drunkard walk. A dog, which had been sprawled in the shade, ran up and licked him all over the face.

The train made no unexpected stops. The air coming through the windows was stifling; a small green overhead fan was no help at all. It was 39 degrees centigrade outside. Battambang would be cooler, the porter said. It was surrounded by forests.

Momentarily, the compartment became scented like a hothouse: flowers shaped like the spokes of a star dangled from trees along the line. A lovely small wat stood bathed in shadowy light. It was a moment that gave a sense of life in Cambodia before everything in the country went irredeemably wrong.

That point of contemplation passed as quickly as a dream. Whistles rang; Battambang was near. A soldier came into the car and motioned that we were not to exit when the train pulled into the station. We would be told when to move. I shifted seats nearer to the window and watched as the train glided to a halt and the door to the First Class compartment opened. Evidently some politicians had been on the train with us. Like the soldier, they were drunk. They carried with them, as a kind of jester, a drunken girl with a thin wild face who flapped her hands and crowed like a parrot. One of the politicians handed her a bottle of Angkor and she appeared to swill the warm beer then burst into a high explanatory scream, pointing to the roof, buzzing like a chainsaw.

After all that I had heard about Battambang being the de-facto capital of a Khmer Rouge statelet within Cambodia, about Ieng Sary's big ideas to transform his fief into a model for the rest of the kingdom, the first sight of the city was a letdown. The arrival hall was little more than a shed. In an office off of it blank rectangular patches edged with reddish dust showed where photographs of Lenin and Mao and perhaps Pol Pot had once hung. Now CPP pamphlets and caricatures were taped to the walls and pillars. There was even a colour photograph of Hun Sen, as hard-eyed, carnal, unreliable, and roguish-looking as his royalist enemies portrayed him.

The entrance to the train depot—rough tables, lounging clerks,— was like a Middle East bazaar. A handwritten note on the ticket counter said: *Dearest Tourist. Blessings for You. Welcome to the new Cambodia.* Bits of sticky brown paper dotted the station notice board advising Khmers travelling to meet their families where they should go. A porter with a little brush moustache asked if I needed 'accommodation.' His pronunciation of the word, and his little smile, seemed to turn the query into a sinister joke. When I said no, he didn't push the matter but waved me into the morning glare to face the rapaciousness of Sary's state.

Dust blew everywhere, coating the trees, dimming the colours of cars. Bricks and plaster were the colour of dust; unfinished buildings looked abandoned and crumbling; walls, like abstracts of the time, were scribbled over in Khmer script and stencilled with portraits of Hun Sen.

On the outskirts of Battambang in a field of scrub and wasteland, I saw what looked like a pentacostalist revival meeting tent. That foresaken barren land seemed to exude a wretched, abandoned, and derelict population. Their ragged appearance made me think of the refugees from the Khmer Rouge who once huddled in appalling squalor in camps not far away, just across the Thai border. But then—seeing another tent and another queue—I recognized the signs of an election underway. But parliamentary elections were not to be held for another few months. So I asked one of the monitors. 'Yes, the people will vote for a new prime minister then,' he said with resignation, 'but Sary wants them to know what they are doing. So we are holding a practice election so that people will know what to do when the real vote comes,' he concluded with a sly smile.

Battambang was in an advanced state of decay—its little balconied houses and bars open to the street to catch what breezes might blow down from the hills. In an overrun garden courtyard near the ACE English language school and a cracked, moulded and mildewed pool, doves whispered and crows splashed in a disused fountain. Pop music played desultorily in a little ochre ruined square where a French female tourist wandered round the birdcages hanging outside a shop, cooing secretively to herself. A woman in a nightdress trailed a bucket across a dingy yard. On the other side of the square there was a ruined wat from which gentle moaning chants could be heard. Small Khmer soldiers lounged in grubby uniforms outside its precincts. Their barracks appeared to encircle the wat as if it was something dangerous. Awakened, the soldiers feigned a professional alertness. It did not last long; moments of menacing stares gave way, almost instantly, to the soldiers' normal torpor. Flies rambled on the flat black barrels of their rifles.

Next morning, the Australian doctor that the publican at the Globe had promised to contact was waiting for me at the hotel door. Philippa had small, sun-burned hands and a mane of red hair, deepened by the bottle.

Middle-aged, Philippa had been a Maryknoll nun, serving missions in Indonesia, Bangladesh, even briefly as a novice in East Timor until the invasion by Suharto's Indonesian army forced her to leave. Her nose and chin were pointed; obstinacy and courage were displayed in that chin. She was the type of woman that Khmer men disdained; they preferred petite Madonnas as their ministering angels. Philippa had no illusions about this. 'They shout after me in the street: "there goes the giant bitch."'

'They get that crude?' I exclaimed.

'It's an imprecise translation. But it gives you the flavour; it's really nothing,' she said smiling, setting her chin and jangling the spare pair of eye glasses she wore around her neck habitually. 'Every once in a while a man will stop me on the street and form his thumb and fingers into a circle, then repeatedly stick the index finger of his other hand through the hole, imitating sex. Once he realizes that I understand exactly what he means by this, he'll look me in the eye and shake his head "No". I was not worthy of him.'

Philippa's direct brown eyes were mischievous. She was clothed in a dress as faded and tattered as anything I had seen on women in Phnom Penh. Even the child hookers of the Tuklo district dressed better than Philippa. Rags, however, suited her. Anything else might have made her look dowdy. The only reprieve from that vagrant look was found around her sun-withered wrists, where she wore an amethyst bracelet. 'These stones have brought me luck all my life,' she said as I closed the hotel door behind me, the metal handle blistering from the sun.

In all societies, no matter how broken, there are indestructible people—emergency room doctors with eyes reddened by long hours, airline mechanics numb-fingered in the cold. Philippa was of that breed. She was a woman who had grown up with a love for the difficult and her appetite for it had expanded with the eating. She wanted greater and greater difficulties, and she was determined to make them out of the simplest materials. Small difficulties, little dodges, the trifling intrigues of life, bored her. First, she tired of the freedom of the snug consular life provided by her father; in the convent she tired of the difficulties of routine.

'You were a missionary?' I asked.

'We didn't call ourselves that,' Philippa said with a wry and resolute smile. And she was right of course. Why would anyone call herself a missionary? It suggested imperialism and being eaten.

Her father had been an officer in an Australian infantry unit which fought in the far south of Vietnam during the American war;

later he served as a military attaché in Phnom Penh during the Lon Nol government, the time of Nixon's not-so-secret bombing of Cambodia. Her best girlfriends in high school were Khmers, some the children of Lon Nol's ministers, children who were later to be executed by Pol Pot's regime. Nowadays, she rarely brooked the slightest nonsense from any Khmers, ministers and peasants alike; she put down their demands skillfully, like ill-planned insurrections. Still, she secretly adored them.

Philippa knew all the old NGO hands in Battambang and didn't think much of them: 'all goodwill and training and not an ounce of common sense.' Philippa was not a woman given over much to grand solutions, to the sort of abstract notions that galvanized Youk. Her life was grounded in the specific. Before we met that morning there had been a funeral for one of her nurses, a Khmer woman who had died of a cerebral haemorrhage caused by a blow to the head received in a robbery. Eleven children had died that week, of diarrhea and dehydration, in the squatter camps that ringed Battambang. Many of these were refugees from Khmer Rouge camps who had been set 'free' when Sary defected from Pol Pot. There was no medicine, only that provided by Philippa. There was no running water; no fresh clean water ever since a tank delivered by the Sasakawa Foundation of Japan was dynamited six weeks before.

Two weeks after the dynamiting the rains began. That made matters worse in some ways because the torrents flooded the camp's latrines, but better in another way because people no longer depended on a nearby stream, soupy with bacteria and amoeba and worms. 'We use water collected off the roof now,' said Philippa. 'Much better. It is greenish yellow; the stream water, we only use it for the toilets.' The truth was that, though she was the only western educated doctor in the city, though she fought a solitary battle with malaria and other diseases each day, she never made much headway. Support for her movable clinic was running out; a grant from the Australian government had not yet been renewed; all her work now was paid for out of private donations and from her own funds.

*

SARY'S AIDE, Hay Sarin, was plump, unshaven and probably

unwashed; his hair, however, was well oiled. He was chewing a red mouthful of betel nut and dressed in a popular Asian style you might call American country club suburban: a denim, short-sleeved Ralph Lauren button-down shirt, its long tail hanging out over tan chinos. That casualness was studied, the way politicians'outfits when they are on the hustings are always contrived. Besides, any attempt at a more decorous presentation would have been self-defeating. The former Khmer Rouge guerrillas who formed the backbone of the local government would not have liked to see *their* man getting above his station.

Everywhere we went in Battambang, in outlying villages too, Hay Sarin was hallowed: he was distrusted, feared, and envied as an accomplished minor minister and gangster. Some years before he led Khmer Rouge guerrillas in the forests to the north and east of Battambang, his military command stretching to the temples of Angkor, where over the years he wantonly mined roads, dismembering and mutilating—when he was not killing outright—hundreds of men, women, and children. Whatever responsibility he held for that time of violence had vanished; there was nothing anyone could do about it. Since deserting the Khmer Rouge, Hay's power had increased; everyone in Battambang province had to be friendly, deferential even, toward him, like the dusty little group of minor public officials and peasants who scuttled after his every step.

To anyone who read the signs, Hay's power was tangible, like the pull of a dark star. It was shown in that full mouth of betel nut that made it difficult for him to speak without an indiscriminate spray of scarlet spittle. It showed in his paunch, which was shadowed by a snug grimness to his shirt. That American-style shirt and preppy trousers, the slack, western style of his dress, trumpeted Hay as a man of power and leisure, or at any rate as a man divorced from physical labour. Power was also demonstrated in the way in which he spoke to his aides—he treated them with that laconic contempt which conceals the gratitude powerful people often feel for their junior aides.

Hay's home was really two connected bungalows at the end of an Americanized strip of video shops, electronic goods, liquor stores and a small casino. The house was blank-fronted, with a low, narrow doorway in the middle. A central courtyard surrounded by a wide, raised, covered veranda, stood within. At the back, off the veranda, shaded from the sun, were the family's quarters. It was surprising, after the dust and featurelessness of the lane, to find this ordered domestic courtyard, the cultivation of a small space and preservation of privacy.

After decades in the jungle, Hay was now a man of property, a man becoming used to daily dealings in money and, as a member of the provincial council, a politician and high official of the state. He was among the dozen most important men in Battambang province. People in the street, Philippa informed me, addressed him as 'Excellency.' Hay admitted that he had a share in the ownership of the new casinos opening in Battambang and Paylin, and that he held shares in the Battambang Bank, and owned eleven transport lorries. By hints and inference—Hay admitted nothing openly—it became clear that he received a substantial part of the profits derived from the illegal teak and mahogany logging operations that were turning nearby forests into wastelands. Hay had also secured a 'cut' of the take from gem mines near the Thai border.

He was, moreover, a mighty landowner. Hay owned two thousand prime acres; and, though he did not own people, he may as well have done so: the fate of whole families, even villages, depended on his whims. To these people he was, literally, their master.

Philippa, ever businesslike, explained my purpose: would Hay arrange a meeting for me with Ieng Sary? Governor Sary had been declining to meet with foreigners. No interviews were being granted, not even to Phnom Penh newspapers whose editorial lines favoured the deal struck between Sary and Hun Sen's government; a bargain that allowed Sary to come out of the forests with his followers and rule almost one third of the country. Sary preferred that his own people speak to the press and to television on his behalf, emphasizing his modernity, his courtship of Asian investors, his devotion to his governmental duties, the hard work of Battambang's reconstruction. There was a story circulating in Phnom Penh which said that Sary's relationship with Hun Sen had deteriorated; by trying to plant stories in the papers about his effectiveness in Battambang, Ieng Sary was trying to keep his political options alive.

'Will Sary see me?' I asked.

Philippa translated. It might be arranged, Hay seemed to nod, sticking his tongue in and out like a lizard. Hay would telephone Sary's secretary.

Telephones, secretaries, appointments: the apparatus of a functioning state bureaucracy seemed strange in the employ of a man like Hay. Sary had reinvented himself as a man of the age, a man of modernity; all those who served his administration served his new purposes. The lunge into the past of the Khmer Rouge years had not been *his* idea, or so Sary proclaimed on his rare visits to Phnom Penh. No: he was merely Pol Pot's foreign minister, responsible for diplomatic affairs, nothing more. No crime should be laid at his door, he implied. He might be Pol Pot's brother-in-law, he would not and could not deny it, but where was the crime in that? His mistake, he believed, had been to justify the regime to the world, but that was a mistake in judgment; it wasn't a violation of Khmer law, let alone a crime against humanity.

Hay invited us to look around the courtyard of his home while he called the governor's office. He seemed to be receiving us as guests rather than visitors connected to his official duties. We strolled past laundry drying in the courtyard to a kitchen at the back. The roof sloped low; after the sunlight of the courtyard it was dark, even cool. To the left a woman was making what appeared to be curds, standing over a high clay jar and using one of the most ancient of tools: a cord double-wound around a pole and pulled on each end in turn: it resembled a carpenter's drill from the Tang Dynasty China, of the sort seen in the Musée Guimet in Paris, and also the churning tool I would later see depicted in some of the temple carvings of Angkor. In the servant's gloom to the right an earthen fireplace glowed. In that twilight, brass and silver and metal vessels glimmered on a high shelf; tinned cans of food were ranged on a shelf below. And— another sign of a borrowed modernity—on a Formica counter-top lay a Motorola cellular telephone.

The young woman at the fireplace rose. Well-mannered, she brought her palms together like a child saying her bedtime prayers and bowed slightly, shyly, in the Khmer way. The girl, Hay's daughter, would enter the Royal University of Phnom Penh in the autumn, to study English. But Hay was now too grand to boast of her accomplishments. This he left to others, his admirers and hangers-on. Though lost and modest in the gloom of the kitchen, stooping over the fire and smoke, the girl was her family's hope. Another step away from the long dark decades of guerrilla war.

The kitchen door opened onto the back yard which was ringed by a high concrete wall with razor wire, like a prison. You couldn't really call it a garden because, as so often in Cambodia, order ended where a dwelling ended. Sheltering in the shade in the farthest corner of the grounds, behind a ring of empty jerry cans and broken palettes, was a hushed party of men and women, probably the household servants, playing some kind of card game. One man looked a clear loser, resigned to losing more. The apparent winner, a pygmy in an orange jumper, slapped her cards into the dirt with the droop-mouthed, gluttonous expression of an old lady playing the slot machines in a casino.

Cans and containers were not the only junk about. The dusty ground was scattered with bits and broken pieces of household things—old stereo speakers, an electric can opener, a woman's hand-held electric hair dryer—tossed out but not quite abandoned. Even here, amidst the trash, were things to show with pride. On the roof above the backdoor was a satellite dish. A rich man, this Hay, to have access to the globe via modern technology. No need for him to watch the two or three hours of Khmer state television with its endless repeats of Thai soap operas. Hay also had something else few other Khmers possessed: an outhouse. There it was, a safe distance downwind from his home, visible for all his guests to see.

We re-entered the house into a room being re-floored: thin slabs of stone lay on caked mud. Hay returned and spoke to Philippa. 'How should he introduce you?' she asked. 'Sary does not like journalists you know.'

'That isn't how I want to talk to him anyway; I'm not here for news. I really just want to have a conversation. I want to understand how he survived, to see how he connects yesterday with today in his mind.'

Philippa spoke to Hay. 'I told him to say that you are writing a book. That you are an American writing a book. The American connection may help.'

Hay disappeared, but only for a few moments. Two of his assistants entered the room, waiting with us, watching. When Hay returned, it was clear that nothing had been settled with Sary's office.

There was a large metal desk against the far wall, behind it a high-back chair like a throne. As soon as Hay returned, one assistant brought the chair to the centre of the room for his master to sit upon, which Hay promptly did, as though this was part of the formality of the house. Around the room were seven folding metal chairs, which the assistants placed in a semi-circle below Hay. Chairs were for visitors, and were painted in the same yellow-green colour as the walls, which were otherwise bare of decoration. A tall, dark brown cabinet stood near the door, and the lighting was by three long fluorescent tubes, evenly spaced apart, and running in parallel lines across the ceiling. A black square quartz clock on top of the cabinet was the only ornamental object in that cell.

Tea arrived almost at once. The undergraduate-to-be daughter in the kitchen at the back knew her duties. The tea was brewed in a Khmer way I had seen before: sugar, tea leaves, and condensed milk boiled together into a thick stew, hot and sweet. We drank with considered haste, Hay fastest of all, and soon the daughter was standing above us, ready to snatch the cups from our hands. Each of us held up our cups to surrender them. Hay, calm in his role as host, detaching himself from his zealous daughter, gave a severe look and soon the cups were refilled.

Next, a small melon-like fruit was brought in. Hay halved the melon with a knife he pulled from his trouser pocket, slicing the white speckled flesh. The five of us—Philippa, Hay and myself were joined by the two assistants without their being asked—took pieces of the melon from a single dish. Hay revelled in this serving and sharing. A Khmer moment: a rite the Khmer Rouge perhaps observed in their jungle camps. The assistants, former guerillas, joined the ceremony. Those attendants were also Hay's; Hay was sharing food with 'the people,' but also imposing his ritual generosity upon them.

Hay spat the melon seeds onto the floor. The assistants followed Hay's lead. Eventually, Philippa and I did the same. Abruptly, stabbing his knife into the remainder of the melon, Hay leapt from his seat. He was finished; he had enough of the melon. Burping, he paced the floor then sat on a stool that put his head at a level below ours. In that submissive posture, Hay employed the pose of so many

villagers I had come across—slight, wrinkled, defeated. Yet as he
sat—no longer unknown but, he believed, revealed as a man who
had established his worth and his standing, as host, the provider of
tea (his daughter, her task finished, was slurping and sighing over
her portion), the owner of this house—his personality was exposed.
The small, twinkly eyes that first seemed, in that bantam's round
head, merely the eyes of a cunning peasant—always about to
register respect and obsequiousness combined with mistrust—could
be seen now to be the eyes of a man used to exercising a special type
of authority, an authority that to him and to the people around him
was more real than any authority emanating from Phnom Penh,
perhaps even from Sary. Hay's face was the face of a master, a man
who knew men, wives, whole families from their birth to their death;
a man who held the fates of many in his hands; a man who knew
violence.

It was necessary to go into the villages, suggested Philippa, to
understand the nature of the power Hay exercised. For Hay was
more than a bureaucrat and landowner. In villages where needs were
primitive, Hay, with his lorries to carry rice and maize surpluses to
Battambang and Siem Reap, ruled. And he ruled without question,
with the same suzerainty with which headmen had once ruled by
custom and consent.

Hay's silver Lexus bumped along between a few cultivated fields
and rice paddies; a small brown Nissan with two soldiers bearing
machine guns trailed behind. The sun shone behind saw-tooth
mountains, shooting pale rays like torches into the sky. Hay sat in the
front passenger seat. Every now and then he ordered the driver to
stop so that he could inspect a field, a crop, an irrigation canal.
Peasants rambled in that vacant landscape, smoke drifted upwards
from slash-and-burn fires, the dust of the day settled. It was all
simple and, except for the guns, idyllic.

Hay's home village was not a commune of peasant farmers. Set
below blue mountains, it was divided between people who had land
and people who did not; and the people who had land were divided
into those who were masters of others and those who were not. This
was the age-old feudal pattern, restored by the Khmer Rouge and
maintained by Sary. Under Pol Pot, agriculture was dealt with along

the usual communist-collectivist lines. After the Vietnamese invasion, when the Khmer Rouge became guerrillas once more, a warlord economy developed in areas under their control. By the middle 1980s in the Battambang region, land had haemorrhaged out of the supposedly common hands and into the grasp of powerful Khmer Rouge chieftains. The number of landowners and the structure of land ownership began to approximate the pre-revolutionary pattern, with ordinary Khmer Rouge cadres claiming title to smaller plots and senior leaders becoming the new warlord and landed class.

Hay was *the* lord in his village. Landless peasants in his employ (slaving in his fields and paddies) were like indentured servants; they owed him for the huts in which they lived, their wages, and the percentage of the harvests which they received would probably never cover the ever accumulating 'debts' that they owed to Hay. Of course, Hay acknowledged certain obligations to them. He would lend money for the dowry needed to marry off a daughter; if violence was visited upon them, they could come to Hay for protection and vengeance and maybe even justice. But their debts to Hay, winding around them like a boa, would constrict and never end. Those debts would be passed on to their children, and to their children's children. After the Khmer Rouge years, however, to have a master who allowed you to live in a home that was yours, to till fields and paddies that you knew, to feed and keep your family together, was to feel more security than you had ever known.

In keeping with Sary's public statements, Hay was a broad-minded master. He welcomed new ways and methods of farming. Most landowners—landless peasants too—thought that machines were unnecessary. They were unsuited to the soil; tractors, it was said, could make the land infertile. When people from the UN food program came with new seeds and rice seedlings, Hay insisted that these be tried; when the World Bank came to describe a program to provide small loans for farmers and for women to start businesses, Hay was supportive. He would not stand in anyone's way. Some landowners had tried to thwart new irrigation schemes, until Sary denounced them as wreckers. Other landowners didn't like the idea of their peasants making more money, even if it meant more money for themselves. Everyone, rich and poor, was wary of change.

The 'Pol Pot time' had taught that change was dangerous. Not for Sary, not for Hay; both knew, really knew, the power of change; that change delivered power to those who initiated and manipulated it. So other landowners were careful not to cross Hay. They consulted him, they looked for his guidance and followed his lead. While we were there, two local rice farmers approached Hay like supplicants. Hay stuck out his jaw as he listened, but his face buckled, and an expression vulture-like but sentimental came over it. If Sary's official goal was to increase food production, or expand the irrigation system, landowners and desperate peasants would have to go along; they would have to keep their ideas about servants or bound labour to themselves. Their village was part of Sary's new order, an order leading to no one knew where.

It was impossible for me to think of Sary and Hay, ex-Khmer Rouge apparatchiks, as liberators. But Western Cambodia was now ruled by a network of men like them, and it was changing, visibly. They were linked to each other not only by the bonds of Khmer Rouge savagery, but continued to solidify their new caste through intermarriage, as they had in their guerrilla days. Just as Sary's ties to Pol Pot were both ideological and through marriage, so the men in Sary's administration were bound through marriages to each other. Hay's wife was the sister of a deputy governor of Battambang. Hay's university-bound daughter would be a prize for one of the younger generation of men in the network. One day she would exchange her work in her father's home for work in another just like it, and she would be conscious of her connections.

Waiting, and drinking from coconuts as we watched Hay work his local magic, a woman approached, walking along a bombed wall encased in shadow. She was wearing a straight green dress, cut like a pillowcase, which stretched from her shoulders to her bare shins. She was a Khmer, perhaps some mixture of French and Khmer, tall and lank and young. She came close and grinned, looking with the curiosity of a late-arriving child at the remains of a birthday party. She winked and we both sidled around the edge of the group.

'Is he helping you at all?' she whispered, nodding toward Hay.

'Doesn't seem to be. Not for what I wanted, to meet Ieng Sary. That's not going to happen. But I'm not unhappy.'

Her name was Chandra. She was a Khmer who arrived from Phnom Penh with a team from the Halo Trust, a group of volunteers (many ex-American and British soldiers) removing minefields throughout Cambodia. Philippa and Chandra had known each other for three years, long enough to have established a grave companion-ableness between themselves, a courtesy and good humour that made them seem civilization's last stand in the Battambang and Paylin provinces. They presented a sense, not only of grace under pressure, but of grace under siege.

Chandra had a level gaze and a veneer of vitality in her eyes. There were crescents of grey dirt under her fingernails and dust gave a dull sheen to her skin. Her breasts were small and firm and her arms slim and solid. She had slashed the sleeves of her dress to allow air to circulate under her arms.

Philippa and Chandra had met through the mine-clearing program. So many Khmers seemed to have trouble with their artificial limbs—previously those plastic arms and legs had been imported as discards from the West; nowadays, however, they were made at a factory in a central district of Phnom Penh, the biggest plant in that city. There were still new mine victims each week. The Halo Trust helped not only to remove mines but assisted the victims of mine explosions to become accustomed to their new arms and to make new lives for themselves. Chandra's job was to work with villagers.

'How long have you known Pip?' she asked.

'All of one day,' I said.

I mentioned that clearing mines was an odd job for a Khmer girl. She lowered her eyes and blushed.

'I don't really do what you think I do, though of course I know how. What I do is act as a liaison with villagers, teaching children how to recognize mines, recruiting people for training in removing them, that type of thing.'

'It can't be easy.'

'You'd be surprised. It is easier than you think. The trust pays money, in dollars, and people know that their villages cannot prosper if they don't reclaim lands that have been mined. So you have a lot of motives at work.'

'And the children?'

'We have a lot more trouble with them. If you are a boy or girl with nothing, a *bombi* looks like a toy.'

Day settled into evening which, in turn, settled into a silvered calm when we saw a streak of dust along the line of the road. It was Philippa, who had left me with Hay some hours before to continue her rounds but was now returning to have an outdoor barbecue picnic for dinner and take us back to Battambang as agreed.

She drove up at the wheel of a white Toyota Land Cruiser, through the humps, and parked about twenty yards short of the village. Two brawny women, Janie and Claire, squeezed themselves out of the cab and there were four thin Khmer men behind. They jumped down, brushed off the dust of the day, stretched and flexed their arms and legs.

'You're late,' Chandra shouted playfully.

Philippa's cheeks were creased with tiredness.

'You would have been late too,' she harrumphed.

Since leaving us she had driven 150 kilometres; treated twenty men with malaria and a boy with a snake bite; dosed a baby for dysentery; drawn an abscessed tooth from an old woman; sewn up a twelve year old prostitute who had been beaten by her pimp; sewn up the pimp, who'd been beaten by the other girls and boys in his stable.

'Now, I'm starving.'

Chandra fetched from the Toyota a bucket filled with cold beer, a large bowl of rice, and some dried shrimp pancakes. There had been a plan to cook a kind of shish kebab here, but when one of the women fetched a cooler from the back of the Land-Cruiser and opened it, the meat was swimming in blood-coloured water. The ice melted during the day.

While deciding what to do a Khmer woman emerged from a thicket of bushes. She came right up to us, grinning with the curiosity of a grotesque bird at the ruins of our food. We watched her, silence mounting like a bill that would have to be paid. Her nose and mouth appeared clumsily formed, the upper lip savage, the lower no better than a line; she looked unfinished. Emaciated, she seemed boneless, like Turkish taffy.

'She wants it,' Chandra said, her voice running low like a secret. The woman's eyes remained fixed on the meat in a lethal stare. From somewhere within those dark eyes whiteness flickered; her inner absence struggling to swim to the surface.

'We better give it to her,' said Philippa, curtly. 'If we throw it on the ground, she'll only pick it up after we leave. Give it to her.'

Chandra nodded in assent toward the Khmer woman, who snatched the chicken and chicken parts. Then the woman stood and grinned broadly. She spoke a few laughing words. Chandra appeared to understand only a little of what was said. All the while the woman's eyes remained fixed on the rest of our food. In the deep, young, liquid pupils of her eyes, sunken in their hollows, was a dull crimson core. Arms and legs stuck out of her garment; they were no more substantial than tumours on sticks. Pregnant, her belly swelled under her sarong like a pot. She walked firmly, with a solid thump of a step. As she moved away, you could see blue-bellied flies tacked on her forehead and her neck. At a safe distance, she stopped, turned, and smiled at us with wonder.

'She'll stay and watch until we are gone,' said Philippa.

From that distance the woman's head seemed like a flattened knob on her bony shoulders. She put out her hand and begged for money.

Chandra shook her head: No. 'She won't go away,' said Chandra.

Those beggar's eyes darted from one to the other of us, following our conversation like a dog. She pushed out her belly and laughed at it.

She pointed at me and signalled for me to come to her.

'You haven't spoken to her?' asked Chandra.

The deep single line of Philippa's frown creased in her forehead. 'You see what has happened to her? For more meat she'd do it with you now, even in her condition.' Philippa stared at the woman with a look secretive, intense, almost fearful.

'We should go,' said Chandra protectively. The only way to rid ourselves of the woman was to leave. We moved toward our cars and Chandra's motorcycle. The woman stood watching, with the same vacuous black grin. The same blue-bellied flies seemed to be glued to her head; she did not notice them. A mosaic of bees fed on the remnants of our food.

On the drive back to Battambang, Chandra abruptly pulled her

Honda off the road. As she shut the engine small birds skimmed out from a bank of reedy grass and flew low across the gravel. An old woman had stumbled and fallen while leading three gaunt Brahma cows to a pen behind a concrete and cinder block bungalow. Her cry for help queened like a crow's over that mute landscape. She was dark, tawny like a gypsy, and with a gypsy's canny eyes, bird bright, arrowing and shivering. Taking the old lady by the elbow, I helped her to the side of the road where there was a rock for her to sit as Chandra wiped away a trickle of blood from below her nose.

The old woman's face was fine and sharp, incised by the sun and ingrained with the scrupulous beeswax polished graining of old wood. Her voice, the chirp of a bird. I smiled at her appearance. She saw me smiling and smiled back. She seemed to know everything, as an old hen sees all things in the barnyard. Maybe she had seen everything; in that place, she may well have seen every horror that man can inflict on other men and women. After a few moments, she gestured that she wanted to rise, and I helped her to her feet. Lifting her was no effort. As light as a husk, she seemed like a figure carved from cork. It was like holding starvation in your hands.

XI

La Voie Royale

IT WAS ANOTHER four or five hours journey—'if you're lucky'—to Paylin, I was informed. If I wanted to get there, I should set out early, before eight but better before six. And don't take a motorcycle. Everyone told me that. You can perhaps get away with it during daylight hours in Phnom Penh, but I'd learned what a close run thing that can be. Here, you went by car with a driver, preferably one that you trusted but at the least someone who works for people you know. And try and get a car with tinted windows so that no one can see that you are foreign. Do that, and they'll think you are one of Sary's boys. You'll be left alone.

The road to Paylin, a small provincial capital ninety kilometres or so from Battambang and a mere ten or eleven kilometres from the Thailand border, was a straightish band of crushed stone and rutted earth with, strips of red dirt and straggling weeds wilting in the dry heat on either side. A wilderness of pale scrub and trees drooped at times over the roadside, the trunks as gnarled and bent as many of the villagers we whisked past. The land was used in the modern Khmer way: burned, cultivated, abandoned. Everything looked desolate, but that solitude was broken every now and then by little settlements in scraped brown yards, with little plantings of maize or banana or sugar cane about the huts.

A military truck, bouncing through the potholes, overtook us about twenty kilometres into the journey. Filled with CPP militiamen who seemed to strut even as they sat, the lorry churned up the dust of the unpaved road. It trundled by and soon disappeared from sight. Half-an-hour later, we caught up with it. One of the lorry's axles had cracked, and soldiers were jumping down from the open back onto the road. Our timing was lucky: in a few minutes the entrepreneurial zeal of those ill-disciplined troops would take over and they would begin stopping cars and demanding bribes.

As it happens, I had become resigned to frequent searches, resigned to being stopped in the middle of nowhere, to getting out of a car or off the back of a motorcycle and presenting identification— remembering each time to carefully reach into my pockets, my movements calculated not to startle the soldiers, many of whom seemed barely pubescent as they clutched their Kalashnikovs—and wait while the car or motorcycle was searched.

We arrived in Paylin after midday in appalling heat. Only once in Phnom Penh had I experienced anything like it, but Phnom Penh was freshened by tender breezes off the Mekong and Bassac rivers, and from winds blowing over the length of the Tonle Sap. To know how hellishly hot the world can be, you must experience Paylin—white bleached streets running off between concrete shacks, one or two with satellite dishes aiming upward into a blazing sky that renders the nearby green hills phosphorescent. Businesses faced each other across what was less a square than a dusty widening of the road. Soldiers were billeted somewhere nearby; a few of them were kicking a soccer ball, idly, among their leaning rifles. Otherwise Paylin was like a city of the dead, no civilians were to be seen, the ground barren, as if sown with salt.

It was the barbed wire that you really noticed hovering over buildings, sliced between the branches of trees. Razor wire like that always communicates a message: *be on guard, you have entered a different world.* It imprinted on my mind everything I needed to know about the place, and did so relentlessly, for my own good.

Quick students, we tried to avoid attention. Chandra bought two Coca-Colas and we drank them as I made surreptitious notes. Save for the soldiers, there was no one about in this hideout for defectors from the Khmer Rouge. The first signs of life came from vultures skulking on either side of the main road through the centre of town, their grey idiot heads and serrated wings hopping in little powdery clouds. They were joined on the street by underfed cattle, mongrel dogs, and armoured-plated all-terrain vehicles, fitted with reinforced steel and bullet-proof tinted plexiglass.

Signs of Cambodia's approaching elections were everywhere. Looking at the posters you could see that this would be the sort of election Khmers have known for three decades, meaning that the government intended for there to be no choice. You could vote for Hun Sen's CPP, headed here by Ieng Sary and his son or else. Motley policemen stood at the entrance to the local hotel and watched us edge up and park. Their Che Guevara outfits—the dark sunglasses, the holstered guns, the red and white check bandanas—general issue gear of revolutionaries circa 1968. Their incongruity in the 'Kingdom of Cambodia' seemed not only absurd, but irritating. Chandra said gently, 'ignore them. They are like the threatening clowns you see in the circus. Nothing more.' She was not to know that the metaphor was not reassuring. My friend Norman Manea has written on the clown as a figure of savagery, treachery, and terror; given his history—a survivor of the Nazi camps, of Ceausescu's gulag—Chandra's metaphor offered no comfort.

Here was Paylin—Sary's second city, once the capital of the Khmer Rouge's isolated, malarial, and puritanically atheist statelet, the base from which they waged guerrilla war against the Vietnamese occupiers, and later Hun Sen's regime. On the run from the Vietnamese, in Paylin Pol Pot tried to level every wat; every monk was hunted down or shot, except for a few who hid for years in the forests and swamps, venturing out only among the local tribes people at night. Small patrols of Khmer Rouge soldiers even crossed into Thailand once or twice when hunting down an escaping monk. A Taiwanese Buddhist leader who had come to Paylin in the mid-1980s to report on the state of the faith was shot down in the street. The few notes he had taken, I was told by a monk who had come up from Phnom Penh after Sary crossed over to Hun Sen's side, recorded a hideous sense of impotence, of horrors that could not be confronted by the comforts of faith. At the time of my visit, Pol Pot was supposedly under house arrest—dying of a checklist of diseases: cancer, malaria, angina—somewhere in the swamps north of Anlong Veng, yet his anticlerical zeal could still be felt in a curious sort of half-life.*

* Succumbing (or so the impromptu autopsy said) to a heart attack at age

That first afternoon I listened to monks droning their prayers in snarling, resonant voices. Their incantations had a hypnotizing effect. But their monotonous groaning, like a prayer wheel, existed in a vacuum. It was like the hum of a factory, or of propaganda droning over loudspeakers, something that created the hallucinatory spell, not of faith, but of communal rule.

As Chandra and I approached a hotel I noticed three soldiers herding a young peasant boy into the back of a canvas-shrouded truck, a pistol pressed into the boy's back. I walked straight into the lobby, not wanting to see any of this.

Chandra returned for dinner a few hours later. She wanted to take me out before dark to get a feel for the town. Her first choice for sightseeing was curious: the brothel area. She drove the borrowed motorcycle down its narrow lanes: the lights, the handpainted signboards, the shanties, the young girls and boys sitting out, some sprawled on string beds in shadows at the side of the lanes; the piles of sopping rubbish, the smell of open sewers; child prostitutes and their pimps and johns and moneylenders all on dreary display.

The daily life of the area was proceeding: a troop lorry passing through the lane—a dark place, and usually without motor traffic—hardly caused a stir. In a bright light at the end of the lane, on a raised platform covered with wires and loudspeakers, two drunken soldiers were singing some Michael Jackson song to a karaoke machine. No one paid attention to them; I received all the stares. When we passed

seventy-three), Pol Pot died on April 15, 1998. His funeral was fittingly ignominious. On April 18th, three days dead and boxed in a rough plank coffin, Pol Pot's body was heaped onto a pyre composed of used tyres, scrap wood, and discarded furniture—his own mattress and chair—which was then doused in gasoline, set ablaze, and reduced to ashes. '*Burned Like Old Rubbish*' chirped the 'Phnom Penh Post.' Six months previously, Pol Pot had been toppled in a power struggle, after he had ordered his longtime comrade, Son Sen, and eleven members of his family murdered and repeatedly run over by a truck. He had been sentenced by a 'People's Tribunal' (the proceedings filmed and distributed around the world by the freelance journalist Nate Thayer) to life imprisonment. But that punishment appears to have amounted to little more than a forced retirement, with the dictator pensioned off to his hut with his wife and teen-age daughter and feeling misunderstood.] 'My conscience is clean,' he told Nate Thayer. 'Everything I have done and contributed is for the nation and people and race of Cambodia.'

one brothel, two young girls, they could not have been more than twelve, emerged from the shadows. I wanted to get away; those miniature Lolitas with their black, dead eyes were following us. At the end of the lane, near a brighter main road, Chandra said that they would stop following; but they did not. She thought it better if she went to talk and explain matters to them. It did not work. Those girls would not go away until we left.

The governor of Paylin was to hold court for a few dozen people in a small, shaded garden, untended, near the back of the municipal building that was the seat of his provincial government. The grounds were crowded with politicians, civil servants, and local traders. With their resignation and passivity, you had a feeling that they were awaiting orders from their impresario, an unseen man whom all must obey.

They were waiting for Ieng Vuth, son of Ieng Sary, to appear. One hunched, simpering fellow in sneakers was dressed in green trousers and a polyester shirt in a red check pattern. He was a teacher pining to run the new Hun Sen grammar school currently under construction. He had come to Vuth to plead for the job. Besides such favour seekers, there were a dozen security guards with guns on their hips, their holsters and cartridge belts prominent. Battle scars on the face of one guard mingled with the dark colours of religious tattoos. Ieng Sary had issued an order restricting the right to carry guns to government employees, and members of his army. But rules didn't operate any more successfully in Paylin than in Phnom Penh. Within the yard it was steaming hot, and the audience waited patiently, one hour, two hours, three, waiting to get something: money, an appointment, a permission, a promise, a pardon, a reprieve.

One trader came all the way from the former Khmer Rouge stronghold of Anlong Veng, which government troops recaptured days before. The Khmer Rouge were in their death throes. In a last frenzy, desperate schemes had appeared, the Khmer Rouge violence becoming more and more grotesque. Traitors to the movement were butchered in their homes, the assassins practically children. Some became sickened by their acts; afterwards they sat in the dirt outside the homes of the victims and wept. New mass graves were also reported. The last fighting remnants of the Khmer Rouge, commanded by the peg-legged general Ta Mok, were slaughtering camp followers before a final surrender in the impassable Koy Forest.

Suddenly, everyone in that garden stiffened and stood to attention. From out of a dusty blue Mercedes came the governor; among the officials, he was the only man without a gun. Beams of sunlight broke through the peepul trees onto his brow: his face, was otherwise swallowed in shadow. As soon as Vuth moved into the courtyard the teacher rushed toward him, offering exaggerated gestures of respect. Vuth nodded soothingly to the wretched man with that sort of vacant aplomb that is authority's analogue to courtesy. Vuth looked at everything with political distance, like the dead-eyed gaze of a blind man. The teacher's public exhibition was extraordinary. Perhaps Vuth regarded it as too public; anyway, the governor gave no indication that he felt harassed. The anxious-eyed teacher became less servile. Moving away from the man. Vuth stood in full light. His face, except for that politician's beam, appeared like that of any peasant. Formidably silent, Vuth was grave with his sense of self-destiny, diligently resolved to act out the position of authority bestowed on him by his father. Crooked teeth stood out like a flaw in his character.

Royalty and Communist politburo men make their way through a crowd, usually speaking only to select supplicants. Vuth was more modern than that. Like a politician on the hustings, he moved from man to man and woman to woman, working the room, radiating energy. No humour touched his smile, which seemed to have been stitched across his face like the line of a stuffed bear.

The government chairs set out on a stone patio were ugly and heavy; their bamboo or whicker bleached and dulled by the sun. Big rolled up awnings, green in colour, were the only decorative features on the building, and they added to the bare, dull, bureaucratic feeling of the place.

Vuth found the chair set out for him and sat like royalty, a few locals seated themselves at his feet. He surveyed the crowd, holding a cup of green tea in one hand, his free hand extended like the Pope's. An obstinate look creased his face. From time to time, a seated young woman would look up to Ieng Vuth, make eye contact, then scribble a note in a small diary.

The son, I feared, would be as elusive as the father. I had prepared some formal questions to explain my visit—the sort of foolish, insipid questions newspaper reporters are supposed to ask— about the Khmer Rouge and whether or not the movement was dead, and about the coming elections and the role of the Sary family in them. When the receptionist moved next to the governor to explain what I wanted, I saw Vuth turn toward me, muttering with his expressions 'not another one.' When Chandra conveyed to the receptionist the questions I intended to ask, Vuth, overhearing, looked annoyed. He didn't want to answer questions. Not yet, there was a time for everything. Then, pondering, he told Chandra that he would answer my questions in writing; we didn't have to speak at all. I had to wait another ten minutes for the receptionist to speak to explain that a conversation was what was needed. Rejection, I believed, was still certain.

As we waited for his response, the receptionist escorted us around the grounds as other secretaries, pretty, nubile and faintly insolent, handed food to the assemblage. There was lawn furniture that might have come from a jumble sale, an occasional teak table, and a poster of the King glued to the back wall—an old photograph, the King looking innocent and youthful and playful, as he did when he starred in a movie with Marlon Brando decades ago, *The Ugly American*. This reception area was, I imagined, like the unkempt garden of a ministry building in a European capital ruined by war, used once again as a sign of approaching normalcy.

Vuth's political health depended on the strength of his father in Battambang. Not many months back old Sary had been politically sick; politicians from Phnom Penh ceased to visit—Hun Sen was said to be preparing a change of allegiance, readying a deal with another ex-Khmer Rouge leader. Only a few old Khmer Rouge men came to see Sary in his illness. All the time old Sary commanded his own private army of eight thousand former Khmer Rouge guerrillas; so long as he continued to pay them, they would be loyal. Guns were all that mattered here.

Secretaries brought us food—cut fruit, shrimp pancakes, rice— and Vuth watched me eat with his dark, scarred courtesy. Chandra ate as if she had not tasted food for some time; in complete absorption. I began to think that as we were eating, some assistant was probably inside typing up pat answers to my questions, which we would be given and then sent off. Nothing about Vuth, however, was going to be as simple as all that. We finished eating and mingled with the others in the garden—the governor had disappeared, but that petitioning crowd loitered.

It was another hour before Vuth reappeared. Marching through the crowd he made his way toward me. 'Are you here looking for the Khmer Rouge?' he asked with the practised nonchalance of a politician dealing with a scandal. 'The Khmer Rouge doesn't exist anymore. Period. The Khmer Rouge is over. What they did is over. They are our ghosts, nothing more.' Cambodia, it seemed, not only did not have the resources to deal with the legacy of the Khmer Rouge, it didn't have the desire. The country's future had already arrived, it was here now, in the shantytowns, those spontaneous communities that needed Vuth's guidance and discipline. All that his authority could add to the lives of his wards, however, was regulation haphazardly deployed. Maybe trash collection could be added; maybe electricity could be guaranteed for some. Shantytowns might, in effect, begin to be planned, but Vuth could not promise anything. Only by such benign neglect could the people leaving the land be controlled and accommodated. With that, he was finished with me.

That evening Chandra took me for a final meal in what was supposed to be Paylin's best restaurant. Manners in that thieves' den were correct. A teenage prostitute—obviously Khmer but, even so, here all whores were called Vietnamese 'taxi girls'—was annoying a dark mouthed man by rumpling his hair. He slapped her across the face, then examined his hand. The nail on his little finger was an inch long, curved like a talon. Otherwise, most of the customers were indistinguishable, silent and sullen.

Watching that girl skulk away made me think about how little women in Cambodia had to hope for from life. The bargains which they could strike for money or love would always be meagre. Chandra, too, as I looked at her, had acquired the always available smile of so many Khmer women. In the half-light of that bar her face was sharp, her voice intense. Her longings were so vast that barely a part of them could be acknowledged. Perhaps it was exactly this, the injudiciousness of her gaze and need for luck, that would make me remember Chandra after I was gone. Her life had no solution. It was like a crime that could not be undone.

*

AT HALF past eight the bus from Battambang to Siem Reap stopped at a small town hall in the middle of an old colonial era square of one and two storey stucco and stone houses. Attempts were being made to make the place look like a resort development. There were air-conditioned lounges. At one end of the square a decayed municipal garden was being restored, and the base of a statue to King Norodom, King Sihanouk's father, was having new stone facing applied. Squatting outside a bar, two farmers were drinking palm juice from a Fanta bottle and munching sliced papaya. An old woman huddled over her kettle. Inside the bar were paintings of King Sihanouk and his wife Queen Monineath, he wearing a brightly coloured sash and looking an old libertine, she sporting a hairstyle recalling Queen Elizabeth in its frumpiness; another photograph was of Sihanouk alone, looking younger and whimsically treacherous. Nearby was a third photographic portrait, this of Hun Sen, with sunglasses shielding his glass eye. Who held pride of place was uncertain: the iconography of the 'democratic' Kingdom of Cambodia was complicated.

Decades after Vietnam's invading army chased Pol Pot's Khmer Rouge into the jungles near Thailand, the temples of Angkor—the supreme symbol of Indo-Khmer civilization, of its ambitions and tragedies—were at last being renovated and restored. White vans from the UN's World Historical Monuments Project trundled along roads overhung with banners that proclaimed '*Plant Trees Not Mines*' and '*Mines are Unpredictable.*' The curious thing about those warnings was that they were written in English, meaning that they were not helpful in a land where most people were illiterate even in their own language of Khmer.

The results of the mines could be spotted along the roadsides; women hopping about on one leg, children without arms, legless men rolling themselves on wooden crates to which bicycle wheels had been attached. One peg-legged woman was selling coconuts; tacked to a wall within her wattle hut—two chickens were tumbling in its dust—was a yellowing, mildewed portrait of Diana, Princess of Wales, wearing a gleaming tiara and in blue chiffon, the patron saint of mine victims.

Such posters were on display throughout Cambodia. How was this adoration of Diana to be understood? The Khmers had their own king and queen; they had any number of soap opera heroines on television. Those idols were too close, however, too tangible; Diana was untouchable and unknowable.

For hundreds of years, the Khmers lived without heroes. They began to get champions late, provided by the French in schoolbooks and public ceremonies. Paris even provided a king and a royal court. Then, with independence, as political life developed, the Khmer peasantry acquired leaders, military men, guerrilla fighters, most of all the nimble Sihanouk with his marathon tap dance of neutrality between America and North Vietnam. For those early leaders who were the Khmer's own, the Khmers had more than adulation. They wished those leaders to represent them, and in more than a political way. They wished their leaders to be powerful and glorious. Glory in the leader revealed glory in the people. Ordinary ideas of morality and propriety didn't apply. A leader wasn't required to be modest or correct; those were the virtues of another world. A leader was, instead, invested with responsibility to be grand, larger than life, for the sake of all the Khmers.

Something like that sort of adulation was at work within the Khmer cult of Diana.

The motorcycle ride along the gentle top of the plateau toward Angkor's complex of temples was a journey of expectation. In the shade of giant trees there was cooling air like spring water against a morning sun. I passed the bleached skeleton of a rhesus monkey. Packs of mongrel dogs and a few cattle lay motionless in the heat under thorny trees. Like those listless beasts, I found myself swerving instinctively toward whatever patch of shade I could see.

Tourists, a few scattered monks, straggling members of Hun Sen's army and party militia, four amputees in a mule cart, pretty young peasant girls hawking sliced pineapples: all infested Angkor Wat, its beehive domes looming over a landscape of jungle and bush.

Immediately on entering the temple compound, the familiar nuisances of global tourism appeared: those grinning buskers and hustlers are the same everywhere. The few pre-packaged tour groups sauntering about also seemed as natural in that castaway landscape as religious pilgrims once did a millennium ago. When crossing Angkor Wat's west causeway above a moat of brackish water (what diseases and parasites were infecting the children swimming below?), on spotting me, emaciated men carrying old-fashioned cameras straightened themselves like Marine recruits and barked to attention: '*ten hut!*'

I carried no detailed guide to the monuments. My plan was to make only an aesthetic investigation. I cannot say now what treasures of detail I missed: tragic carvings, ceilings gloomy with the burden of their beauty, stones on which men had chiselled their desires and then died.

Cloisters and courtyards were crammed with village people, camping in the open below the grey stone beehive towers, sprawling on the ground or on tattered hammocks. Small, cadaverous, filthy, poor, their blank village faces filled the temples with indifference. Walking past and over so many of them, it was difficult to see more than the exterior beauties, the broad effects and sights. Angkor was a monument turned slum.

Except for its massive and splendid walls and central towers, Angkor Wat looked flimsy. Much of its stonework was so worn that it had a lichenous shape and seemed as much vegetable as mineral. A large part of the temple's West Gate had collapsed in the monsoon rains a year before. It made me wonder how the temple, neglected for centuries, survived a thousand seasons of such torrents. Angkor reminded me of many of the American-era buildings I had seen in Vietnam; buildings which, due to their hasty construction, also demanded constant repair. Angkor, I was told, had also been built hurriedly over the centuries—and it looked it. UN restoration men darted about the temple grounds in their white vans from one emergency restoration site to another.

The nitty-gritty of construction 'seems to have been a bothersome necessity,' to the Khmers, wrote the French archeologist

Henri Parmentier early last century. Parmentier was one of that group of academic freebooters sent out from Paris to 'rediscover' the glories of Khmer civilization at the time of the Great War. The stone cutting, says Parmentier (whose writings inspired the young Malraux to set off in 1922 on the Indochinese journey that began his career and his legend) was 'done without great care, rushed into being so as to achieve the only thing that mattered, the final form.'

But you could not take in all of the forms of Angkor Wat and the neighbouring, Buddhist-inspired Angkor Thom all at once; it took hours in that furnace just to navigate the two vast compounds criss-crossed by canals and *barays* (reservoirs). Not even the light could be grasped easily or taken for granted: it was a potent presence in itself. In London, New York and Paris, light appears as merely a temporary arrangement of varying degrees of substance and shadow. In Angkor, it had an absolute quality. Under a cloudless midday sky, temple after temple looked as if it were floating in some lake or sea that was on fire.

The first pleasure that sight of the temples gave soon surrendered to awe and a sort of melancholy. Constructed from locally quarried pinkish, grey, and golden stones—their size varied from temple to temple, helping preservationists to date them—the monuments seemed not like planned architecture but like sudden molten projections out of the earth. Tilted here, slanted there, sometimes in rubble, their surfaces knobbled like clay wasp nests, the scrambled establishments were among the greatest overstatements of Hindu genius to be found anywhere, for the lands of Indochina were Hindu in the first millennium. Angkor's hundreds of tapered towers and corbelled roofs, many topped by carved stone lotus flowers, stared and blinked in the violent sun.

Medieval Europe's great cathedrals were built to commemorate the death and resurrection of a lone god: even the most garish Baroque churches in, say, Prague or Rome, remain stone premoni-tions of the end of man. Hinduism's architectural genius was for human excess, excesses not only of austerity but of sensual decoration, of the flesh in the here and now—and hereafter too. Above all, because the stone statuary brings even today so much of the Hindu world to our eyes, Angkor provides tremendous access to a vanished ethic of life. No other faith has Hinduism's consuming preoccupation with physical delight. Even in the art of ancient Greece true sensuality seems a passing mood. In Hindu life and art, as manifested in Angkor, the feeling is continuous. Death and sex are festivals celebrated in the faces and stories of numberless gods; their stone presences within Angkor have the force not only of a carnal realism, but of a timeless and ceaseless life and death struggle.

As you look at the stone carvings within crumbling towers, whether earthly or religious, sombre or spicy, you see an enormous volume of emotion contained within each minutely watched figure. How meticulous Angkor's anonymous Hindu—and later Buddhist—sculptors were about every detail, always on the watch to convey the telling dramatic insight, the clue to a god's character, the spring to action. The faces and bodies of the gods are caught at moments of movement from one state to another. Those long ago sculptors were not at all slavish to dogma; they were, instead, readers of human nature, insistent on imprinting its waywardness on the celestial. Their playful views of faith seemed to me a kind of creative scepticism, and very modern.

On first sight of the line of stone giants guarding the south gate to Angkor Thom, for example, you saw merely a patient copyist of conventional Buddhist images. Look at them more closely, and you saw a sculpture of reflections, the smiles on all those giants became at times arrogant, at times knowing—sometimes even a gentle smirk creased the dark stone. At one time, fifty-two mammoth *deva* lined that causeway, itself elevated on a dyke above Angkor Thom's south perimeter; each colossus stood on braced legs—huge, misanthropic sentinels for the tower of gold standing—alas, no longer; plundered, it disappeared centuries ago—at the centre of the temple.

Even the huge faces of Buddha inside Angkor Thom's temples were like no other statues of that tranquil god-man that I had ever seen. Not content with a sublime grandeur, those anonymous sculptors captured something entirely unexpected. The Buddha of their carvings seems enraptured in a trance not of benevolence, but of vigilance; it was as if, through observation, the hard grains of faith and time had been transformed into a stone image of wariness. Each monumental stone face of Buddha was a kind of frozen moment; one at the point of passing into another moment. Humanity, the sculptures hinted, was not only a spiritual passage, as the Buddha proclaimed, but something held together by light and time. Each sculptured deity, in whatever state of repair or ruin, watched the world with all the concentration of which a human ego was capable. Here, settled in stone, was the heroic, ancient Khmer definition of living: it was to see. *I look, therefore I am.* Everywhere was that marriage of eye and spirit.

The ravenous hungers of those gods, Hindu or Buddhist, I was told, were struck deliberately. The soldier kings—part monk, part bureaucrat, part warrior—of the great age of Khmer civilization (between the 9th and 13th centuries) who built Angkor held in disdain the hierarchical simplicity of China's Confucian civilization with which Hinduism (and later Buddhism) was in deadly competition. Temples were built as a range of sacred mountains dedicated to a series of disputatious, warring gods; the whole complex all rushed into being bit by bit with a relentless, military spirit. And despite the powerful affirmations of the physical, the sense of death was also present; present as a fact and not as the shadow of a fear, and thus as intense as the ravening for life. Life and death existed only in absolute terms.

Chou Ta-Kuan, an ambassador in 1296 from Kublai Khan to the Khmer court of King Srindravarman, captured the sense of awe and disquiet that the Khmer kings cultivated in their temples. 'Although this is a land of barbarians,' he wrote, 'they know how to treat a king.' Srindravarman paraded about his temples and palaces in a gold palinquin, seated behind curtains which, at the blast of a conch horn, girls would suddenly appear to part the silk curtains and reveal a glimpse of the king on his tiger-skin throne. On looking once, briefly, the assembled people would then beat their heads on the ground until the conch horns ceased and the royal exhibition was over.

Chou recites, feigning disgust, some of the more barbaric habits of Srindravarman's court. He loathed the open displays of royal favour bestowed upon court homosexuals, who struck the novice ambassador as particularly predatory in their solicitings of the young Chinese men in his embassy. He condemned the faithlessness of Khmer wives, who could not or would not remain faithful beyond a fortnight's separation from their husbands. Perhaps because lascivious, Chaucerian monks were standard types in Confucian literature, Chou seemed particularly fascinated by tales of the ritual deflowering of virgins by the probing fingers of specially anointed Angkor monks.

In the Bayon temple within the complex of Angkor Thom, the largest and most ambitious of the temples, built in the 12th century by King Jayavarman VII, there are fifty-four intricately carved towers capped by gigantic heads of Buddha—one for each province of the ancient Khmer kingdom—each looking inward, like sentinels, to where there once stood a tower of gold which held within it Jayavarman's golden Buddha. It was in the temple's mixture of faiths that the beginnings of the Khmer disaster were to be found. Jayavarman's effort to fuse the Hinduism of his royal line with the Buddhist fever then sweeping Asia, was a replay of the fierce struggles that marked Hinduism's advance into Indochina five hundred years earlier. Seeing so many mutilated people wandering the temples, squatting in shadows, that story of spiritual-conquest-made-flesh also seemed to me a prophecy of the murderous rampages of the mid-20th century, when colonialism, capitalism, and communism seesawed for control here. Cambodia had lived for long periods of its history in a condition of active or passive civil war. Beyond the dream-like vistas of Angkor you felt the history of a country struggling against its own natural anarchy. No Buddhist conception of denial and law, no Hindu conception of pleasure and pain, not even Pol Pot's chiliastic vision, had ever been really strong enough to control the Khmer's natural anarchism.

Centuries of feuding faiths and shifting occupations created a society composed of three groups of people: enemies, conquerors, and—the majority—collaborators, those who through force or self-protection assumed the rituals and habits of whatever side had somehow become dominant. First Taoists became Hindus, then Hindus became Buddhists, then Buddhists became Roman Catholics, Catholics became communists, communists became capitalists or whatever it was that Khmers might consider themselves today. In serial occupations the Khmers, as if by osmosis, came over the years to see everyone as a potential internal enemy, fifth-columnist or secret party cadre. 'We kill only when we all believe', Youk once told me in Phnom Penh. But the more any

Khmer spoke of their country's ancient unity, the more they revealed how utterly absent it was. Passive acceptance of official doctrines might be the daily social command at any period in the country's history, but was the recent convert really a secret acolyte of Shiva, Buddha, Christ, Nixon, Ho Chi Minh, Pol Pot, Sihanouk or Hun Sen?

Only people lacking born-in-the-bone unity place so fateful an emphasis on it. In doing so, they corrupt the idea and make it into a coercive uniformity, one needing to be watched over by inquisitions, tribunals, and committees of public safety. Cities rebel, the faithful are militarized, fever spreads, a new faith is put down or an old one laid low. So the patterns of Khmer history were repeated over the centuries. In this sense, Pol Pot's genocide of the Khmer middle classes was not at all aberrant, but merely a crazed affirmation of the national ideal: the practical and rational elements of Khmer society expunged in the name of the new true faith. Fanaticism, cruelty and decadence were, to some small extent, engraved in the faiths vying for attention within Angkor's architecture. The pocked facades, even when screened by green creepers or leviathan parasite trees, could not hide the theocratic frown. In the stones of Angkor the Khmers appear as a people who are either one thing or the other, black or white, as if the years of Pol Pot were just another blow that had somehow short-circuited their senses and their intelligence. They were smiling fatalists, either resigned to the law that was imposed upon them, or who rejected and fought against it. Nothing in between.

And what of that royal line, the kings who built Angkor? As centuries of war and harsh internal rule mounted, by a kind of tragic retribution they became unfit for the rational tasks of governance. King Sihanouk, second in the royal line after the French engineered restoration, was perhaps their apogee. Over the centuries the Khmer kings could win battles, impose ravenous taxes and confiscate crops, but they could not work. For a thousand years the disciplined humanism of the Confucian states to Cambodia's north and east had seemed a weakness to the Khmer rulers. Instead of falling into China's orbit, they sought to distance themselves from that great power by aligning with and mimicking each rising faith that came along. Angkor carried the signs of that improvisation, that dexterity, and that tragedy. So monumental an effort at synthesis exhausted the Khmer impulse, fatally so. The Buddhist-Hindu fusion that Angkor proclaimed was, like all attempts to graft one faith upon another and all half-way reforms, really a dead end, one that decayed into barbarism.

For five hundred years Angkor Wat maintained its vibrant slave markets, its temple prostitutes. Even into the 15th century it remained huge, splendid, but in desperate need of administrators, artists, craftsmen; construction and preservation of the temples was using up all the energies and talents of the land. When the upstart Thai people finally conquered the Angkor kingdom, and Khmer civilization was smashed, more than bayons and temples lay in ruins. All the talent, energy, and intellectual capital of the kingdom was dispersed into the fields and then extinguished. And the conquerors, by creating a desert out of what had been the Angkor garden, invited their own subsequent defeat. Again and again over the centuries the land of the dead Khmer kingdom was trampled over.

Today, that defeat showed in the finality of the destruction of Angkor and in the acknowledged 'backwardness' (even by today's Khmer standards) of the region, which now seemed a place without a history. The connections of local Khmers lay elsewhere: in the squalor of Siem Reap not far from the temples. Over the past decade, much money had been spent on the Angkor region by international aid agencies. Land mines were cleared; new schools—all of them seem to have been named for Hun Sen—were constructed. An extensive irrigation scheme was in the works to make use of the ancient bayon-based irrigation system of Angkor.

But that land which was once a land of heroic, visionary builders was now a vast human deficiency. So thorough were the Khmer Rouge in their work that the Angkor-Siem Reap provincial government needed to encourage migrants from other parts of the country. It was in dire need of technicians of all sorts, artisans; it craved people with the simplest of skills; it even lacked hotel waitresses and busboys, many of whom fled Phnom Penh for what they thought would be a better life here. All that Angkor seemed to have been left after the flight of the Khmer Rouge was a brightly coloured, unimportantly active peasantry that could not even begin to comprehend the idea of change as anything but violence: violence like the young toughs slipping in and out of the ruined stones of the more remote temples such as Banteay Srei, waiting to pounce on isolated tourists.

It was at Angkor, which at the end of my visit seemed less awesome than the idea of it had seemed at the start of my journey, no longer speaking of a fabulous past but of a depleted, stifling present, that I began to wonder about the intellectual, moral, and spiritual uprooting of Khmer civilization, a depletion that began not with Pol Pot or the American bombings but with the myriad invasions and conquests of the last thousand years. What happened to Angkor happened, in varying degrees, across Indochina. In Phnom Penh, ruin lay upon more recent ruin; in Saigon, Hué, and Da Nang the instant decrepitude of the Soviet era lay atop American ruins that sat on top of French ruins.

In the history books of the last decades, in the accounts of wars and imperial conquests, Indochina's mental exhaustion passes largely unnoticed; the cultural compromises of a millennium pass in nothingness, for the ferocity of a Ho Chi Minh or Pol Pot are all that can be recalled. We absorb and outlast our conquerors, many Vietnamese had told me, and I suspect that those Khmers who survived the abominations of the Pol Pot era would agree with that sentiment; that is, if they had any capacity to reflect on their past. At Angkor, I wondered if in the habit of spiritual withdrawal, of running away and retreating again and again in order to survive, the people of Indochina only succeeded in making themselves intellectually smaller and ever more vulnerable.

Indochina's current turbulence was not due to foreign invasion or attempted conquest or ideological rage; it was generated from within. The peoples of Indochina could no longer respond to external threats in their old ways, by retreating deeper into their archaism. The borrowed ideas and borrowed institutions that they imposed upon themselves in order to meet the challenge of the world, however, worked like anything else taken on credit: the borrower's distress precluded any real rooting of those ideas and institutions. So the crisis of Cambodia, and to a lesser extent the crisis of all Indochina, was not merely a reflection of political and economic trouble. The larger crisis was of fractured civilizations that were, at long last, becoming aware of their inadequacies, but which lacked—fatally so—the intellectual resources to confront that recognition.

*

DUSK CAME quickly. Across a heaven of terrifying Toledo blue, huge clouds moved north, dark as the sea. Cooking pots clanked in the forests surrounding the temple precincts. Voices carried in the swollen air.

In those hoarding woodlands around Angkor there seemed to be deep belts of a watching, predatory silence. A few monkeys could be heard screaming at the tops of trees, dense as velvet; in the cries of monkeys and birds you became deafened and exasperated and longed to swim in silence. Suddenly, when everything did become silent you were unnerved once more. Silence hit like a hammer. Then, more abruptly, lightning sheeted the temples and lit flares in the encircling woods. There was an abortive crack of thunder, a peal snapped and cut short like wood splitting. Rain came down straight and dense, making the foliage ring like a tin roof. The wind moved like ocean waves through the trees. That drenching downpour, brief as it was, washed away some of the dirt around Angkor Wat's collapsed eastern wall. As the rain petered out, in darkness a crew of Chinese workmen from the Institute of Archaeology in Beijing hustled to pile back the earth, reinforcing it with wooden planks. They constructed a strange apparatus, four strong poles guyed to the ground from which blue floodlights illuminated the ruins.

In the temple precincts of Angkor Wat there were no trees, only a grey dimming sea of lawn on either side of a crushed stone path leading to the temple complex. Out of the shadows came a man holding hands with a rhesus monkey; both monkey and man stopped and stared at me. The temple lay in gloom, so I walked slowly into its quadrangles. Far to the right I saw a light scratching the shade like a pin. Despite the inky blackness, I got off the path and groped my way toward that light through a rutted field. At last I saw the tower and the form of a building where light was escaping. The temple appeared to have been abandoned in the blackness left behind by the storm. No sound could be heard save for the crackling minimalist chorus of bats whirring above. Opaque night. It was like being under the influence of a powerful narcotic.

My eyes groped the darkness for sight of some steps and an archway toward the light. As I stood, the air suddenly twisted into the spiralling caterwaul of a chicken. A sharp, forlorn cry. Where there were chickens, I told myself, there were families. I felt my way along the temple wall until I found some stairs leading toward a low level of the building and a partly lit passage. The cloister was in darkness but I heard voices from a room within. I might have been in a stable or a workshop, for I knocked into a bench before coming to stone steps rising into a long narrow room. The air was thick with body smells and tobacco smoke. The darkness was striped with a dirty yellow light and the confused shadows cast by it. A man came out of the inner to the outer darkness and shouted.

'Are you crazy? What are you doing here at this hour?' he said, in German-accented English.

'My last night. I'm just trying to remember everything.'

'Ass. You better come and have a beer. We can give you something to eat, too.' A woman now appeared in the passage with a flashlight in her hand; its beam splintered the walls with shadows, like a window starred by a stone. I entered the passage and when she shut down the light I saw a long row of stage lights and cameras as on a film set.

The German wasn't a German but a Czech who had lived and taught in Cologne ever since Soviet tanks had crushed Alexander Dubcek's Prague Spring in 1968. His name was Jaroslav Poncar and he was photographing, by means of a specially adopted Swiss-made Seitz panoramic camera, the hundreds of metres of scroll-like bas-reliefs etched in the walls of the long galleries and pavilions of Angkor Wat. That photographic record, also including detailed studies of the 1,850 sandstone sculptures of the sylph-like goddess Aspara, was likely to be the most detailed documentation Angkor Wat would ever receive. 'You could say,' he quipped pointing at one bas-reliefs which he titled 'Churning the Milk Ocean', 'that these are the comic strips of the gods.'

'What are you doing here?' I asked him.

'The wall engravings. I am photographing them. All of them. The conditions here, the conditions they are in. Who knows how long they will last? Storms like tonight are eating them away.'

The woman reached into a cooler and tossed me a cold Angkor beer. The coolness of the bottle pierced like a knife. Jaroslav was a small, lean, braided whip sort of man with large, calf-like eyes and he carried a pack on his back that was strapped so high that it appeared to make a hunchback out of him.

I asked him whether the government supported his work, and Jaro laughed sadly. Once, he said, the deputy minister of culture came to visit, and the talk touched on the subject of the Khmer identity. '"To be a Khmer," he told me, "was something without meaning,"' said Jaro. The man was only in his thirties, of the post-Pol Pot generation really, but he no longer knew what he was; he didn't know anything about the old Hindu gods celebrated here. His Buddhism was almost as bad. He thought that his grandmother, had she survived Pol Pot, might understand what she was seeing here; she wouldn't need to have anyone explain to her the significance of the beehive towers or the *aspara* carvings. 'The minister, he was only a tourist. He saw only an architectural monument that might pull in some money for the government. He had lost the key to a whole world of belief and feeling, and was cut off completely from his past.'

At first, Jaro's talk seemed fanciful exaggeration. The minister, it seemed, was annoyed by all the hustling peasants who were encircling them as they spoke. He ordered his guards, rifles at the ready, to shoo them away. 'It is not an easy thing to say,' the minister mumbled to me, 'but this is what kindness gets you. If we put people in their place, they would have to stay there.' That last statement, Jaro believed, explained some of the current Khmer frenzy. The minister's idea of Cambodia simply could not accommodate the Khmer people. It was an idea of his country that, for all its determination to preserve Angkor Wat—and the man *was* determined, his career depended on it—answered only his own, private, personal needs. The man was a minister and he was completely insecure. Even as one of the leaders of the state he was not secure enough to imagine a new Khmer dynamic, some social energy that could incorporate all of the peasant poor, that infestation, those defilers of the temples.

For the minister, Khmer identity was not something developing or changing, perhaps not even something salvageable; it was something fixed only in an idealization of his own personal background, the past that he somehow lost and which no one else knew about. Identity was related to the set of beliefs that his grandmother must have held, it was related to a knowledge of the Buddha, a code, an entire social fabric and civilization. Pol Pot's rupture with the past had meant the loss of that civilization, the loss of the fundamental idea of Cambodia, and the loss of any motive for real, innovative social action. Such feelings of purposelessness were real: government here, civilization here, was simply the act of holding on.

*

AT THE END of anything that really matters to you, a feeling of inconsequence, Kundera's unbearable lightness of being, takes hold. Preparing to fly from Siem Reap to Bangkok, and then on to Tokyo and New York, I felt again what I had felt on my arrival at Tan Son Nhut: a deadening sense of being lost, of being an outsider.

I wondered if I had done enough, seen enough; had been too reliant on others, or too unskilled. Certain things, I knew, I would remember forever. They might become discoloured a bit by time, like coins in the pocket of a forgotten suit, and some details might be transformed or rearranged so as to reveal others. But I wondered, when I began to try and make a whole concert out of the events of the months of my journey, if everything would fall apart in my hands, like an old newspaper. After all, the past enters all of us and disappears, except that somewhere within, like diamonds, there exist fragments that refuse to be consumed.

Momentarily, I felt contempt for myself. But then I remembered the tastes, the rioting yellow motorcycle headlights of Saigon, the silent huts along the Mekong, the dusty Phnom Penh mornings, the thoughts of everything that had happened, and the notebooks that confirmed them and made them imperishable. Time with its clumsy thumb would blur nothing. Everything was stored away, like an inheritance.

My last evening in Angkor, my last night in Cambodia and in

Indochina, was spent in the almost empty dining room of the Grand Hôtel d'Angkor, a restored Raffles-like pile (the owners also operated that famous remnant of the British empire in Singapore) at the entrance to the wide avenue leading to Angkor Wat. It was a large hall, a yawning historic fake in colonial style made shabby by time. The only other person in the room that night was a Royal Cambodian Army general, who seemed almost a caricature of an officer having a hearty meal before the final throw of the dice in a coup: massively built, colourfully decorated, crew-cut, tight-lipped behind his sunglasses. He lifted his chin stiffly on spying me, his black eyebrows rising like a pair of startled swallows. Staring with resentment, he stayed in the room only long enough to finish his drink.

I ordered a chilled Pernand-Vergellesse that arrived with ice in a silver tureen and was poured into a crystal glass. Despite this elegance, the room seemed strangely threatening. No one was going in or out. A mist hung across the middle of the hall like breath left behind for years. Although the chandeliers were lit, the light fell yellowish and weak. Damp called forth a smell made of floorboards, disinfectants, the sweet, sooty cellulose effluence of the jungle. Walls were of a cream turned ochre, the heavy draperies looked as if they had come out of years of storage and gave off a faint muskiness when touched. Still air, the scent of a killing boredom instantly recognized, like mould. In the ceiling fixtures the bulbs were of clear glass.

On the tables were white brocaded silk tablecloths, hand-woven. For every stalk of steamed vegetables served—the menu so opulent that you could order seasonal white asparagus from France—there appeared another battery of plated flatware, platters and *vinaigrette* sauce boats, and also another battery of 'waiters.' Little boys, they could not have been more than twelve or thirteen years old, dressed in long white smocks, each taught to serve as if they were in Paris at La Coupole.

Long, unhurried hours: the immemorial procession of a French meal. I lingered in exhaustion and delight. Outside, the wind was swirling dust into palm trees. Beehive temples were absorbed into an indigo sky. One dark boy, fidgeting with his white gloves, picked up an empty wine bottle from a table, fitted it precisely into a wine holder and marched toward the kitchen holding it stiffly before him. He glanced covertly at the *maître d'hôtel* for a nod of approval. The *maître d'hôtel* was a veteran of the place. For him, the real Grand Hôtel ended decades ago; all of this was some sort of corrupted half-life. It seemed to me, not then but later, that I had never before seen, and would perhaps never see again, the residue of European custom so pointlessly observed.

In that twilight of rehearsed graciousness, Angkor seemed the summary of a nation and its hoarded cultures: the zenith of Hinduism's political and spiritual expansion, the simulacrum of Buddhism's ascetic drama, and a living mausoleum of French achievement.

To arrive at an understanding of a country trapped in time, of a place static, eternally vulnerable to the outside world and cultural conquest, was to begin to acquire something of that feeling of the void I had sensed everywhere across Indochina. It was to begin to fall, willingly or not, into the region's remorseless dream of past lives: when dead ancestors watched and protected, and when your greatest enemy was your future self.